COLD CASE JURY
TRUE CRIME COLLECTION

POISONED
AT THE PRIORY

ANTONY M BROWN

MIRROR BOOKS

First published by Mirror Books in 2020

Mirror Books is part of Reach plc
10 Lower Thames Street
London EC3R 6EN

www.mirrorbooks.co.uk

ISBN 978-1-912624-79-9

Typeset by Danny Lyle

Printed and bound in Great Britain by
CPI Group (UK) Ltd, Croydon, CR0 4YY

1 3 5 7 9 10 8 6 4 2

Mirror Books *presents*

The fourth crime for the Cold Case Jury

POISONED AT THE PRIORY

After finishing this book,
readers are invited to deliver
their own verdicts at the
Cold Case Jury website
coldcasejury.com

ACKNOWLEDGEMENTS

This book would not have been written without the help and support of my wife Carla, for her plentiful edits, suggestions and discussions. I would also like to thank everyone at Mirror Books for getting this book into your hands, especially Jo Sollis for her unwavering support in publishing this series and Julie Adams for her artistry with the covers.

CONTENTS

PART TWO: The Evidence

PART THREE: The Verdict

ABOUT COLD CASE JURY

BEST SERVED COLD

I agree with George Orwell, who famously lamented the decline of the English murder. He thought original murders were virtually extinct by the first half of the 20th century, and that brutality had replaced ingenuity in pursuance of the ultimate crime. Gone were the days of assiduous poisonings, carefully laid traps and mysterious killings without apparent motive. These were now the preserve of thrillers, movies and, of course, dear Aunt Agatha. Fact had lost its frisson to fiction and reality was left somehow diminished.

There is a quality to a bygone murder that seems to set it apart from its modern counterparts. It was an era of etiquette and arsenic, of afternoon tea with a spoonful of malice. Modern Britain is too open, too honest even, to create the social conditions of the past that drove some to commit murder, often with an insidious craft that flummoxed the authorities of the day.

This last point is important. Like revenge, a venerable murder is best served cold. Unsolved. These are the intriguing cases that have several plausible solutions and have bequeathed us enough evidence to let us debate what probably happened. These are the masterpieces of murder, to quote the title of an Edmund Pearson book, the dark art that would be hung upon the cold walls of a Tate Criminal Gallery. These are the cases for the Cold Case Jury.

Does this mean that these crimes were perpetrated by the Machiavellis of murder? No, an unsolved crime from Orwell's golden age of murder does not imply its criminals were more deviously clever than today's. Undoubtedly some were, but the truth is that many of these cold cases would be solved by today's higher standards of professionalism and scientific methods of detection. Even the assassination of President Kennedy in 1963, arguably the most analysed murder of the last century, spawned a vast conspiracy theory industry largely because of a flawed autopsy. Whether this was by malign influence or honourable incompetence is a quicksand best avoided here. My point is that, had the autopsy retrieved the bullet fragments from the President's brain, subsequent forensic analysis would have revealed the type of gun that terminated a presidency that bright November day and the shadows of doubt, as well as an industry, might have disappeared.

So, am I re-investigating these cold cases, unearthing fresh evidence or presenting new theories to shed new light on old crimes? Sometimes, yes, but my overriding goal is to present the reader with an interesting case for which the verdict is open to doubt. My task is to take the reader back in time to witness the events leading up to a violent or suspicious death; reconstruct how it occurred according to the different theories; and present evidence to the reader as in a real court. I hope to bring these crimes back to life, showing how the drama might have unfolded, emphasising the timeless interplay of the people involved and presenting the historical stage on which they acted. In recon-structing events I prefer to use narrative's present tense – dialogue. Some of it is verbatim, drawn from trial or inquest testimony. The rest is more a work of imagination, yet always governed by the facts and theories of the case, connecting the evidential dots by plausible lines of narrative.

I hope I am also an impartial advocate – the Cold Case Advocate, if you like. My aim is to show the strengths and weaknesses of each theory, and then you have your say. I'm hoping you will give your verdict on the Cold Case Jury website. Over time, an overall verdict of the Cold Case Jury will emerge for each case.

My final task is to present my views on the case. But my view is only one.

The verdict always lies with you, the jury.

PREFACE

SECOND-HAND CHANCE

My interest in true crime mysteries arose from a love of the Sherlock Holmes stories as a student. I always wondered if there were any real-life cases from the same historical period that matched the fictional ones for their interest and puzzlement. Years later, chance events led to the Cold Case Jury series of books.

I stumbled upon a copy of *How Charles Bravo Died* by Yseult Bridges for sale in a Winchester second-hand bookshop. I liked the intriguing nature of the case, and I spent several minutes browsing through its pages. Although it was reasonably priced, I could not convince myself to buy it. I replaced the small book on the shelf and thought nothing more of it until a few days later.

It was again by chance that I stumbled across another copy of this book at a car boot sale, possibly in a better condition than the first. I gave the stall holder his full asking price: 20 pence. A superstitious mind might say fate had placed this book in my path.

I was captivated by the story and its puzzle. I discovered and read other books on the poisoning at Balham Priory in 1876. I had my own opinions on the case and was curious as to what others thought. I found myself explaining the Balham Mystery, retelling the story in my own way, but after a while I ran out of new listeners and gradually it passed from my mind.

Several years later, almost on a whim, I enrolled on an evening course at the University of Southampton called 'Telling True Stories', run by author Iain Gately. I always remember Iain telling us that good writers let their readers work things out for themselves, summarised by the rule "two and two, not four". For example, if you have two people in a scene and another couple joins them, you do not need to tell the reader there are four people. From this, came the idea to write about true crime mysteries in which the reader has the chance to decide things for themselves; it applied the rule to an entire concept. Although not the first to be published in my Cold Case Jury series, the Bravo case was the initial book I drafted, and it has now been thoroughly updated and expanded.

The result is in your hands.

Antony M. Brown, *October 2019.*

PART ONE

THE STORY

This is the true story of the agonising death of Charles Bravo in 1876.

It led to one of the most infamous Coroner's inquests ever held in Britain.

In 1875, Queen Victoria was on the throne and Benjamin Disraeli was in Downing Street. Joseph Bazalgette was knighted after completing London's sewer system, *The Times* published its first weather map, while Captain Webb was the first person to swim the English Channel.

And, in Balham, to the south west of London…

Chapter 1

A CASUAL PROPHECY

Tuesday 7 December 1875

Regulars at the Bedford Hotel paid no attention as the 11:50 thundered along the West London and Crystal Palace line. In the tap room, a customer by the wooden bar raised his voice to compensate for the clattering hooves of the iron horse on the adjacent bridge.

"It ain't fair," he said, his wiry fingers clasping a ceramic mug of porter.

"What happened then, George?" his companion asked.

"Mrs Ricardo asked me to take her into town in the landau. We were in Bond Street and a wine cart pulled out in front of us. Pulled out, just like that. I steered the horses to the right but…" He shook his head. "The carriages hit. I got the blame, of course."

"And Mrs Ricardo asked you to leave?"

"Yeah, last Friday with a month's notice." George Griffith hesitated, his mood shifting from melancholy to resentment. "But the missus ain't the problem. It's him! He's the one who wants me gone."

"Mr Bravo?"

"Yeah, he told her that I wasn't a safe driver and I had to go. What choice did she 'ave? She could hardly disobey her husband-to-be." Griffith downed some of his ale. "You know he forced her to destroy

3

one of the hounds after it bit him on the arm? I was the one who had to shoot the wretched thing. He also made her sack her maid. Too many servants, he said. As if she's counting the pennies!"

"Well, he's the man of the house now, layin' down the law. Nothin' wrong with that."

"Yeah, but the missus won't like it. She's been used to havin' her own way."

"So yer outta work now?"

"Yeah, but I might 'ave found a new missus."

"What, 'ere in Balham?"

"No, Herne Bay in Kent, but I wouldn't have to move anywhere if it weren't for this marriage."

The ears of the fresh-faced hotel manager pricked up, and he lumbered over. "Hey George, haven't you gone to the wedding?"

"Nah, I'm on my way to Wandsworth, Mr Stringer," Griffith replied. "The County Court."

"You in trouble?" Stringer asked, concerned.

"Oh, I had a summons. An unpaid bill, nothing serious. I really ought to be on my way." He picked up a grey cap from the stool and placed it neatly on his head. "If you see the missus, make sure she has plenty of brandy before the wedding, won't you?"

Stringer frowned quizzically. "Mrs Ricardo?"

"It'll be Mrs Bravo later today, for better or worse." Downing the last of his porter in a few audible gulps, Griffith wiped his mouth with the back of his hand. He headed for the door, glancing over his shoulder. "Poor fella, I wouldn't want to be in his shoes. He won't live four month."

*

The barroom prophecy was eerily prescient: Charles Bravo died in agony just a little over four months after his wedding to

4

Florence Ricardo. Not only had George Griffith apparently foreseen Mr Bravo's untimely death, but also when it would occur. And there was more. The post-mortem identified that Mr Bravo had been poisoned by the same chemical used by Griffith to manage equine parasites as part of his duties as a coachman. Further, one of his former employers was an eminent doctor who had an illicit affair with Mrs Ricardo before she left him for her younger but short-lived husband.

How had Griffith known what was to happen? Not surprisingly, he found himself at the eye of the storm when it raged a few months later. A key witness at the sensational inquest into the death of Charles Bravo, he was asked about his wedding-day premonition, his links to the deadly poison and the jilted lover. But we will come to this – and much more – later.

This case is unusually baffling because the body of evidence, mainly from the inquest testimony, appears to support equally the different theories of how Charles Bravo met his death. Indeed, since the fateful night over a century ago, many books have been published on the case, with each author sifting the evidence to support their particular view of events. I intend to take a different approach. I'm inviting every reader to take a seat on the Cold Case Jury.

In Part One, I will take you back in time to reconstruct the events surrounding Charles Bravo's death and the different versions of how he might have died according to the various theories. One is the view of Agatha Christie, and you will be able to read her solution in her own words for the very first time.

In Part Two, you can see original evidence, some of which has never been published before, including police reports, witness statements and extracts from the first-ever book on the case written by a doctor just months after the poisoning.

Finally, in Part Three, I offer my opinion on who was responsible for the infamous death of Charles Bravo, but it is your opinion that matters. As in a real court of law, the verdict always rests with you, the jury. I hope you will enter your decision at the Cold Case Jury website, where you can also see a poll of how your fellow jurors have voted. The result should be a fascinating verdict in the court of public opinion on a death that has mystified for well over a century.

The case revolves around the young and privileged bride, Florence Ricardo, and her broken relationships. Before we turn back the hands of time, we need to discover her background and the antecedent events that led to the death of her husband. And this first takes us to the other side of the world.

Florence was born on 5 September 1845 in Sydney, Australia, into wealth. Her grandfather had left Scotland for the new continent 20 years earlier and had made a fortune from wool. After his death in 1851, Florence's parents, Robert and Ann Campbell, took their inheritance and ever-growing family and returned to Britain. In 1859, Robert Campbell purchased the run-down Buscot Park, an estate of 3,500 acres nestled to the west of Oxford and south of the Cotswolds. Over the next few years, and at vast expense, the imposing, Neoclassical-style mansion was completely refurbished, and became Florence's home until her marriage to Lieutenant Alexander Ricardo of the Grenadier Guards. The young couple had met in Canada, on one of her family's foreign tours. The groom was the son of Lady Catherine Duff and John Ricardo, the late Liberal MP, founder of the Electric Telegraph Company and director of the London and Westminster Bank. At just 21 years of age, Alexander was wealthy and well connected, and the Campbells thoroughly approved of the match.

At 10:30am on 21 September 1864, the wedding party left the grandeur of Buscot House in eight carriages, each drawn by a pair of horses. As the entourage wound its way through the grounds of the estate, it passed under a series of floral arches, each bearing messages of good wishes to the young couple. At Buscot Church, a large concourse of onlookers witnessed the arrival of the bride. Florence's rounded face of delicate features and glorious cascade of auburn hair was hidden by a veil of white tulle and festooned by orange blossom. She was followed into the church by a trail of nine bridesmaids, including her two younger sisters, Alice and Edith.

After the ceremony, the married couple left the church along a flower-strewn path flanked by a choir of 18 local school girls, dressed in pink frocks and straw bonnets. As the smiling couple slowly walked to their waiting carriage and future, the choir sang *Bridal Wishes.* Certainly, 19-year-old Mrs Florence Ricardo had the "wealth for all her days" as the hymn suggested, but she was to cruelly discover it would not buy her love or happiness. For her marriage was on a path lined not with flowers and petals, but secrets and scandal.

After the honeymoon on the Rhine, the couple leased Hockham Hall in Norfolk. Florence later described the next three years as the happiest of her life, but it was not to last. Alexander was promoted to Captain, despite his propensity for excess, especially his drinking. When he left the army in 1867, his dipsomania was increasingly evident, at least to Florence. Now a couple of leisure, enjoying London society, visiting country estates, touring abroad and throwing hunting parties, the idle time only exacerbated Alexander's love for alcohol, and his bouts of drunkenness became more frequent.

Even though they were wealthy, their income was not unlimited. Indeed, most of it was derived from interest on trust capital, and the principal would only pass to the couple on the death of their parents. Their increasing expenditure appears to be the reason they failed to renew the lease on Hockham Hall in 1868 and moved to Somerset. Alexander also attempted to abstain from drinking, which he managed for several months only, before again succumbing to temptation. And it was not his only vice. He had a mistress in London, and persistent rumours suggested he had other extra-marital interests elsewhere.

A year later, when Alexander's mother died, the couple's financial position improved, and they moved to Bournemouth. The change of scene did nothing to change the man. In fact, his drinking problem was observed by everyone close to the couple, including Florence's mother, who noted drily that he "was drinking more than usual and more than was beneficial to him". By April 1870, the domestic situation deteriorated to such a pitiful extent that Florence's own health began to suffer and she sought guidance from her mother. A temporary separation was arranged, whereby Captain Ricardo stayed at the St James Hotel in Piccadilly, London, while Florence rested and recuperated at Malvern, where she took the opportunity to soothe her nerves and anxiety under the care of a trusted family doctor.

Florence had known Dr James Gully since she was eight years old, when she was first treated by him for a minor complaint. Born into a wealthy family, Gully had spent the first years of his life in Jamaica before being educated in Britain and France, pursuing an interest in medicine. In 1840, he married Frances Kibble, a widow 16 years his senior. Unfortunately, his wife's mental health deteriorated over the ensuing years, and they lived apart. Rejecting orthodox medical methods, Gully began a homeopathic and hydropathic practice at the spa town of Malvern in 1842. Both the practice and the town began to thrive when celebrities, including Tennyson, Dickens and Darwin, made their way to the "water doctors" for treatment.

When Florence entered his consulting room in May 1870, Dr
Gully was 62 years old. His eminence, wealth and charisma
compensated for his less-than-imposing physical appearance.
His sympathetic and caring manner was the antidote to Florence's
toxic marriage, and his patient was now an attractive and
free-spirited young woman in need of his help. Despite the age
difference of almost 38 years, there was an undoubted spark of
attraction between them. She was the promise of a nubile young
love long denied; he the attentive and wiser companion she
craved. Both knew that any future relationship would shatter
virtually every ethical and social norm of the day, but forbidden
fruit always tastes the sweetest.

If either had harboured hopes of a secret relationship during
those halcyon days, Alexander Ricardo was a reminder of how
difficult it would be. The Captain soon wrote to his wife, promising
to give up the booze and nights away, and he arrived at Malvern in
the middle of May. The couple rented a nearby cottage, Orwell
Lodge. The time they spent together did little to invigorate the
marriage and within three weeks Alexander had left, heading back
to London to indulge his desires to excess again. Florence grew
increasingly fond of Dr Gully: attentive, considerate and learned,
he was the opposite of her boorish husband.

Later that summer, Alexander was treated for *delirium
tremens*, the potent withdrawal symptoms from alcohol. He
returned to Malvern, Florence hoping that its serenity and Dr
Gully's care might save her husband from his demons. It was a
forlorn hope. A few months later, after Alexander was physically
violent towards his wife, Mrs Campbell took her daughter back
to the sanctuary of Buscot Park. Reality had killed the promise
of the fairy-tale wedding to a dashing captain, and now Florence
needed her parents to face the truth: her marriage was irrepara-
bly broken. Although Florence was determined not to be chained

any longer, her father was equally adamant: marriage was sacrosanct, separation unconscionable.

At the time, divorce was almost impossible for women. The Matrimonial Causes Act of 1857 had introduced divorce by civil court decree in England but its aim was to protect the "reverence of the nuptial tie" by limiting the grounds of dissolution. A husband was permitted a divorce by showing a single instance of adultery, yet the same right was not afforded to the wife, who had to show the adultery was also incestuous or bigamous, or was compounded by cruelty or desertion. This inequality would persist for decades.

Florence sought a legal separation, yet even this was problematic. Her father, resolute that she should continue her duties as a wife, withheld the interest she received from him as part of her marriage settlement. Headstrong Florence would not be cowed, leaving the luxury of her parents' estate to stay with friends in London, where she took legal action against her father – and won. Naturally, relations rapidly soured, yet Florence pressed on, knowing that she could count on the support of Dr Gully. Already Florence's confidante and benefactor, he became her saviour when he agreed to act as a trustee for the deed of separation. Under the agreement drawn up on 31 March 1871, Florence would receive £1,200 a year from her husband, who promptly left for the continent.

With Gully's role in facilitating Florence's legal separation, suspicions that he was something more than her doctor cast dark shadows over Buscot Park, and familial relations deteriorated further. Less than a month later, Florence received the shocking news that Captain Ricardo had died in Cologne, a few days before his 28th birthday. The cause of death was presumed to be alcoholic poisoning.

Although love had turned her back on Florence, fortune smiled again when it transpired that her late husband had failed to amend his Will, leaving Florence as the sole beneficiary of his estate worth £40,000 – millions in today's money. Released from her noxious marriage, Florence Ricardo was free to open a new chapter in her young and privileged existence. It might have led to any number of wonderful life stories but, like a moth helplessly drawn to a flickering flame, she embarked on one that would have a tragic ending.

It is unclear whether Florence Ricardo and Dr Gully started their affair while she was married, an allegation she later denied vehemently, but the couple were certainly intimate in the months following her husband's death. Gully had already announced he was retiring from practice at the end of the year, an indication of a passion for something other than medicine, and he relocated to the same street in Streatham where Florence was now living, an obvious sign of its object.

Although accompanied by two servants, the couple's vacation in Italy in early 1872 was an unconventional travel arrangement. And even if the relationship had been platonic, it appeared otherwise, and appearances were everything to Victorian sensibilities. Florence's strained relationship with her family, and particularly her father, now snapped. Apart from the occasional letter from her mother pleading with her daughter to change her ways, Florence had no contact with her family for nearly three years. A sign of the fracture could be seen at Buscot Park, where Robert Campbell had built a six-mile railway to ferry beet and other farm produce from his estate using three small locomotives. Two engines were named after his younger daughters, Edith and Alice. Conspicuously, the third was called "Emily".

Aware of the problems her relationship with Dr Gully was posing, Florence Ricardo decided to hire a chaperone and confidante, someone who could offer female advice and support as well as give her greater respectability, shielding her from the gossip that inevitably followed when Dr Gully was seen visiting her alone. In August 1872, Florence employed 45-year-old Jane Cox as her resident companion.

Jane Cannon Cox had a pale complexion and dark hair, which was scraped back from the temples and tied into a chignon just past the crown. Mrs Cox's shrewd intellect, resourcefulness and powers of observation were often disguised by her timid and hesitant discourse. She always thought carefully before speaking circumspectly. Reliable and loyal, she had the ideal qualities for the role. For her it was a plum job, no specified duties but paying extremely well – £80 per year, five times the market rate for a maid. She must have believed her fortunes were picking up.

Unlike Florence, Jane Cox had always fought for her modest foothold in the world. In her early twenties, she was a governess for several years before marrying civil engineer Phillip Cox in 1858. A son was born two years later and in 1861 they moved to Jamaica, where two more sons completed the family. While working in the West Indies, Philip Cox became close friends with Michael Solomon, brother-in-law to Mr Joseph Bravo, a successful island merchant now living in luxury in London. Fate was spinning the web of connections so important to our drama.

Unfortunately, tragedy struck. After ten years of marriage, Philip Cox died, leaving Jane a widow with little money and three young sons, whose welfare was now her paramount concern. She had little choice but to return to England, where she invested the little capital she had in a property in Notting Hill Gate, London, which she let out. With financial assistance from Joseph Bravo, she managed to send her two eldest to a boarding school for "the sons of impoverished gentleman". To make ends meet she became daily governess to the children of Mr and Mrs Brooks in

Streatham. She must have felt her life had been a cruel game of snakes and ladders, taking her back to where she had started out 20 years previously. In fact, the appointment was another of fate's connections. Mr George Brooks was Florence Ricardo's solicitor, with whom Florence had stayed for almost a year after leaving her husband and falling out with her family. It was here the two women met and became friendly.

From the outset, Mrs Cox would have known about the entanglement of Dr Gully and Florence. He had called for her at the Brooks' house on many occasions. In fact, when Mrs Brooks had caught them "cuddling on the sofa", Florence was asked to leave. She rented a villa in Streatham, where Mrs Cox later joined her. And so did Dr Gully, his visits now more frequent than ever as he rented a house almost opposite. Florence would later claim that Mrs Cox had no idea of how intimate her relationship with Dr Gully had become, but this is hardly credible. Mrs Cox might have been as silent as a tomb in her discretion, even with Florence, but she was no fool.

The affair reached its passionate zenith a year later when the two lovers went to Kissingen, Bavaria, for six weeks in August 1873. Ostensibly this was to continue Florence's water treatment under the direction of Dr Gully. Florence took her maid with her, leaving the capable Mrs Cox to manage the household in her absence. Florence was completely content during these languid summer months, but storm clouds were gathering.

Chapter 2
BITTER TROUBLES

A few weeks after returning from her Bavarian break, Florence Ricardo fell seriously ill. It was described to the servants as "an unusual natural illness" and "a kind of tumour" which Dr Gully had removed. Later, Florence claimed she had suffered a miscarriage; in all probability, the homeopathic doctor performed an abortion. There was no other option. If it became known that Florence was pregnant, neither of them would have survived the pernicious scandal that would have enveloped them like a poisonous fog. Whatever the suspicions of Mrs Cox, she kept them to herself, and diligently nursed her mistress back to health. Florence would later say, "I had acute physical suffering... I owe my life to Mrs Cox's attendance on me." Indeed, the two women now became close friends on first name terms.

According to Florence, although the friendship with Dr Gully remained strong, the "improper intimacy" now ceased. No doubt she could not risk another pregnancy, fearing she would not survive the inevitable abortion. A few months later she orchestrated another change: she moved her household from Streatham to nearby Balham.

Today, Balham is a highly desirable area of south London, popular with City high-flyers attracted to good properties,

14

schools and transport links. But back in March 1874 it was a quiet locality surrounded by swathes of open countryside dissected by the West London and Crystal Palace railway. As trains approached the provincial station at Balham Hill, passengers peering out of the sooty carriage windows would have seen in the distance an imposing white house surrounded by trees and manicured gardens. The castellated, gothic-style building was Balham Priory, which Florence was renting from George Byng, MP. Further down the Bedford Hill Road was a row of six semi-detached houses, one of which was taken by Dr Gully and sentimentally named 'Orwell Lodge', a reminder of the cottage Florence had occupied at Malvern four years earlier when their attachment began.

At this time, Mrs Cox received a letter from her aunt Margaret in Jamaica {see *Exhibit 10*}, informing her that she had changed her Will, leaving properties by St Ann's Bay, nestled on the island's north shore, to Mrs Cox's eldest, Leslie. This piece of good news for Jane has important implications in what follows. Indeed, all the major elements of our drama are now present, save for one. He enters our story nine months later, when Mrs Cox arranged for Florence to call on her benefactor, Joseph Bravo, who had been a friend of her late husband's and had provided financial assistance to Jane when she returned to England. It was at Joseph Bravo's palatial Kensington residence, shortly before Christmas 1874, that Florence first met 29-year-old Charles Bravo.

He was born Charles Turner, most probably in Jamaica, although his origins are obscure. He had two sisters, Alice and Ellen, both of whom were plagued by serious medical problems. Alice was described as a "deaf mute", her sister "mentally defective" and institutionalised. After his father's death while Charles was still young, his mother Mary Turner married Joseph

Bravo, an island merchant who had made his fortune trading colonial goods such as tea and coffee. He proved to be a great stepfather, affording Charles every opportunity, including an education at Oxford. On reaching his maturity, Charles Turner adopted his stepfather's surname, and it was as Charles Bravo that he was called to the bar in 1868. Described as someone with "ordinary ability and more than ordinary ambition", a career in law was never an end in itself, however – only a stepping stone to his ultimate goal of entering Parliament.

Charles was the same age as Florence, but looked older on account of his high forehead and muttonchop whiskers that framed his prominent, deep-set eyes and thin mouth. The law was an ideal calling for someone who, even according to his friends, was calculating and rarely moved by sentiment. He had two sides to his character, the hard-nosed and the high-spirited. His stepfather liked to use his wealth to exert control over others, including the affairs of his stepson, and Charles had been conditioned with the materialistic outlook of someone obsessed with money. His over-protective mother had attended to his smallest want and her every word had instilled in her son the belief that he was special and the best. So it is of little surprise that Charles was impulsive and prone to violent outbursts of temper when he did not get his way, and could be overbearing and arrogant, with a sharp tongue. By every account, Charles Bravo was outspoken to a fault. But he was also persuasive, affable, cheery and attentive to others. Members of his household would later testify he was a considerate employer.

We do not know what transpired when Charles entered the elegant drawing room while Florence was enjoying afternoon tea with the Bravos, but it was certainly not love at first sight. For one thing, both had existing romantic attachments. Florence was still involved, at least emotionally, with Dr Gully while

Charles kept a mistress in Maidenhead with whom he had fathered a child. Both relationships were problematic and secretive. They made no effort to see each other again.

In March 1875, Florence and Dr Gully again toured Italy, this time accompanied by Mrs Cox. Her presence did little to appease the concerns of Florence's parents or diminish the piquant gossip circulating in polite society.

This was not the only problem gnawing at Florence's conscience. During the summer, Mrs Campbell fell seriously ill at Buscot. The bitter family estrangement prevented Florence from visiting her mother. She knew the only way to seek a family reconciliation was to break all ties with Dr Gully, and this she resolved to do. Not wishing to spoil his holiday abroad with friends, she decided to tell her former lover of his expulsion from her life on his return. Her sensitivity in delaying the bombshell communication cannot disguise her single-mindedness in abandoning her loyal friend and supporter so abruptly. It revealed a glint of steel within her decadent and impulsive heart.

There was another reason for the complete separation from her former paramour. In September 1875, while spending a two week retreat in Brighton with Mrs Cox, Florence happened to meet again none other than Charles Bravo walking along the famous promenade. It seems unlikely this was by complete chance; some behind-the-scenes arrangements were undoubtedly made to ensure both were in Brighton at the same time. Over the next week, they met every day, and remarkably there was subliminal talk of marriage. For Charles Bravo, marrying into wealth offered patriarchal independence and a means to fund his Parliamentary ambitions. For Florence, it represented social redemption and a shortcut back to respectability. Lack of emotional rapport appeared to be no object to a marriage of mutual benefit. It made Florence's conversation with Dr Gully even more pressing. He was duly informed of the termination of their friendship and requested he leave Balham. The doctor told Florence not to rush into marriage and to become properly acquainted with the young man and his family.

Days later, when Gully was told that Florence had accepted Charles Bravo's proposal of marriage, he wrote an angry letter to her. She fired back with her pen, stating bluntly that she "must never see his face again". Gully instructed his butler never to admit either Florence or her companion into his house. Florence disclosed the full details of her relationship with her old lover to her young admirer and, after some thought, Bravo agreed to press ahead with the marriage – but only after making Florence solemnly promise that she would never again see Dr Gully, or even mention his name. She agreed and, moving at remarkable haste, the couple's engagement was announced in early November 1875, less than five weeks after the promenade encounter.

Dr Gully was therefore bemused when he was given a message to urgently meet Florence at the coach house a week before the wedding day. If he hoped the marriage was about to be called off, he was bitterly disappointed. During the clandestine rendezvous, Florence had the temerity to ask his advice about the terms of the marriage settlement Charles was demanding.

Prior to the Married Women's Property Act of 1870, marriage was a form of female incarceration. A wife immediately relinquished control of most assets, such as her income, stocks, inheritance, and furniture to her husband. The new law allowed married women to independently retain their income and own stocks, but it was mute on the ownership of furniture and other possessions after marriage. Charles refused to marry unless her household possessions were transferred to him: "I cannot contemplate a marriage which doesn't make me master in my own house," he told Florence.

PART ONE

"I cannot place myself in the position of having to sit at a table or upon a chair which doesn't belong to me."

The settlement would entail Florence legally relinquishing all her possessions – furniture, carriages, horses, jewellery, art and even her clothes – to Charles, who would be free to dispose of them at any time and in any manner he wished. Despite bringing little to the marriage financially, save for his relatively meagre salary of £200, the agreement would hand Charles enormous leverage in the relationship. Yet such was the sense of entitlement in this misogynistic age, every man would have demanded the same and all would have agreed that Charles was sensibly exercising his lawful rights over a woman. Dr Gully was no different. He advised her "not to squabble about the furniture… it was a small price to pay for happiness". He also wished the marriage well, although one suspects he also took secret satisfaction from knowing that Florence was facing the consequences of her hasty decision. She had made her bed, and now her husband owned it.

Despite her disgust at the settlement, Florence agreed, and married Charles Bravo at All Saints Church in Kensington on 7 December 1875. Like a rash heralding an illness, tell-tale signs of impending marital problems soon appeared. On the honeymoon in Brighton, Charles sought out Dr Dill, one of Florence's doctors whose counsel she trusted on all matters connected to her welfare, and told him she was drinking too much sherry. After Brighton, the couple spent some time at the Bravo residence in Kensington, where it was obvious that Charles' mother, absent from the wedding, did not hold Florence in high esteem.

After a pleasant stay at Buscot Park, the couple returned to Balham Priory in early January. Three days later, on 9 January 1876, Florence sent a telegram to her parents informing them she was expecting her first child already. In his book, *Death at The Priory* (2001), James Ruddick suggests it had been a shotgun wedding; Florence could not face the ignominy of bearing a child out of wedlock or endure another abortion, so Charles was able to force her hand in the marriage. There is little to support this view. If she felt she had no choice in the matter, Florence would hardly have sought the counsel of Dr Gully just days before the wedding.

Later in January, the complications of Florence's past began to poison the young marriage. Charles received an anonymous letter accusing him of marrying for money and informing him that Florence had been Dr Gully's mistress. Charles was enraged beyond reason: "If you had not told me before our marriage of your acquaintance with Dr Gully I should have been on the sea tonight!" He demanded that Mrs Cox look at the handwriting to determine whether the doctor had written the note. She stated he had not. Interestingly, it seems Charles did not trust his wife to give a truthful answer to his question.

The letter was immediately thrown into the fire, leaving the identity of the writer unknown. It was almost certainly George Griffith, the former coachman who had also suffered when Charles Bravo arrived at The Priory. His sacking forced both him and his wife to leave the comfortable residence of the coach house. Griffith was bitter and prepared to cause trouble, albeit anonymously.

The letter was an ominous sign, presaging a series of real difficulties in the marriage. The first followed swiftly: Florence lost the baby at the end of January. In addition, arguments broke out like wildfires, typically on the occasions when his desire for control clashed with her desire to write a cheque. Bravo's acute parsimony was fuelled by his parents, who constantly encouraged him to reduce household overheads. As early as the following month a dispute became so heated it ended with Florence fleeing to Buscot Park and Charles retreating to Kensington. From his parents' house he wrote a conciliatory letter to his wife on 15 February 1876:

Looking back on the 10 weeks of our marriage, I feel that many of my words, although kindly meant, were unduly harsh. In future my rebukes, if it is necessary to say anything, which God forbid, shall be given with the utmost tenderness... I hold you to be the best of wives. We have had bitter troubles, but I trust in times to come the sweet peace of our lives will not be disturbed by memories like these.

The "bitter troubles" might refer to the financial arguments, the miscarriage or both. Later Florence claimed the rifts were caused by her husband's constant moaning about her relationship with Dr Gully. With Charles insisting that the doctor had no reason to stay in Balham any longer, he might have become edgy and incensed by his lingering presence near to The Priory. After all, there could be no greater threat to a cold, calculated marriage than the flame of true love burning so closely. But Dr Gully was going nowhere. Maybe he knew the marriage would not last long.

The young couple returned to The Priory a few days after Florence received his letter, but the peace was short lived. In early March, Florence wanted to book a trip to Worthing, believing the sea air would help with the nausea she had been experiencing. In his typically overbearing manner, Charles told her it was an unnecessary expense. His mother joined the fray, writing a letter to her daughter-in-law in which she objected to the trip for the same reason. This was the last straw for Florence, who lost her temper and threatened to write his mother such a letter that she would never interfere again. Charles exploded with rage and struck his wife, vowing to leave The Priory and never return. Like a child unable to control his emotions, he burst into tears and pleaded forgiveness.

The second fight ended the same way as the first: Florence sought sanctuary with her family in Oxfordshire, Charles withdrew to his in London, and then some sweet words persuaded

Florence to return a week later. On account of work, Charles returned to The Priory a few days after his wife, but not before he wrote again on 15 March 1876. The rosy letter, full of gushing sentiments, could not disguise a nasty thorn: "My father has promised us the barouche on condition we put down the cobs. By giving up the cobs and Mrs Cox we can save £400 a year and be as comfortable." We can imagine Florence's reaction on reading those lines: if she surrendered dear "Janie" and her beloved ponies, the annexation of her personal life would be complete.

Despite heaping praise on Mrs Cox on several occasions, in his letter Charles had revealed his true intentions. Had Mrs Cox read it, her worst fears would have been confirmed: Charles was not going to tolerate three in his marriage for much longer. The timing was particularly troublesome. After corresponding with her aunt in Jamaica for over a year about the property in St Ann's Bay, Mrs Cox had recently received another letter, this time imploring her to travel to Jamaica "as soon as possible". With her health failing, and no longer able to attend to matters, Margaret Cox had reason to believe Jane's son's inheritance might be usurped should she pass away soon.

This placed Jane in a quandary. She refused to take her family to Jamaica, knowing it would end the education of her boys for which she had sacrificed so much. She was also reluctant to go by herself because she feared for her job at The Priory while she was away. Without the well-paying position she would no longer be able to afford the school fees. She needed guidance.

Mrs Cox first sought the counsel of Joseph Bravo, who urged her to follow her aunt's advice and travel immediately. If she also wanted reassurance that her position at The Priory would be safe in her absence, she received none. She responded by saying it was not convenient to travel on account of her boys. Still perturbed, she sought a second opinion, this time from a trusted friend of over 20 years, Mrs Harford, who also advised her to go to

Jamaica. Mrs Cox realised she had little choice but to visit her aunt, although she still needed to find a way of safeguarding her position and the welfare of her boys during her absence.

At roughly this time – the exact date is unknown – Charles fell ill. On travelling to London one morning he vomited profusely and subsequently suffered violent diarrhoea. The suspected attack of gastroenteritis was extremely unusual for Charles, who had a robust constitution. He soon recovered but, in light of what is to follow, this trivial episode may be significant.

Florence's troubles were not over. On 6 April 1876, she had another miscarriage and fell seriously ill. Mrs Cox dutifully nursed her again. Charles was banished to the spare room while Florence convalesced. He refused to call her local doctor, Mr Harrison, insisting his surgeon cousin, Mr Bell, was perfectly capable of attending to her. Mr Bell advised her to take a break; the rest and bracing sea air would do her good, he suggested. Florence decided to convalesce in Worthing for two weeks after Easter, and was planning ahead. "I need not tell you," she wrote to her parents, "how thoroughly delighted Charlie and I will be to welcome you here on our return."

Five days later, Mrs Cox showed her aunt's letter to Florence and Charles. They advised her to go to Jamaica and offered to look after her boys until her return. If this provided relief for Jane, her anxiety could only have increased when Charles added, "And we will consider your arrangements on your return." It could only mean one thing: her situation at The Priory would change. At worst, she would be handed her notice.

On 14 April 1876, Good Friday, Florence continued to rest, although she was not the only person suffering. Charles was tormented by bouts of neuralgia and toothache, frequently rubbing his gums with laudanum and chloroform to alleviate the pain. Out of sorts and restless, he continually popped in and out of the morning room, where Florence was trying to rest after lunch. Exasperated, Florence ordered him out, to which Charles took offence, sulking upstairs alone.

On Easter Sunday, Charles wrote to his mother:

I passed the whole of yesterday most pleasantly. I rode Cremorne from 9:30 to 11, and on Victor afterwards by the side of Florence while she took an airing in the family coach. We went to see if we could persuade the school to let Mrs Cox's babes pass the holy season with us. We could not, but they are to come on Monday...

The same day, Florence also wrote to her mother:

Charlie is looking forward to a game of lawn tennis. I never saw him look so well. The country is life to him, and he walks about with a book under his arm as happy as a king... The flowers here are in great profusion and lovely...

On Easter Monday, Charles played tennis with Mrs Cox's boys and then delighted in showing some friends round his estate, as he was fond of calling The Priory. He agreed to lunch with one the following day in London. From their letters, the marriage of good calculation now appeared a congenial one. Indeed, Florence would later testify they were "happy as the day is long" when his interfering mother left them alone.

Florence was looking forward to her break. In her letter to her mother, Florence wrote "We leave here (D. V.) on Thursday for Worthing." A suitable furnished house had not yet been taken, but the capable Mrs Cox would head to the south coast the next day to do just that. The acronym in parentheses stood for "Deo Volente", Latin for "God willing". But God willed no such thing. Instead of recuperating by the sea, Florence would be keeping vigil by the bed of her dying husband.

Chapter 3

A BOLT FROM THE BLUE

Members of the Cold Case Jury, Charles Bravo's hasty marriage found him entangled in the web of Florence's past. He was sharing the marital home with his wife's companion – who feared losing her comfortable position – and living in the shadow of his wife's former lover, who felt sorely betrayed. His obsession for financial retrenchment, provoked by the interfering sniping of his own parents, had led to the sacking of two servants, one of whom felt bitterly aggrieved at his high-handed treatment. And, in only four months, the fragile marriage had been ruptured by two major quarrels and riven by the pain of two miscarriages. Something had to give.

We now turn back the hands of time to witness the chain of events that led to the cruel death of Charles Bravo. The reconstruction below, and the others that follow, closely adhere to the detailed testimony of all those involved, including the servants and doctors who tried to save his life, published by *The Daily Telegraph*, *The Daily News*, *The Morning Post* and *The Times*. Some of the stated times are estimates, but are based on a thorough assessment of all the evidence. Indeed, I believe the reconstructions constitute the most accurate timeline published on the case.

Tuesday 18 April 1876

10:15am. At the end of a sweeping driveway lined with mature trees fresh with spring's new leaf, a two-horse carriage waited outside the arched porch of Balham Priory. The overcast sky above the castellated roof felt sullen and pressing. To the North the weather looked ominous with dark, brooding clouds.

"I hope it's not going to rain," Charles Bravo remarked, his boots crunching on the shingle as he approached the black carriage, its roof folded back, exposing the comfortable interior.

"I think it will hold off, sir," Edward Smith replied, promptly pulling open the door of the landau.

"It better do," Bravo replied in a tone that suggested he would hold his footman responsible otherwise. Sitting down, he added: "I just loathe town when it's raining."

A few moments later, Florence stopped by the front door. "I presume Mrs Cox has left for Worthing already, Rowe?"

"Yes, Mrs Bravo, about an hour ago. She asked me to tell you that she hopes to be back before dinner." Closing the doors, Rowe muttered softly: "If not, she will have to slum it and eat with the rest of us in the kitchen."

Florence joined her husband in the carriage, sitting opposite. "It still hasn't warmed up, has it?" she shivered, placing her hands in a fur hand muff.

Overhearing, Smith asked, "Shall I close the carriage top, ma'am?"

"No, I'm feeling a little faint, and the fresh air will do me good."

"If you're not well, perhaps you should not come," Bravo said, sounding annoyed.

"But you wished me to come, Charlie. I've got up especially."

"I don't want you fainting." His tone was unsympathetic, her illness an inconvenience. "Leave it open," he told Smith and then shouted to the coachman seated at the front: "Let's get going before the weather turns! Stratford Place."

"Yes, sir," Charles Parton replied, flicking the reins. Smith clambered onto the standing board at the rear of the carriage as it pulled away to the sound of gently clopping hooves. Leaving the well-tended grounds of The Priory, the carriage headed along a narrow lane bursting with luxuriant undergrowth.

"Would you like me to wait in town for you?" Florence asked.

"No, you're still not fully recovered. Head back when you're done shopping. I'll get the afternoon express from Victoria after luncheon." The landau rocked viciously to one side as a wheel fell into a pot hole. "Blast these drivers! Can't they see where they're going?" They turned into Bedford Hill Road. "When are you going to Worthing?"

"Thursday morning. Will you be coming?"

"I told my mother we would take a small house," he responded, ignoring her question. "We could really do without the unnecessary expense."

Florence held her tongue. Her mother-in-law was steadfastly opposed to the trip on account of the cost, which they could easily afford. She knew it was really about control. "Janie knows that. I'm sure it will not be too dear." The more pertinent question was whether he would dare stand up to his domineering mother. "I do hope you will come, Charlie."

"I doubt it."

Florence looked hurt. "Why not?"

He paused, before replying tersely, "I think it'll be better for your health."

"I would like you to come. I should be unhappy otherwise."

Bravo looked away sulkily, and said no more on the subject. When they approached a row of six semi-detached houses to their right, Florence turned her head and looked the other way. As the carriage trundled by the last, Orwell Lodge, Bravo turned to his wife. "Did you see anybody?" he asked pointedly.

Her heart sank. "No, I wasn't looking."

"The old wretch!" he grumbled to himself. The carriage fell under the shadow of the arched railway bridge by Balham station and continued its journey towards the city.

1:30pm. Smith jumped down from the footman's seat as the landau slowed outside The Priory. Inside the carriage, Florence was clutching several shopping bags, one branded Benson's of Bond Street. She had first accompanied Charles to the Westminster Bank in Stratford Place where he had deposited a £500 cheque from her and, after dropping him off at Jermyn Street, she had proceeded to Bond Street and Haymarket to buy some gifts for herself and her husband.

Smith opened the carriage door. "Bring the bags," Florence instructed, stepping out.

"Welcome back, ma'am," the butler announced, one hand swept behind his straight back. His tall, lean frame stood to one side in the porch, holding open the door.

"Tell Stone I'll take lunch now, Rowe. And decant some champagne, too."

"Yes, ma'am," he replied. "A good trip?"

"Yes, although we turned back when it started to sleet!" Florence handed Rowe her coat. "But thankfully it stopped, and we turned around again. I'm a bit tired and quite famished," she said, heading for the morning room.

"Shall I'll bring you a sherry while you wait for luncheon to be served?"

"Yes, do."

Florence entered the morning room, falling into the chaise longue by the piano. Despite its name, this was where she relaxed most afternoons. As the fashions of the day dictated, every wall and surface was crammed with artwork, ornate porcelain and intricate glasswork. Sinking into the tasselled cushions, she slipped off her shoes and waited for the sherry.

PART ONE

4:35pm. Bravo stepped out of the carriage, paid the driver and strode into the porch. "Where can I find Mrs Bravo, Rowe?"

"The morning room, sir," the butler replied, closing the door.

Reclined comfortably on the chaise longue, Florence was reading a leather-bound volume of Shakespeare's sonnets. She looked up. "Charlie! You're back!" Closing her book, she placed it on a small table next to an empty wine glass. "How was your day?"

"The Turkish baths were invigorating and it's always a jolly lunch with your uncle!" he replied cheerfully.

"Go up to your bedroom and see what I have bought for you." He was surprised and intrigued by her excited tone. She smiled, waving him upstairs. He returned holding a box of Cavendish tobacco. "This isn't my normal tobacco," he said, "but thank you." He walked over and kissed Florence on the forehead. "It is just like you to be so considerate, getting all the things I like. I'll smoke this in the garden, I think."

Outside, he wandered through the manicured lawns punctuated with trees and rose beds to the stable yard. "Have you exercised the cobs today, Younger?"

The groom stopped brushing the flank of a small grey and straightened up. "No, sir."

"You know what?" He slipped his wife's gift in his jacket pocket. "The weather looks brighter. I'll take one out."

"If I may say, sir, I wouldn't ride today. They were both exercised hard yesterday and they're a bit skittish, especially Cremorne."

Bravo's expression darkened. "Don't tell me what I can do with my own horses, man!"

"Sorry, sir."

"Saddle up Cremorne right away! I'm going to change into my riding breeches."

"Yes, sir."

"And I might take Victor out afterwards, too," he added belligerently, turning towards the house.

6:20pm. Drawn and grimacing in pain, Charles Bravo was half slumped against the mane of his cob as it ambled into the courtyard, steam rising from its hindquarters. "Goddamn it, Parton!" he shouted out to his coachman. "Cremorne bolted with me for five miles. I couldn't stop him galloping." He winced as he straightened his back in the saddle. "You could knock me down with a feather!"

Parton took hold of the reins with one hand and affectionately patted the horse's muzzle with the other. "You've ridden with a snaffle, sir", he said shaking his head. "You want a curb bit. It'll pull harder in the mouth. A good tug on the reins will stop a little cob."

Bravo looked disdainfully from his mount. He was not an accomplished rider and disliked to be reminded of the fact, however elliptically. Resting on Parton's shoulder, Bravo slid off his saddle in great discomfort. Waiving away Parton's offer to help him further, he hobbled the short distance from the stables to The Priory and made his way to the morning room. He used the last of his energy to push open the door and staggered across to the chintz armchair, into which he slumped, breathless and wrought with pain. He glanced across the room and saw Florence prostrate on the chaise longue, snoozing off the afternoon's sherry and champagne.

On his rounds to check the fires were lit for the evening, Rowe opened the door of the morning room. Surprised to see Florence asleep on the couch, he stopped in his tracks. Hunched forward in the chair, his face pale and drawn, Bravo did not look up. Rowe noticed the large fire burning in the grate, and discreetly pulled the door to; he would return later.

6:25pm. On hearing Charles moan with the pain, Florence opened her eyes and slowly sat up. She noticed he was still in his riding breeches. "What's the matter, Charlie?"

"Cremorne has got a right temper. He bolted as soon as I got through the gate. As far as Mitcham Common." Charles rubbed his side. "My hat was blown clean off my head but I couldn't dismount – my legs felt like stone. I was so weary I even had trouble getting a shilling out of my pocket to pay the lad that fetched my hat."

"You look dreadful."

"I feel worse. I've never been so stiff in my life."

"Would you like a brandy or some Burgundy?" Bravo shook his head as he leaned further forward in the armchair, as if to be sick. "You should take a bath, Charlie," Florence said, rising from her chair. "Let me arrange one for you."

"No, I'll ring for someone." Like an elderly man, he slowly rotated his body in the armchair and pulled the tasselled cord next to the fireplace. "I'm so exhausted. I should have smoked that tobacco instead."

6:35pm. Rowe appeared. "You rang, sir?"

"Could you get a servant to run me a bath, Rowe?"

"Yes, sir. Shall I light the fire in your room, as well?"

"Yes, of course," Florence replied.

6:45pm. "The bath is ready now, sir," Rowe announced, entering the morning room. Leaning heavily against his loyal servant for support, Charles laboriously made his way to the hipbath in his bedroom with Florence following behind. "I hope the cob didn't throw you, sir," Rowe said.

Charles stopped and looked at his butler indignantly, "Of course not!" Rowe lowered him to the side of his bed, where Charles perched for a few moments, still in discomfort, but enjoying the warmth of the young fire. Rowe knelt down and pulled off Bravo's boots.

As he got up, Bravo winced and placed his hand on his side. He shuffled towards the bath. "Tell Mary Ann this water will do me very well in the morning."

"Yes, sir."

"Thank you, Rowe." Florence said, gliding into the room. The butler nodded and quietly withdrew.

"I forgot to mention, I met Frederick in town this afternoon," Charles muttered. "He walked with me to Victoria." He grimaced as a pain forked down his left flank like lightening. "I invited him over to play tennis tomorrow evening. Assuming I'm able to lift a racket!"

Florence furrowed her brow, trying to picture the face. "Frederick?"

"McCalmont. You know, from my chambers."

"Yes, of course. How you love to entertain your friends, Charlie! But you need to get your bath." She left her husband to undress and headed towards her dressing room across the landing to get ready for dinner. Downstairs she heard the clock ring out the three-quarter hour chime. "When will Janie be back?" she wondered.

7:20pm. While Jane Cox walked the short distance from Balham Station, a sense of normality was returning to The Priory. Charles emerged from his bedroom onto the landing, where his young and petite housekeeper was lighting the gas lamps. "Good evening, Mary Ann."

"Oh, you gave me a start, sir!" she replied, laughing lightly. "Are you feeling any better?"

"Yes, I'm all right now."

He proceeded across the landing to the top of the stairs, where he stopped and turned around. "Don't throw out the bathwater. I'll re-use it tomorrow morning." He then descended for the morning room.

After lighting the gas lamps, Mary Ann Keeber slipped into Charles Bravo's bedroom to tidy up. As usual, she opened the small casement window on the far side of the bedroom and filled up the water bottle on the table standing at the foot of his bed.

7:25pm. Mrs Cox hurriedly climbed the stairs clutching a bag. Wearing her usual black bustled dress and tinted circular glasses on the bridge of her nose, she looked like a scurrying beetle.

"Janie?" a voice called out as she reached the top of the stairs. She turned right for Mrs Bravo's dressing room and found Florence seated at her dressing table. Mary Ann Keeber, who also doubled up as her maid, was brushing her cascade of hair.

"Sorry I'm late," she said, catching her breath. "I caught the five o'clock express and had to change at Clapham, and there was not a cab to be found in Balham. I had to walk back."

"You've made it in time for dinner, at least," Florence replied, talking into the mirror.

"You're dressed," Mrs Cox observed with surprise.

"I'm having dinner downstairs tonight."

"But you must be exhausted after your trip to town. You really ought to be in bed, Florence."

"No, I will take dinner with you both. I've promised Charlie to go to bed straight after."

"So long as you do, Florence." With that, Mrs Cox left for her room to quickly freshen up.

7:35pm. Dinner was called a few minutes later than usual. Rowe and Smith stood like sentries by the mahogany sideboard on which there was a roast leg of lamb, stewed whiting, bloater paste, vegetables, eggs and toast. As the three sat down at the large dining table, Mrs Cox slid a letter to Charles. "I met the postman on the drive as I was walking home," she explained.

Bravo glanced at the handwriting on the envelope. "It's from my father, by the look of it." He ripped it open and unfolded two letters. A short note from his father accompanied a letter from his stockbrokers, Messrs Alexander & Co. "I'll have the lamb and bloater paste on toast, Rowe." The ladies tucked into their meals, each having fish and some lamb accompanied by a generous glass of Marsala.

"My father should attend his own affairs and learn not to meddle in mine!" Charles blurted out angrily. Rowe silently moved to Charles' side to pour a glass of Burgundy.

"What's the matter, Charlie?" Florence inquired softly.

"My broker inadvertently sent a letter to my father who opened it. He's forwarded it to me with his own note about affairs that are nothing to do with him!" He moved his head to one side, as if trying to alleviate a neck pain. "Well, I'm going to write him a shirty letter and see how he likes it!"

"What did he say?"

"He dislikes Stock Exchange trading; says it's no way to make money."

It was not the full story. Charles had purchased £1000 worth of Caledonian Railway shares the week before at 119½ and the stock had lost two pence in a few days. He decided not to risk any further decline and sold, making a £20 loss. The transaction was typical of him – trying to turn a quick profit of £10 or £20. Yet his track record showed he was as likely to suffer a loss, which he loathed as vehemently as his father.

"But he doesn't have to be shirty about it," he mumbled. The loss, and especially his father's knowledge of it, added to his physical discomfort. He was in a waspish mood.

7:45pm. Her appetite diminished, Florence gently placed the knife and fork on her plate, but indicated she wanted more wine. "Did you take a house at Worthing?"

"I did." Mrs Cox proceeded to describe the house and its location, as Rowe topped up the drinks of both women. Placing a photograph on the table, she clarified: "It shows the vicinity but not the house itself."

Charles glanced at the grainy image of a man standing by a horse and cart in a road by the Worthing seafront. "The usual pony and trap, I see," he remarked dismissively. "Well, I shall not be going." He flicked the picture back into the centre of the table.

Mrs Cox looked disapprovingly at him over the top of her spectacles. "Oh," she said in such a rebuking tone it shocked the butler.

8pm. Florence motioned to Rowe that she wanted more wine. Charles glared reprovingly as each woman partook of another glass. "Charles had a terrible ride this afternoon," Florence remarked to her companion. "Cremorne bolted."

"It didn't throw me," Charles interjected.

"You were so exhausted, Charlie. You looked like death."

Grumpily, Charles muttered under his breath. The prickly atmosphere did not improve when the three retired to the morning room after dinner, Charles still nursing his aching body and complaining about the letter.

9:10pm. Charles looked at the clock: "Florence, remember your promise? It's gone nine."

"Yes, Charlie, you're right," his wife replied, getting up from the armchair next to her husband.

"The servants will still be having supper," Mrs Cox observed, putting her embroidery aside. "Would you like me to assist you?"

"Yes, thank you, Janie."

The two women left Charles in the morning room. At the foot of the stairs Florence turned and asked her companion for a glass of diluted Marsala. Mrs Cox headed to the dining room to pour the drink and soon joined Florence in her dressing room.

9:30pm. In the kitchen, the kettle wailed on the range. Wrapping a towel around the handle, Mary Ann took it from the heat and filled two small copper cans with the boiling water. Sealing them, she carried them upstairs. She left one on the landing, which she would later take to Mrs Cox's room, and knocked on the door of Mrs Bravo's dressing room.

"Come in!" Florence called out. The housemaid opened the door and found Mrs Bravo at her dressing table, ready for bed, with Mrs Cox leaning against the mantelpiece.

"Mrs Bravo, I have your hot water." She placed the small can by the wash basin to provide warm water for Florence's nightly ablutions.

"Mary Ann, fetch me a little Marsala will you?" Florence handed her the tumbler containing the dregs of the wine Mrs Cox had fetched minutes earlier. The housemaid took the glass and descended the stairs.

9:35pm. Leaving the dining room, Mary Ann encountered Charles in the hall. Distant and off-colour, he stared at the full glass of wine in her hand but said nothing, which was unlike his usual affable manner. Still in discomfort, he ponderously climbed the stairs, the maid following discreetly behind. Seeing him make a beeline for Mrs Bravo's dressing room, Keeber decided it best to place the wine in Florence's bedroom. Moments later, Charles walked across the landing into his room, closing the door. Florence went to hers, Mrs Cox trailing behind like a bridesmaid. Continuing her chores, Mary Ann popped into the vacated dressing room to put away Florence's clothes.

9:45pm. Her dreary duties nearing their end, Mary Ann knocked on Florence's door. "Yes?" It was Mrs Cox's voice. She first opened a green baize door and then an inner door. Inside the sanctum of the bedroom, Florence was recumbent, apparently asleep, Mrs Cox seated by the bed, her back to the door. She asked quietly, "Is that all for tonight?"

"Have you brought up the little tray?" Mrs Cox asked, turning around.

"Yes, it's over there." She pointed to a tray on which there was a teapot and some bread and butter, Florence's usual nightly refreshments.

"I think that will be all, Mary Ann. Remember to take the dogs downstairs, won't you?"

Mary Ann approached the prostrate bundle of fur by the fire. "C'mon boy," she said softly, prodding him awake. The Skye terrier reluctantly got up. She glanced around the room. "Where's Mrs Dot?"

"Oh, I believe she might have gone up to my room."

Exiting the bedroom, Mary Ann closed the inner door. As the small terrier scampered down the stairs, she turned, walked the few paces to the corner of the landing and pulled open a small door adjacent to Charles' bedroom. Standing there at the bottom of a narrow flight of stairs leading to the second floor, where Mrs Cox had her room, she gently called up for the other terrier.

The young maid must have thought it was merely her last task of another day at The Priory, but the stillness enveloping the household like a rolling mist was about to suddenly evaporate. By now a massive dose of poison had been absorbed into the bloodstream of Charles Bravo and its devastating effects were about to be unleashed.

Chapter 4
ON PAIN OF DEATH

Charles threw open his bedroom door and yelled loudly in sheer panic, "Florence! Florence! Hot water!" Mary Ann immediately spun around and saw him dressed in his nightshirt, pallid and nauseous-looking. She hurried to Florence's bedroom, finding the scene inside exactly as it was moments before; it seemed the cries of Charles Bravo had gone unheard.

"Mr Bravo is ill! Come quick!"

Mrs Cox rose from the chair, moved swiftly across the small landing and into Charles Bravo's bedroom. Mary Ann followed, but lingered at the doorway, unable to shake a lifetime's deference. Ashen-faced and covered in pearls of sweat, Charles was standing by the open window on the far side of the bedroom. When Mrs Cox reached him he screamed, "Hot water! Hot water!"

Mrs Cox's nursing instincts now took control of the situation. "Fetch some hot water! Be quick!" she ordered Mary Ann, who ran to the kitchen to boil some water. Bravo leaned out and vomited violently onto the roof below. He pulled back from the casement and turned to face Mrs Cox. His eyes rolled upwards as consciousness fled, he sank to his knees and then came down like a felled tree at her feet. Mrs Cox managed to prop his head and shoulders against the side of the chest of drawers and swiftly descended the stairs to the butler's pantry, a small office adjacent to the morning room. She urgently instructed Rowe: "Get Parton to fetch Mr Harrison! Mr Bravo's ill!"

9:50pm. Mary Ann returned to the bedroom with the hot water can. Mrs Cox was leaning over Charles, rubbing his chest. "Get some mustard!" she fired off next without looking up. Mary Ann rushed back to the kitchen and, on her return, Mrs Cox told her to mix some with the hot water in a basin. "Keep his feet in it and rub them hard," she added with the authority of a doctor.

She next directed Mary Ann to mix some more mustard and water in a tumbler. With his head pulled back, they managed to tip a small amount through Charles' clenched teeth, but most flowed out like a yellow brook onto his nightshirt. Mary Ann was told to make some coffee, which again was poured between the lips of the insentient patient with as much success as before. Bravo eventually vomited, but there was no sign of returning consciousness. "Go to my room and get my spirit of camphor," Mrs Cox ordered.

10pm. "It's not there," the maid said breathlessly when she returned to the bedroom a few minutes later.

Without looking up, Mrs Cox barked: "Try Mrs Bravo's medicine chest!"

When Mary Ann entered the bedroom, she found Mrs Bravo lying in bed, her back turned to the door. As silently as she could, the housemaid urgently rummaged through the bottles and jars in the chest without success. As she was about to leave she decided to rouse her mistress. She approached the bed and touched Florence lightly on the arm: "Mrs Bravo, you must get up!"

Florence woke easily. "What is it?" she enquired, sitting up. "What's the matter?"

"It's Mr Bravo. He's been taken ill."

Out of bed in an instant, Florence was helped into her dressing gown by Mary Ann. She took the few steps across the landing and into the adjacent bedroom while Mary Ann headed back up to Mrs Cox's room in one last effort to find the camphor. Florence was shocked at what she saw. Her inert husband was slumped on the floor with Mrs Cox bent over him rubbing his chest vigorously. "Oh dear Lord!" she exclaimed. "He looks like death!" She sobbed as she crouched down by him and held his flaccid hand. "We cannot keep him on this cold floor."

Mrs Cox realised they would not be able to lift his dead weight onto the bed. She pulled the bedroom chair to near where Mr Bravo was lying. The under-housemaid was called to the room and, when Mary Ann returned triumphantly holding the camphor, the four women managed to drag Charles' limp body onto it, his head drooping to one side and his arms hanging loosely like a rag doll.

"Has the doctor been summoned?" Florence asked.

"Yes, Rowe has sent Parton to fetch Mr Harrison," Mrs Cox replied.

"Mr Harrison! He lives nearly two miles away!"

"Well, I thought Mr Bravo would prefer to be seen by the family doctor," Mrs Cox explained, but Florence was already running out of the room. She flew down the stairs in a growing state of anxiety.

"Rowe!" she screamed, crying as she ran. "Rowe, fetch someone! Mr Bravo is ill. He's dying!"

The butler had just returned from the lodge after raising the coachman. "Parton has taken the carriage to get Mr Harrison…"

"No! No! Get someone from Balham. Get anyone! Do something, Rowe!" she cried hysterically.

"I'll get Dr Moore right away, ma'am."

10:25pm. Dr Joseph Moore, a congenial, egg-faced man with bushy mutton-chop whiskers, was whisked into the bedroom, which had been tidied and cleaned in expectation of his visit. Insensible and slumped in the chair with his head limply rolled to one side, Bravo looked like he had just been taken down from the gallows. The ever-busy Mrs Cox was still rubbing liniment on his exposed chest.

"I don't know what's wrong with my husband," Florence explained anxiously as Dr Moore began his examination. "The only thing I can think of is that he had a rough ride this afternoon when the cob bolted with him."

"Yes, your butler mentioned that, but that would scarcely cause this. Is there anything else you can think of that would account for his collapse?" As he spoke, Moore pulled back Bravo's eyelids; the pupils were dilated.

"He was also worrying over stocks this evening…" Florence's voice was tremulous.

"I heard him call out," Mrs Cox replied, "and came in here. He complained of great pain in his stomach, so I gave mustard to make him sick."

"Perhaps they used a coppery pan to cook his lunch in town," Florence continued, quite distracted. "I heard a man in Epsom was poisoned like this last year."

The doctor placed his hand on Charles' neck to feel for a pulse. It was almost imperceptible, the heart's action near suspended. Gravely concerned it would soon give out completely, and with Rowe's assistance, he moved Charles onto the bed and gave the patient a rectal injection of brandy to sustain the heart.

"You don't apprehend anything serious, do you doctor?" Florence asked.

"I do, Mrs Bravo. I fear your husband is seriously ill." He paused and said bluntly. "Mrs Bravo, it is my opinion that your husband will not recover." Florence burst into tears.

41

11:15pm. Rowe opened the heavy front door to see Parton on the doorstep holding a lantern. Standing next to him was a young man with penetrating eyes and a horseshoe moustache. Relieved to see a familiar face, Mrs Cox greeted Mr Harrison warmly as he stepped inside. "I'm so glad you're here," she said earnestly.

"What's the matter?" he asked.

"I heard Mr Bravo call out for hot water and went to his bedroom," she explained. As they walked, she described Bravo's collapse and her treatment.

"So, you gave Mr Bravo a mustard emetic, coffee and applied some spirits of camphor," Harrison recapped.

"Yes, I fancy he has taken chloroform," Cox added. "I smelt it when he was sick." Harrison nodded but said nothing as they reached the top of the stairs. The door to Mr Bravo's bedroom swung open and Florence greeted him. Placing his medical bag on the floor, he introduced himself to Dr Moore, who was standing at the end of the bed. After consulting his colleague, Mr Harrison proceeded to examine Charles and discovered the same symptoms – the patient was unconscious with laboured breathing, dilated pupils, cold skin and virtually no pulse. Finally, he leaned over the prostrate Mr Bravo, placing his nose near the patient's face.

"I smell no chloroform," he announced. "Have you?" he asked of Moore, who shook his head.

"It could be a cardiac vessel has given way, as Dr Moore suggests," Harrison said after his examination. "There's certainly internal inflammation, but I am at a loss as to the precise cause." He took Mrs Cox discretely to one side. "I fear he will not last a further hour."

Florence, seeing the pitiful state of her husband, curled up on to the bed next to him, placing her head on his chest. "Do speak to me, Charlie. Do."

11:25pm. "I think Mrs Bravo is falling asleep," Harrison said, concerned.

"She's very tired," Mrs Cox replied. "She's recovering from illness herself."

"She might compromise his breathing. We ought to get her up."

"Florence, Florence," Mrs Cox called out softly, gently shaking her mistress by the arm. "You need to come with me. Let's go to your dressing room."

11:55pm. Loosening his tie, Harrison moved to the small table at the foot of the bed, picking up the half-full water bottle. He poured a quantity into the clean tumbler sitting next to it. As he quenched his thirst, Florence returned to the bedroom.

"Is there any change in my husband's condition?" she asked anxiously.

Moore shook his head. "I'm afraid not, Mrs Bravo."

"Can we get another opinion?"

Moore looked to his colleague. Finishing his drink, Harrison replied gravely: "Your husband's condition is extremely serious, Mrs Bravo, you should not get your hopes up."

"We must do something," she pleaded, struggling to hold back tears. "He values the opinion of his cousin Mr Bell more than anyone. They're like brothers."

"All right, as you wish." Harrison knew Royes Bell was a Harley Street surgeon and doubted he would be able to advance the diagnosis, so added tactfully, "Tell him, if he wishes to bring a physician whose opinion he respects, that would be helpful."

Wednesday 19 April 1876

In the early hours of the new day, rain fell, washing away parts of the vomited matter on the leads outside Mr Bravo's bedroom window. Inside, there was a silent vigil. There had been no change in Bravo's condition apart from when he groaned almost indiscernibly, "No… laudanum… no… laudanum." Like trapped bubbles surfacing from the deep, the words were a sign of life. And hope. In the hall the grandfather clock regularly punctured the heavy silence, chiming like the tolling of a church bell. One o'clock… one-thirty… two o'clock… two-thirty…

2:35am. Mrs Cox first heard the clatter of hooves of the returning carriage. Informing the doctors that Mr Bell had arrived, she hurried downstairs to meet him. Royes Bell had picked up Dr George Johnson, senior physician at King's College Hospital, on his way to The Priory. Mrs Cox ushered them into the crowded bedroom.

Bell introduced himself and the sombre-looking Dr Johnson to the attending doctors. As the most senior medical man, Johnson now took charge of the case. The condition of the patient remained serious but there were modest signs of improvement: his pupils were normal size and, most significantly, he was now drowsy rather than unconscious.

2:45am. Charles thrashed the sheets with his legs. Within minutes, full consciousness and agonising pain both returned. He vomited blood-stained mucus and made such violent efforts to get out of bed that the doctors had trouble restraining him. "Close stool!" he screamed repeatedly. He was helped onto the chamber pot, and after agonised straining, passed a considerable quantity of blood.

After examining the discharge, Johnson cleared the room except for the other doctors. "He is suffering from an irritant poison," he announced quietly to his colleagues. "I suspect arsenic." There was silence as everyone understood the likely implication.

Bravo let out a shrill, ear-piercing scream that filled the entire house. The deadly poison in his body was now taking its dreadful toll, producing severe abdominal pain and violent nausea; it was like being shackled to the deck of a small ship tossed upon high seas while mercilessly tortured. Apart from the occasional respite, this was how Charles Bravo would spend the remainder of the little time left to him.

3am. Dr Moore responded to the gentle knock at the bedroom door. Mrs Cox stood in the doorway. After exchanging a few words, he approached Mr Bell. "Mrs Cox would like to speak with you." Mr Bell nodded and walked out of the bedroom, closing the door behind him.

He followed Mrs Cox across the landing into a discreet corner. She spoke calmly and softly. "When Mr Bravo was taken ill, he said to me, 'I have taken poison, don't tell Florence.'"

"What?" Bell sounded incredulous. "What poison?"

"He didn't say. Immediately after he said this to me he vomited and then collapsed."

"Have you told any of the doctors about this?"

"No."

Bell was clearly irritated. Trying to keep his voice down, he said: "It's no good sending for doctors if you let them work in the dark!" Mrs Cox looked uncomfortable, resettling the spectacles on her nose. "Wait here," he added tersely. A few moments later he returned with Dr Johnson and Mr Harrison. "Please tell the doctors what you told me." Mrs Cox repeated her statement.

"Is that all he said?" Johnson asked.

"Yes."

"Did you ask what he had taken and why?"

"No, he told me nothing more than that. I thought I could smell chloroform on him."

Johnson and Bell returned to the sickroom. Annoyed, Harrison remained with Mrs Cox. "Why didn't you tell me before?"

"I thought I did, Mr Harrison."

"You certainly did not," he fired back. "You told me you were sure he had taken chloroform."

3:10am. Back in the sickroom the doctors continued questioning Bravo. Although the patient was in obvious pain and distress, he was lucid and reasoned. Mrs Cox's statement implied Charles knew what he took, possibly as a suicide attempt, and the doctors now focused on this.

"What have you taken, Mr Bravo?" Johnson asked directly.

"I rubbed my gums with laudanum for my neuralgia."

"No," Johnson responded, shaking his head gently, "laudanum will not explain your symptoms."

"Well, I have taken nothing else."

"We hear you told Mrs Cox that you've taken poison. What's the meaning of this?"

"I don't remember having spoken of taking poison," Bravo replied indifferently.

Dissatisfied, Johnson pressed further. "But you have taken poison?"

"I only rubbed my gums with laudanum. I may have swallowed some."

"Please tell us what you've taken, Charlie," Bell interjected.

"I have taken nothing but laudanum."

"But that will not explain your symptoms," Johnson restated.

"Well, I don't know what it is."

"Are there poisons in the house?" Moore asked.

"Yes. Laudanum, chloroform... there may be rat poison in the stables..." Bravo screamed and writhed in agony. "Oh Lord, help me!" He then vomited some mucus deeply tinged with blood.

Convinced his symptoms were consistent with an irritant poison, the doctors needed to identify it quickly. A search was conducted of the room. On the fireplace, Harrison found a labelled bottle of laudanum, a third full, a blue-fluted one of chloroform, which was empty save for a single drop, and camphor liniment. None of which could explain the patient's symptoms. Dr Johnson instructed that any newly passed matter was to be kept for analysis.

3:30am. Finding Mrs Cox in the dressing room, Johnson pressed her for more details. "Can you tell me anything more about what Mr Bravo said to you earlier? Are you quite sure he said he had taken poison?"

"Yes, he said, 'I have taken poison, don't tell Florence.' He said no more."

Johnson was suddenly aware of Florence sitting next to Mrs Cox and regretted his *faux pas*. Turning to her companion, Florence asked impassively: "Did he say he had taken poison?"

"Yes, he did." Mrs Cox caught the quizzical look in Johnson's eye as he pondered Florence's response. "You're exhausted, Florence. You need rest. Come, lie down." Florence was gently ushered into her bedroom by her companion.

In the sickroom, Bell suggested to his cousin that some laudanum might alleviate his pain. "No!" Bravo retorted. "No laudanum." His tone was surprisingly adamant.

"It might make you feel better," Dr Moore added sympathetically.

Bravo screamed, clutching his stomach. "Nothing is going to make me better. I'm booked!"

10am. The traumatic events of the long night had taken their toll on the household. Having only snatched two hours of disrupted sleep, Florence was red-eyed with exhaustion and worry. The same was true of Mrs Cox, who had not even found the time to change out of her clothes from her Worthing trip. Rowe and Mary Ann both appeared weary and drawn, having retired to bed in the early hours only to resume their daily duties shortly after sunrise.

Although still enduring bouts of agonising pain, Charles had at least experienced a few hours of respite from his torture. "Good morning, sir," Mary Ann said, appearing by his bed. "Mrs Bravo asked me to tidy your room."

"Oh yes, come in, Mary Ann." His voice was weak, his face deathly pale.

"Are you feeling any better?"

"Not much. We shall not have our trip to Worthing now, Mary Ann."

"I hope we shall."

"No," he replied gravely. "My next trip will be to Streatham churchyard." Mary Ann was not sure how to respond. She drew back the curtains of the large window overlooking the western lawn, and opened the casement window. She did not notice the vomit still lying on the lead tiles from when Bravo was first sick.

An emotionally drained Florence smiled as she entered the room and held her husband's hand. "I've sent a telegram to your parents, Charlie. They should be here this afternoon."

Bravo looked up. "What a bother I am to you, Florence."

"Oh, it's no trouble, is it, Mary Ann?"

"No," the maid replied, rather surprised to be asked.

"When you bury me, make no fuss."

"Don't speak like that, Charlie."

"I don't want any fuss," he repeated. "No ostrich feathers and flowers and that sort of thing."

"If that's your wish," she replied, sobbing.

11am. "Oh, Royes, shall I ever recover?" Bravo asked his cousin in despair before writhing in excruciating pain, which was unbearable even after a morphine suppository.

"I hope so, Charlie, but you are very ill indeed." Noticing the patient was lucid, and hoping to elicit more details about what he had taken, Bell enquired: "Is there anything on your mind?"

"No." After a pause, Bravo added: "I have not led a religious life. Please will you read some prayers to me?"

Florence fetched the prayer book from her bedroom, but Bell's voice faltered as soon as he began to read. "I don't think I can, Charlie. I'm sorry." After saying a quick prayer asking for mercy on them all, Charles announced he wanted to make a will.

"Is it necessary, Charlie?" Bell remonstrated, still overcome with emotion.

"I wish to make a will," he insisted. After writing materials were brought to the room, Charles dictated that he left everything he possessed to Florence, who was appointed as the sole executrix. He held Florence's hand. "Please give my watch to Royes. He has been most attentive."

"Yes, of course, Charlie."

"Royes, if I die before mother arrives, please tell her from me to be kind to Florence. She has been the best of wives to me. And you must remarry," he said to Florence, "but not a word of the past next time. And please be kind to Katie; she will have no father in the world after I'm gone. Kiss me, my wife."

Tearful, Florence kissed him gently on his cheek. "What have you taken, Charlie? What have you done to make yourself so ill?"

Wracked again by stabbings of dreadful pain, he screamed: "Oh, Christ have mercy on me!"

3:30pm. The sound of the carriage on the gravel drive had brought Florence and Rowe to the porch, the large oak doors already open for the visitors. Mary Bravo stepped inside first. "We left as soon as we received your telegram." Her cold tone matched her stony face.

"You said Charles is dangerously ill?" Joseph Bravo followed behind his wife, removing his hat and passing it to Rowe.

"Dreadfully so, I fear." Florence's voice quivered with emotion. "He has an internal inflammation and is in such agony."

Amelia Bushell, Mary Bravo's long-serving maid, silently slipped into the hall behind her employers like a shadow and smiled sympathetically. "You look so very tired, Florence. What a dreadful strain this must be."

Before Florence could respond, Mary Bravo interjected. "I think it best if we now take charge of the nursing, don't you?" Her tone was like a headmistress admonishing an indolent pupil. "Amelia and I know the constitution of my son better than anyone." It was the typical, brusque interference Florence had experienced during her short marriage. Like a cuckoo, her mother-in-law was pushing her out of her husband's life, even when he was dying.

"And you need some rest," Amelia added diplomatically.

Wanting to keep the peace for her husband's sake, she replied wearily, "Of course. Rowe will show you up." Like a deposed monarch, Florence now spent long periods exiled in Mrs Cox's bedroom, resting.

5pm. After the regime change, Dr Johnson returned to find the Bravos in the bedroom with Mr Bell. He shared some important news: a chemical analysis of the discharge he had taken away in the early hours of the morning had detected no arsenic. He collected further samples for more testing, but overlooked the vomit still lying on the leads outside the bedroom window.

Thursday 20 April 1876

By dawn of the following day, the condition of the patient had deteriorated. It was evident to everyone in the emotionally fraught household that Dr Moore's initial prognosis was fearfully accurate: Charles was not going to recover. With the consent of Mr Bell, distressed Florence asked for yet another medical opinion, this time the most respected physician in England: Sir William Gull, one of Queen Victoria's doctors. She hurriedly penned a note:

Dear Sir, my husband is dangerously ill. Could you come as soon as possible to see him? My father, Mr Campbell, will be so grateful if you can come at once. I need not tell you how grateful I should be to you.

Yours truly, Florence Bravo

Mrs Cox, still dressed in the clothes from her trip to Worthing, immediately took the carriage into London to deliver the message. The eminent doctor replied that he would call in the evening. Dr Johnson returned in the early afternoon with yet another colleague, Mr Henry Smith, Charles' uncle, who had known Charles since he was a boy. Johnson suggested it looked like suicide, but Smith doubted that Charles would ever take his own life. Johnson then left to accompany Dr Gull to The Priory, briefing him during their journey.

6:30pm. Like a famous actor playing a cameo at the denouement of a tragedy, Sir William Gull took centre stage as he strode into the sickroom. With his powerful personality and intellect, he would have risen to the top in any profession. His eminence, commanding presence and posture – looking slightly downwards, chin tucked in, with an arm often behind his back – made him the Napoleon of medicine.

"This is not disease," Gull pronounced after his cursory examination of Charles. He looked directly at the patient. "You are poisoned." If Charles had any doubt about his condition or its cause, Gull had stripped it bare with those three words. "Pray, tell us how you came by it?"

"I took it myself," Charles replied indifferently.

"What did you take?"

"Laudanum."

"You've taken more than laudanum!" Gull replied accusingly. For leverage, he then added: "If you tell us what it was, we may be able to administer an antidote." He paused. "No, that would not be fair. I fear nothing can save you." Like a snail withdrawing into its shell, Charles turned to face the other away.

6:45pm. The doctors gathered in Mrs Bravo's dressing room to consult confidentially in hushed and sombre voices. "The patient is undoubtedly suffering from an irritant poison, possibly in conjunction with laudanum," Gull stated. "Whatever he has taken, it seems he has taken it himself."

"There is someone you should see," Dr Johnson said, summoning Mrs Cox inside. "This is the lady to whom Mr Bravo said he had taken poison."

"Do you know what he has taken, Sir William?" she asked.

"The symptoms point towards an irritant poison of some kind," he replied confidently, "but he will only acknowledge laudanum."

"Can you not get him to say what he has really taken?"

"I really cannot press a dying man further. Now tell me what happened." After Mrs Cox had retold her story, he asked: "You say he was sick out of the window?"

"Yes."

He turned to Johnson. "Let that be collected. Make sure a clean, silver spoon is used and the contents sealed in a jar."

From the bedroom Charles shouted: "I want to see Sir William! Fetch Dr Gull!" The doctors returned to his side. If they were anticipating Charles making an important announcement, they were disappointed. "Sir William, I must tell you that I've told you the truth and nothing but the truth."

"Mr Bravo, what you've told me does not account for your symptoms," Gull responded. "There must be something else. You must consider the gravity of your situation."

"I know I am going to appear before my maker. I have told them all so," he said looking around the room, "but they won't believe it."

"Under the present circumstances I do not wish to press you much, but if we could know what you have taken we might be able to relieve you."

Bravo was resolute. "I took nothing but laudanum for my toothache. Like this." He lifted his hand and weakly rubbed his finger across the gum of his lower jaw. "I've only taken laudanum," his voice rising with emotion despite his exhaustion. "If it wasn't, so help me God, I don't know what it was!"

"Charles, tell us where you got it," Florence implored him.

"Out of your little bottle, Florence. If there was anything else in it, I don't know what it was." He let out a cry of agony.

Johnson interjected: "If you die without telling us more than we know at present, someone may be accused of poisoning you."

"I'm aware of that, but I can tell you nothing more. Is there any hope for me, Sir William?"

"Mr Bravo, it would be wrong to give you hope when there is none." Gull took his pulse. "There's very little life left in you," he declared. "You're half-dead now."

"Oh Lord, have mercy on me!"

7:15pm. Having done little but confirm that there was no hope for Charles, Sir William Gull left The Priory. In the bedroom, the emotional floodgates opened as Charles gathered everybody around. He reached out to Florence, who tenderly held his hand. "Our Father, who art in Heaven…" he began, everyone joining in.

After reciting the Lord's Prayer, an exhausted Charles lay back and closed his eyes to find respite from his appalling symptoms. He drifted into unconsciousness – and peace.

Friday 21 April 1876

5:20am. Half an hour before sunrise, the lazy light of first dawn brightened the eastern horizon. To those keeping vigil in the bedroom it was still the depths of night. The dancing flames of several candles threw eerie shadows on the wall and ceiling, and in the yellow light the patient's waxen face was like a death mask. His laboured breathing became shallower, and then stopped. Charles Bravo had finally surrendered to the poison.

10am. In the butler's pantry, Rowe was making up his books for the past two days. It was a task he typically performed before retiring to bed each night, but recent events had disrupted the routines of everyone in the household. He dipped his pen in the ink well on his desk and made an entry in his cellar book for Tuesday 18 April: two bottles of sherry and one of Burgundy decanted.

The small bell on the wall jangled. Leaving his desk, he walked slowly to the front door and opened it to a smartly dressed young man. "Good morning!" The visitor's greeting was sprightly. "My name's McCalmont. I work at Mr Bravo's chambers, and I've heard the poor chap's unwell."

"He fell ill on Tuesday evening, sir, and with great regret, I must inform you that Mr Bravo died a few hours ago."

"What!" The news was disorientating, like a blow to the head. "I… we were due to play tennis… it rained… um…" McCalmont rubbed his brow, his hand shaking. "He was so well, Tuesday."

"The entire household is in shock. I will tell Mrs Bravo you called, sir."

*

Members of the Cold Case Jury, let's step back to better understand some of the events that occurred over the three days leading to the death of Charles Bravo. The first point to note is that Charles collapsed just hours after the cob had bolted with him, an episode that had a profound effect on his physical and mental state. You should consider whether this incident occurring so soon before the poisoning was sheer coincidence or a factor in his death. In particular, was it used as a smokescreen by a murderer hoping to conceal the true cause of death? We will explore this again when we consider the theories of how he met his end.

The next issue is the behaviour of Charles Bravo immediately before his collapse. In Victorian times hot water was widely used as an emetic; it was drunk to induce vomiting and empty the stomach. Indeed, the medical journal *The Lancet* of August 1876 stated that Bravo's urgent demand for hot water is firm evidence that the victim believed he had ingested poison, an important point that will have to be explained by any theory of how he died.

We also saw how the capable Mrs Cox sprang into action, but there are questions over her conduct. Why did she not wake Mrs Bravo? Through Mrs Bravo's absence and by sending Mary Ann on serial errands, she was alone with the victim for those critical first minutes. *The Lancet* observed that her remedy of a mustard emetic, camphor and strong coffee was the textbook treatment for a case of poisoning, and not a natural one for merely the symptoms of vomiting and faintness. The medical journal inferred that Mrs Cox knew Charles Bravo had been poisoned. Of course, she claimed he had told her he had taken poison, but the inference is important if Mrs Cox's account is questioned later.

Dr Joseph Moore was the first responder. His account of what happened when he arrived is revealing, and has been overlooked by almost every writer on the case. Mrs Cox told him: she heard Charles scream out and then went to his room, where he told her he was *complaining of stomach pain*. Yet, Mrs Cox would later deny she heard Charles shouting and rushed to his aid only after the housemaid had raised the alarm. Mrs Cox's remark to Dr Moore is also at odds with her statements to Mr Bell and Dr Johnson: Charles told her only that he *had taken poison* before he collapsed.

George Harrison was the second doctor on the scene. He also remembered Mrs Cox telling him that she heard Mr Bravo call out for hot water before going to his bedroom. Additionally, she told him of her belief that Bravo had taken chloroform, something she withheld from Dr Moore. A surgeon in practice at Streatham Hill, Mr Harrison had attended to both Florence and Mrs Cox for some years, and understandably the cautious Mrs Cox felt more comfortable discussing intimate matters with someone she knew, which accounts for her divulging more information to him. However, she neglected to mention Bravo's statement to her about taking poison, an astounding omission.

Why did Mrs Cox not tell the doctors sooner of the "poison confession"? This is a central question affecting the whole complexion of the case, and is something to keep in mind. Mrs Cox is clearly a person of interest, but you should refrain from rushing to judgement until we have gathered all the facts. For now, I would like to draw your attention to the curious reaction of Charles Bravo on being questioned by Dr Johnson that he had told Mrs Cox he had taken poison. He showed no surprise or disbelief, but gave an evasive response: "I don't remember having spoken of taking poison." It was a peculiarly indifferent reaction. Surely, if the allegation were untrue, he would have retorted, "I did no such thing!" or something similar. Notice that he does not deny taking poison, only that he does not remember speaking of it. The answer is guarded and nuanced, all the more surprising given that he was in pain. He continues to deny taking anything other than laudanum to every doctor but, according to Dr Moore, Bravo declared that he would never recover. Was this because he was in great pain and feared the worst, or an indication he knew that he had ingested a lethal poison?

Similarly, what do you think of Florence's reaction when she first learned of Mrs Cox's statement? Dr Johnson later testified he was "rather astonished that Mrs Bravo did not display more feeling than she did". Was she not shocked to learn her husband had poisoned himself? Was she not hurt he had confided in Mrs Cox, but she was to be kept in the dark? There was no flicker of emotion, no demand to know more. Rather, she only wanted confirmation he had said it.

The drama is far from over, and we shall return to The Priory later. Now, we need to uncover the surprising events after Charles Bravo's death. The most immediate concern of the medical professionals was to determine its precise cause. In asking for the vomit to be collected from the roof, Gull played a vital role in this respect. Indeed, *The Lancet* was critical of the other doctors for not collecting it sooner; if they had, there might have been time to ask the victim how he came to ingest a massive dose of an unusual poison.

Chapter 5
POISONED CHALICES

The post-mortem was performed on Saturday 22 April 1876 by Joseph Payne and observed by Dr Johnson, Mr Harrison and Mr Bell. The examination showed a well-nourished male with no signs of major disease. However, when pressure was applied to the chest, a considerable quantity of frothy blood oozed from the mouth. Although the large intestine contained blood clots and ulcerated pustules, the mouth, oesophagus and stomach were free from inflammation, a finding typically present when an irritant poison has been ingested. The doctors were left a little perplexed, hoping the chemical analysis would cast a definitive light on what killed Charles Bravo.

Professor Redwood, an analytic chemist for over 30 years, was tasked with finding the poison. He tested small portions of the vomit collected from the roof for two commonly used poisons, arsenic and mercury, but did not discover either. Although there were trace amounts of lead, the eminent chemist realised this would not have accounted for Bravo's death. He subsequently tested for antimony, a substance as toxic as arsenic and ten times more so than lead. And the results were definite: the vomit contained antimony.

He concluded that the antimony was probably ingested in the form of tartar emetic, a yellowish, crystalline powder soluble in water. The resulting solution has a faint metallic taste easily masked by other flavours. In small doses of less than a grain it is a diaphoretic, promoting sweating that lowers the body's temperature. In larger doses of several grains it is an emetic: violent vomiting typically follows 15 minutes later. This quality of antimony has been known for centuries. In the Middle Ages, wine was poured into a goblet made of antimony, a tiny quantity of which leached into the wine. Drunk after a night of gluttony, the wine produced almost immediate nausea and emptied the stomach. It was also used in the early 19th century as a treatment for alcoholism. A few grains were placed in the alcoholic drink, making the addict sick. The hope was that the drinker would associate sickness with alcohol and avoid it.

Large doses of tartar emetic cause vomiting, diarrhoea and acute abdominal pain. However, not all the antimony may be expelled through vomiting and, once absorbed into the body, the metalloid will affect the operation of the liver, kidneys and especially the heart, and may lead to unconsciousness, coma and death.

From the amount of antimony discovered, Professor Redwood estimated that the collected vomit contained 10 grains of tartar emetic. He concluded that "a very large dose of the antimonial salt was taken, which would probably account for all the symptoms observed in the case." Prior to 1876, there was no recorded case of murder or suicide by a large, single dose of antimony. After all, a strong emetic is not a good choice for a poison: all of it may be expelled before any can be absorbed. For a determined poisoner, using antimony would be like a sniper playing Russian roulette.

Redwood also tested Florence's "little bottle" of laudanum, used by Bravo on his gums, but no trace of antimony was found inside. How such a large dose of antimony was ingested by Charles Bravo remained a mystery; it was now a matter for the Coroner to investigate.

The findings of Redwood's analysis were not submitted to the Coroner for several days, but this did not prevent the news of Bravo's suspected suicide spreading like wildfire among friends and colleagues. Indeed, the reaction from everyone who knew him was invariably the same: the spirited character of Charles Bravo would never take his own life.

But this opinion was not universally shared. Mr Robert Campbell, Florence's father, knew that if a suicide verdict was not returned at the inquest, suspicion would stalk his daughter's household like a pack of wolves. Behind the scenes, he moved quickly to pull the strings that his position and wealth allowed. The first step was to make sure the inquest was held at The Priory. Although arranging an inquest at a residence was quite routine, it ensured the Coroner would be well looked after. Mrs Cox hurriedly dispatched a note to Mr William Carter, the coroner for East Surrey: "Mrs Charles Bravo writes to say that she wishes the inquest to be held at The Priory, where she will have refreshments provided for the jury." Carter also agreed that Florence should not give evidence, on account of her exhaustion from grief and illness. Finally, although anyone was free to attend, invitations to the press were conveniently overlooked.

Mr Carter duly empanelled a jury, which assembled in the dining room at The Priory on Tuesday 25 April 1876. Several of Bravo's legal colleagues attended. One of them, Mr Reid, took notes, greatly adding to the paucity of official documentation. The jurors were first led to the bedroom, where the body of Charles Bravo lay in a coffin lined with white satin and lilies, and Joseph Bravo confirmed the body was that of his stepson. The next witness called was Mrs Cox. A key character in the tragedy, we need to examine her evidence and the reaction to it. Although no detailed notes were taken by the Coroner, some of her testimony was published by the *British Medical Journal*, possibly based on Reid's notes, from which the following brief reconstruction is drawn.

*

William Carter dabbed his forehead with a handkerchief and motioned to Mrs Cox to take the seat opposite. Dressed in the black of mourning, the slight figure of Mrs Cox took her place at the mahogany dining room table, and rested her gloved hands on the table cloth. Like a phalanx of guards around the perimeter of the room sat members of the jury, other witnesses and friends of Charles Bravo. With Florence spared testifying, Mrs Cox alone was in the spotlight. While Carter had a brief word with a colleague, she glanced through the bay window and across the lawns; she remembered her boys there, laughing and playing tennis with Charles on Easter Monday. Her memories were now echoes of a different life; how everything had changed in just eight days.

"Mrs Cox?" Carter spoke, interrupting her thoughts.

"Oh, yes," she said, turning to face her inquisitor. "I'm ready."

"Please state your full name for the record, and your position."

"My name is Jane Cannon Cox. I am a widow and have been staying now with Mrs Bravo as a companion for nearly four years." Her voice was quiet, her metre slow.

"And you saw Mr Bravo when he was taken ill?"

There was the customary hesitancy before Mrs Cox replied. "Yes, at about 9:30pm last Tuesday night." After another pause: "I found Mr Bravo sick and ill upstairs in his bedroom."

"Had he been like that for some time?"

"Oh, no, he had been up and about that day."

"Why were you in his room?"

"The servant called me to his bedroom. I found him standing by the window, looking very ill." Like a bar's rest following a refrain in music, she paused again. "I asked him, 'What's the matter?' He replied, 'Oh, I have taken poison, but don't tell Florence.'"

A juror leaned forward in his chair. "Did you tell the doctor, when he first arrived, that the deceased had said he had taken poison?"

Mrs Cox stroked the table cloth with her gloved hand, a striking displacement activity of hers. "No, not when he first arrived."

"How long afterwards would you say?"

She ironed out a small crease in the tablecloth. "Perhaps four or five hours."

"What! Four or five hours?" exclaimed a juror indignantly amid murmurs in the room. "Why did you not tell him before?" asked another.

Mrs Cox paused. "I did not think of it."

"If someone close to you was dying," a third added, "who said he had taken poison, would you not have considered it necessary to tell the doctor at once?"

"Well…" started Mrs Cox, still stroking the tablecloth. "Perhaps I might, but I forgot it in the hurry and excitement that was going on."

"Which of the doctors did you tell?" asked the first juror. "Mr Harrison?"

Over his horseshoe moustache, Mr Harrison looked keenly at Mrs Cox: "You didn't tell me he had said that he had taken poison."

"Let the witness answer, please," Carter admonished.

"Then it must have been Dr Moore or one of the other doctors," Mrs Cox replied uneasily, hesitating again. "I cannot say which."

To the jury, it sounded like a blatant evasion. "Which doctor do you think it was?" a juror pressed.

Mrs Cox continued to stroke the tablecloth. "Well, most likely Dr Moore."

Harrison was taken aback – he knew she had not told Dr Moore – but kept his counsel. The line of questioning reached an unsatisfactory anti-climax because, despite being the first doctor on the scene, Dr Moore had not been summoned to give evidence. It appeared an inexplicable oversight – or a convenient one: the only doctors called to testify were Mr Harrison and Mr Bell, both of whom had strong connections to the household.

"Did the deceased say anything else or explain why he took the poison?" Mr Carter inquired.

"No. That's all he said to me. I saw him continually until he expired but he did not explain to me, or in my hearing, how he came to take the poison."

*

Members of the Cold Case Jury, Mrs Cox made an appalling witness, her answers giving the impression she was slithering over something sinister. She had no plausible explanation for her failure to inform the doctors sooner about Charles' confessional statement, and the reaction of the jury could not have made this clearer to her. Indeed, it must have weighed heavily on her mind when the inquest was adjourned for three days in order to receive the results of Professor Redwood's analysis.

The following day, Wednesday 26 April, Mrs Cox was dispatched to arrange lodgings in Brighton, where Florence could rest and recover, and while there, she visited Dr Charles Dill, another of Florence's physicians. He was more than just her doctor – he was more like a counsellor, a Victorian therapist, and knew all about Florence's affair with Dr Gully. This explains why Mrs Cox called on him to drop the biggest bombshell of the case.

She confided that she had been holding back on something important: Charles had actually told her, "I've taken poison *for Dr*

Gully, don't tell Florence". Her revelation transformed Bravo's confessional statement into an oral suicide note complete with motive, implying Charles killed himself so that Florence could go back to the man she really loved – Dr James Gully. It also explained her delay in not telling the doctors sooner: she could not repeat the full statement without publically disclosing the damaging affair and inflicting immeasurable distress on Florence and her family. On the night of the poisoning, she had eventually decided the best course of action was to tell Mr Bell about Bravo's confession, but without the three explosive words. However, it now appeared as though she had fabricated the entire statement, embellishing it to make it more credible.

Dr Dill agreed that to mention Dr Gully would be greatly damaging to Florence, and Mrs Cox returned to The Priory for the second and final day of the inquest on Friday 28 April 1876. Professor Redwood delivered his analysis, placing the cause of death into the public domain. However, it was unclear what had been laced with antimony; there was no poisoned chalice. After a total of nine witnesses had given evidence, the coroner recorded the verdict of the jury: "The deceased died from the effects of a poison – antimony – but we have insufficient evidence to show under what circumstances it came into his body." Clearly, the jurors were unconvinced by the suicide theory, a blow for the Campbell family. However, with the Coroner discharging the jury, it appeared the matter was now closed.

The next day, Charles Bravo's body left The Priory in an open coffin covered with white flowers. Distraught and unwell, Florence laid a wreath on the hearse but did not accompany her husband on his final journey. She solemnly watched from her bedroom window as the entourage slowly made its way from The Priory to Norwood Cemetery. She must have hoped it was the final scene of the tragedy, but it was merely the end of the first act.

The second opened two days later. Edward Willoughby, a barrister friend of Charles who attended both the second day of the inquest and the funeral, went to Scotland Yard to tell them that Charles Bravo was the last person he knew who would commit suicide. On the same day, Joseph Bravo visited the police for the same reason. As a result, Chief Inspector Clarke was detailed with discovering if anyone at The Priory had recently acquired tartar emetic. The Campbells and Bravos now faced each other like entrenched armies, one propounding the theory that Charles had committed suicide, the other attacking the idea as disgraceful nonsense.

On Wednesday 3 May, Florence, her housemaid and loyal companion retreated to Brighton, yet there was no respite from the unfolding nightmare. Those weeks in May saw many visitors call at the rented house – Dr Dill, the Campbell family and, ominously, the Chief Inspector. The most unwelcome visitor was the *Daily Telegraph*, its delivery greeted with increasing trepidation each day. The paper had picked up the Balham poisoning story and, like a salivating bloodhound, was relentlessly following what it clearly believed was a fishy scent. The story that Charles Bravo had "died under mysterious circumstances" broke on Wednesday 10 May. There, in black and white for everyone to read, was the basic story of his death, including the six doctors that attended his deathbed and the role of Mrs Cox.

A day later, Clarke submitted his first and most detailed report. He drew particular attention to the decanted Burgundy as a possible source of the poison, but concluded by saying enquiries were ongoing "to ascertain where the poison was purchased and other particulars". Knowing Clarke's investigation had found nothing significant so far, and no doubt concerned about the news coverage of the case, the Campbell family took action. Florence's solicitor posted an advertisement in several newspapers for three consecutive days offering an eye-watering reward of £500 to anyone who could provide information on the sale of tartar emetic or antimony and "throw satisfactory light on the mode by which Mr Charles Bravo came by his death on 21 April". No one came forward, and the ensuing events now gathered momentum like a runaway rain.

On 18 May the *Telegraph* ran an article by Mr Harrison and Dr Moore, and two days later *The Lancet* published Dr Johnson's account of "The Medical History of the Case". He stated that, according to Mrs Cox, Bravo had said "I have taken *some of that* poison, don't tell Florence". On the same day John Simon, MP for Dewsbury, rose in the House of Commons to ask the Home Secretary whether he was aware of the "unsatisfactory character of the Coroner's inquest on the late Mr Charles Bravo". The government minister replied he was "entirely dissatisfied" and it was being investigated by the Treasury Solicitor, one of the government's top legal officials.

It would be difficult to overestimate the anxiety of Florence Bravo at this time. She knew it was only a matter of time before her affair with Dr Gully would be exhumed like a gruesome corpse by the papers. Hate mail started to arrive for both women, from what we now might term 'trolls', levelling all kinds of accusations and insults. Florence's fragile emotional health started to deteriorate rapidly. The stress on Jane Cox was also enormous. She must have regretted ever mentioning the confessional statement that now placed her at the epicentre of the earthquake. Horrified that newspaper accounts perceived her in the same way as the inquest jury, Mrs Cox wrote anxiously to Mr Harrison to clarify a major point in the case:

My Dear Mr Harrison,

The reports and comments in the papers make me most unhappy. I so wish you would try to remember what I said to you about the poison. It is so dreadful for it to be said that I never mentioned anything about poison until Mr Bell came. I told you I felt sure he had taken chloroform, for I smelt it when he was being sick, but when afterwards you said it was not, I said I felt sure it was chloroform, and the bottle is empty, and he said he had taken either "some poison" or "poison", I forget which...

She added a postscript:

I did not tell Dr Moore because I was expecting you any moment, and I quite thought he would recover from the effects of the chloroform, and he would be angry at my having told he had said he had taken poison.

If Mrs Cox hoped his reply would be helpful, perhaps allowing for some equivocation in the matter, she was mistaken. On 20 May, George Harrison wrote bluntly: "You did not use the word 'poison' to me, nor did you say that he had told you he had taken it..."

On Saturday 27 May the *Telegraph* reported that Mr Stephenson, the Treasury Solicitor, had closed his inquiry after gathering statements from 30 witnesses. It observed wryly: "For various reasons, neither Mrs Bravo nor Mrs Cox, though questioned by police, has been asked to give evidence." There was only one implication: the two women should not be held above suspicion. The growing anxiety in the cornered Campbell family had now reached sheer panic. Florence's father strongly advised both women to give voluntary statements to the Treasury Solicitor. During the next week they synchronised their versions of events with legal help to present a robust case for their belief that Charles Bravo committed suicide.

On Friday 2 June, Florence Bravo and Jane Cox provided separate statements, each of which was signed and witnessed {see *Exhibits 3* and *4*}. They revealed that Charles Bravo was prone to impulsive bursts of passion and anger, sometimes violence, and was constantly jealous of Dr Gully. The testimonies were assiduously consistent and supported the alleged confessional statement made by Charles Bravo to Mrs Cox. Everything appeared to fit together but Mrs Cox's statement was a poisoned chalice. She opened her statement by admitting that she had not stated the full particulars at the first inquest because she had wanted to protect Florence's reputation. She then gave the full confessional statement: "Mrs Cox, I have taken poison for Dr Gully. Don't tell Florence."

After giving their statements the two women returned to Brighton where Florence experienced a "brain fever", a mental meltdown so alarming that Dr Dill thought it prudent to stay with her over several nights. But Mrs Cox was not nursing Florence this time. After four years of service and friendship, Jane Cox had abruptly left the employment of Florence Bravo; it was an irreparable rupture. We can only conjecture as to the precise reason, but the timing cannot be a coincidence.

The Campbell lawyers must have realised the legal significance of Mrs Cox's three additional words. First, if rekindling the flame between Florence and her former paramour was a motivation for her husband to commit suicide and step aside, then it was also a motive for the wife to commit murder and force him out of the way. Second, by declaring that she had not told the whole truth at the inquest, there were now grounds for a new one to be opened. The implications were terrifying: a fresh inquest would entail Florence having to testify and the focus would be on her relationship with Dr Gully. Florence's worst fears, like ravaging harpies surfacing from the darkest depths of her being, were dragging her into the abyss. And her former friend was responsible.

PART ONE

The fears of the lawyers were realised on Monday 26 June, when Sir John Holker, Disraeli's Attorney General, applied to the Queen's Bench at Westminster for the inquest verdict to be quashed and a new inquiry held. After reading out an affidavit from Dr Johnson, the Attorney General stressed that the victim had denied suicide on his deathbed, a point ignored by the Coroner, which amounted to misconduct. He argued it was possible that Charles Bravo had been murdered and a fresh inquest might elicit facts which would justify charging someone. Holker then played his ace, reading out Mrs Cox's statement. "You see, my lords," he concluded, "from her own statement, she deliberately kept information from the jury."

In their summing up, the judges agreed there were sufficient grounds to quash the inquest findings and, as it could not be re-opened because the jury had been discharged, directed the Coroner to hold another with a new jury.

Mr Carter would again preside over the second inquest but now it would be a thorough and searching investigation into the death of the young lawyer. Perhaps this time it would resolve many puzzling features of the case:

- If Charles Bravo wanted to take his own life, why did he ingest antimony and then urgently call for hot water, a common emetic?
- Why did he call out for Florence, yet seconds later tell Mrs Cox that his wife must not know he had taken poison?
- Why was Bravo totally indifferent as to the cause of his agonising symptoms when told by doctors that he was poisoned?
- Why did Florence show no surprise when first told of the confessional statement and appear to be in denial about the cause of her husband's collapse?

POISONED AT THE PRIORY

At 11am on Tuesday 11 July 1876, the new inquest opened in the Bedford Hotel, Balham, a few hundred yards from The Priory. Unlike the first, which was sparsely attended by friends and family, the notoriety of the case drew a huge crowd of onlookers. Inside the hotel, a surveyor was even asked to examine the floor of the billiard room to make sure it could withstand the weight of everyone inside. And unlike the first, reporters and lawyers turned up in numbers. The interests of the five parties – the Crown, Florence Bravo, Jane Cox, Joseph Bravo and Dr James Gully – were represented by no fewer than 10 attorneys.

Around the covered billiard table sat the Coroner, his officials and the lawyers. Underneath a row of large sash windows, reporters sat at a long desk, pens in hands, paper and ink wells in front of them. The 17 members of the jury sat in one corner, to the left of the fireplace and below racks piled high with top hats. Spectators crammed inside wherever they could find space, with many forced to stand in the doorway and hall.

A chastened William Carter addressed the jury, reminding them to dismiss everything they had read or heard about the case. As this was a new inquest, the body again had to be viewed and identified. The entire court took the train to Norwood Cemetery, where the coffin had been removed from its brick vault and placed in a temporary tent. Jurors peered through a glass plate in the lead-lined coffin; the body was decomposed and discoloured, the face barely recognisable. The ghoulish task completed, the court returned to the Bedford Hotel. John Mould, the undertaker, confirmed the body was that of Charles Bravo. The stage was now set.

Over the next three weeks, the lawyers picked over the evidence from almost 40 witnesses like scavenging vultures, each trying to elicit information to suit the interests of their client. In the next chapters, we will take a close look at the key testimony of the most important witnesses. The examination is not strictly chronological {see *Exhibit 9* for a daily summary}. Rather, witnesses with a similar evidentiary perspective are grouped together. This approach will lose none of the drama but enables an easier comparison of testimony. The most important witnesses called during the first week were the doctors and scientists, and it is to the medical evidence that we now turn.

Chapter 6

AN OVERDOSE OF DOCTORS

On the afternoon of Thursday 13 July 1876, the third day of the inquest, a clear blue sky stretched above Balham and the temperature soared to 85°F. The Bedford Hotel had attracted another large crowd, far too many to gain entry and watch the drama inside, so people milled around outside, talking and trying to find some shade.

Inside, Dr George Johnson, the physician who had taken charge of the case, was giving evidence. He stood by the side of the table, which was covered by a sea of top hats and scattered papers, and surrounded by a huddle of lawyers. As he gave his answers in a calm, authoritative manner, the jury on his left keenly listened to his every word. After describing the immediate events after his arrival at The Priory, he was asked when poisoning was suspected. This is where we join the examination.

*

"After you had discussed the case with Dr Moore and Mr Harrison, had the word 'poison' been used?" William Carter asked from the head of the table, flanked by several court officials.

"No," he replied firmly, his tone matching his serious countenance. "When I first saw the patient he was lying in bed in a state of unconsciousness. We consulted together and agreed what should be done, but at this time nothing had been said as to poison. By that time he was becoming conscious."

"Did you ask Mr Bravo with regard to his condition?"

"Not at this time. Mr Bell asked me to go out of the bedroom to hear a statement by Mrs Cox. She said, 'When Mr Bravo was taken ill, he said to me – I have taken some of that poison, but don't tell Florence.'" At the rear of the room, reporters dipped their pens into inkwells, writing furiously.

"Did she name any particular poison?"

"No."

John Gorst MP, the heavily bearded lawyer representing the Crown, removed his monocle. "Did you see Mrs Bravo and Mrs Cox together?"

"Yes," Johnson replied, "when I happened to refer to Mrs Cox's statement that he had taken poison. Mrs Bravo said, 'Did he say that he had taken poison?'"

"Did she address that question to you?" Gorst enquired.

"No, she turned to Mrs Cox, who said, 'Yes, he did.'"

"And what did you think on hearing this exchange?"

"My first feeling was one of regret that I had referred to it. I was surprised that Mrs Bravo was not more astonished at hearing for the first time that her husband had taken poison."

"It was not what you have expected?"

"Scarcely." Johnson loosened his slim bow tie and took a sip of water. The room was hot and stuffy, and also infused with the unmistakable smell of alcohol. Many of the reporters, jurors and lawyers had enjoyed the hotel's hospitality and generous supply of liquor during the lunch break.

"In your experience, have you met with a case of suicide by antimony?" the Coroner asked.

"No, never."

"Suppose the antimony had been taken with the dinner. Would that have delayed its action?"

"Not much. I should think vomiting would occur at the table, but it would depend on the quantity of food."

"If antimony and Burgundy wine were taken together would the poison be much slower?"

"Yes, less energetic than a solution in water."

"Your opinion is that the poison must have been taken shortly before he was sick?"

"Probably."

"Would you go so far as to say it must have been so?"

Johnson paused and avoided answering the question directly. "The rule is that a large dose of antimony would take effect in a quarter of an hour afterwards."

"Are you able to speak of the quantity of antimony taken?"

"It must have been a very large quantity if as much as 10 grains were found outside the window after the rain."

"As much as 30 or 40 grains?"

"I should say 40 grains was the minimum quantity taken."

"If such a quantity had been taken by Mr Bravo in his food at dinner, what would have been the effect?"

"Do you mean how soon he would have vomited?" Johnson asked.

"Yes."

"I should think he would have been ill at the table."

The Coroner nodded to a jury member who had raised his hand. "Is it possible to take as much without tasting it?"

"It depends on how it was given. Antimony does not have much taste."

The Coroner asked: "How long did you remain at The Priory?"

"Nearly three hours. I saw the patient again at three o'clock the same day, and three times on the Thursday. Sir William Gull was there at 6:30pm on the Thursday and he told the patient he was alarmingly ill, and in fact he must consider himself a dying man."

"Was the patient not interviewed a second time by Sir William Gull?" the Coroner probed.

"Sir William Gull was called back into Mr Bravo's bedroom, and he said, 'I am afraid you have not told the whole truth.' Mr Bravo assured him that he had told the truth. I do not remember the exact words, but that is the substance."

"What did you suspect Mr Bravo was suffering from?"

"He was suffering terribly from vomiting, purging and agonising pains. I suspected he might have taken arsenic and took away some fluid for a chemist friend to test, which he did without finding any, arsenic being the only substance he looked for."

"Before the post-mortem, did you believe Mr Bravo had died from poison?"

"I knew it was some irritant poison, and I believed it was some metallic poison."

During the stultifying afternoon, Dr Johnson continued to answer questions from the lawyers in an assured and professional manner. There was little drama, in contrast to the first witness of the following morning. Outside the hotel, a huge crowd had gathered hoping to catch a glimpse of the inquest's star billing. Inside, all eyes were on Sir William Gull when he strode confidently into the billiard room and stood in front of the assembled lawyers. Nods of deference were exchanged like members of a country club acknowledging one another. His countenance exuded self-importance and entitlement. In a booming voice, he stated his name and address. Then the questioning began.

"How did you come to see Mr Bravo?" The Coroner enquired.

"On Thursday 20 April last I received a request in writing to see Mr Bravo." From inside his waistcoat, Gull plucked out a piece of paper which he waved theatrically. "I produce the letter, signed by Florence Bravo."

The letter was taken by the Coroner, who glanced at it before handing it to his officer. Gull continued: "Mrs Cox brought the note to me in my house. In consequence of which, I came to The Priory at Balham. An arrangement was made that I should go with Dr Johnson, and I did so."

George Lewis, a young, fiery lawyer with a resemblance to Nietzsche, sprang to his feet: "When you arrived had he communicated to you the symptoms of the patient?"

"Yes."

"Before you went into Mr Bravo's bedroom you were in entire ignorance of the statements Mr Bravo had made to the doctors?"

"I knew nothing of them."

"Were you also entirely in ignorance of the statement Mrs Cox made, that he had admitted to her that he had taken poison?"

"I believe so." Gull paused. "I have that impression." The affirmation was hardly categorical, suggesting he might have been informed of it by Dr Johnson.

"What did Mr Bravo say to you?"

"He used three expressions. He said to me, 'I took it myself', 'I took nothing but laudanum' and 'Before God, I only took laudanum'."

"Those were the only expressions he used at the first interview?"

"Except crying out with pain and distress, he made no other communication."

"Now, when you went back to Mr Bravo, did he say, in substance, that he had told you the truth?"

"He asked no question about the truth," Gull proclaimed. His confident tone could not disguise the fact that he had evaded answering the question.

"But he did state that he had told you the truth?" the lawyer repeated.

"No," Gull asserted, "he made no statement at all. He merely asked if I thought he was dying."

Lewis pounced on an apparent inconsistency. "Did he not say in the presence of Dr Johnson, 'I have told you the whole truth'?

The question hit a raw nerve: if Bravo had told the whole truth then Gull's opinion that it was a case of suicide was groundless. "I do not remember those words," Gull retorted dismissively, motioning with his hand as if to wave away the question.

"Are you aware that Dr Johnson has been examined?"

Gull's face flushed and he looked at the Coroner: "I cannot be cross-examined in this way!" he asserted haughtily. "It is unbecoming!"

"All you say is that you do not remember?"

"Yes."

"What is it you do not remember?" Lewis asked craftily.

"Ask the question, and I will tell you!" Gull fired back.

"You have said you do not remember?"

"Do not put your questions in that way. It is unfair!" The physician's tone was petulant. "I do not come here to equivocate, but to tell you all I know. You put questions to me as if I wished to equivocate."

Lewis was now stung, the duel becoming personal. "I beg to distinctly say that I never had such a thought."

"Your manner implies that you had," Gull snorted.

"Did Mr Bravo say anything about the truth?"

"He said nothing more."

"Did he, in your presence and in the presence of Dr George Johnson, say, 'I have told you the whole truth'?"

"I do not remember those words," he replied again.

Sir Henry James, who served as Gladstone's Solicitor General and represented the interests of Florence Bravo, leaned forward in his chair. Clean shaven, save for wiry muttonchop whiskers that framed his face, his appearance exuded gravitas. "Did he express to you any surprise at being told he was dying of poison?"

"No, and that surprised me."

"Why?"

"I think if I were to tell anyone here present who might be ill that they were dying of poison he would utter some expression of surprise. If he were cognizant of it he might say nothing, but otherwise I should think he would have made some exclamation."

"From his manner of talking to you did you think he had any suspicion of foul play?"

"No, none at all."

John Gorst rose. "You told this poor fellow he was dying from poison, and as he expressed no surprise you were astonished?"

"Yes."

"Were you aware that exactly the same thing had been told him two days before?"

"No I was not."

"Had not Dr Johnson told you of his having taken laudanum and his suspicion of an irritant poison?"

"Yes, and he said he had tested it for arsenic and found none." He then added churlishly, "That had thrown him off the scent."

Gorst returned to the line of questioning that had made Gull indignant earlier. "Can you remember the dying man saying that he was afraid you did not believe him and that he had spoken the truth?"

"I cannot remember that." He then added defensively, "I think the Court should know that in a case like this, in which I told a man he was poisoned and dying, I took upon myself a grave responsibility. Under these circumstances, things may be said or done which may escape the notice of one so engaged. You must remember, too, I was taken to see a man in disease and I found not a case of disease, but a case of poison, and my attention was likely drawn away from the external circumstances."

When Sir William Gull was excused, the prevailing but largely unspoken view was that the eminent witness had not distinguished himself. In particular, his last comment was inconsistent with the testimony of Dr Johnson, who was recalled a week later. George Lewis, the lawyer for Joseph Bravo, enquired what he and Sir William Gull discussed on the carriage ride to The Priory.

"I described the symptoms and Sir William Gull said, 'That looks like poisoning' and I said 'There can be no question as to that. It is clearly a case of poisoning. There are only two doubtful points: first, what is the exact nature of the poison and second, how did it get into the patient's stomach? I told him everything that I had seen of the case."

"Is it accurate that when Sir William Gull arrived he expected to see a case of disease?"

Johnson looked stunned. "I can hardly conceive that is possible unless he disbelieved all that I had told him, or had forgotten it. May I add that when Sir William Gull saw the patient he did not ask a single question with regard to his symptoms or how long he had been ill. He examined his abdomen and felt his pulse, but as he had heard the history of the case from me I believe he did not ask the patient a single question about his illness. Without knowledge of the previous history of the case he could not have told from merely looking at him he was poisoned. It might have been one of a dozen diseases."

It was an extraordinary statement and more or less accused the Queen's physician of showboating. Looking at his notes, a juryman reminded the court that Sir William had stated that he had been taken to see a man who had disease and not one who had taken poison.

"May I make a remark?" Johnson asked. The Coroner nodded. "It was that statement which astounded me. I could not believe he made it until I read it in four newspapers."

But Dr Johnson also faced some tough questions on his recall. John Murphy QC, counsel for Mrs Cox, was keen to plant the seed of suicide into the minds of the jury. He flicked through his documents, the light reflecting off his bald pate, which was more than compensated by his thick beard and busy hair around the side of his head. "Were you under the impression that it was a case of suicide?"

"I don't know how to answer that question." Johnson was more confident answering questions as to the cause of death as opposed to its manner.

Murphy adjusted his pince-nez. "On the Thursday, on your way down, did you tell Mr Henry Smith that your own impression at the time was that it was a case of suicide?"

"Very likely I might have said so. I don't remember."

Mr Lewis interposed. "Is it your impression now that it is a case of suicide?" Johnson fell silent and did not answer. He clearly harboured doubts about the death being a suicide but to deny it would be to imply that someone in the household was most likely guilty of murder.

Never shy to interject, Sir Henry James came to his aid. "Now you're making him a juryman!"

*

PART ONE

Members of the Cold Case Jury, the differences between Sir William Gull and Dr George Johnson led to a bitter professional dispute, almost a feud. It centred on Gull's claim that he did not know that it was a case of poisoning until he had examined Bravo. His area of expertise was disease and professional etiquette demanded he should have turned down Florence's request if he knew it was a poisoning case. But Johnson insisted he fully briefed Gull on the way to The Priory, telling him the cause was an irritant poison. Gull also gave the impression that he made both the diagnosis and prognosis by simply pulling back the bed sheet and looking at his patient. Further, by his own admission, he spent less than an hour at The Priory, while Dr Johnson visited five times in three days.

The disagreement was severe enough for the men to appear before the Censors of the College of Physicians, which diplomatically found in favour of neither. *The Lancet* was less cautious, saying it found the contradictions in Gull's testimony "too flagrant to be capable of reconciliation." Of the two, the more probative views about the cause of Bravo's death came from Dr Johnson. Under questioning from Henry James, he also confirmed that Gull had asked Bravo, "Whatever you took you took it yourself?" To which Bravo had replied "Yes." This might account for Dr Johnson's initial view that it was a suicide.

The testimony of other doctors added to the picture painted by Dr Johnson. Mr Henry Smith, a fellow of the College of Surgeons who knew Charles Bravo well, said he was easily moved to excitement, particularly during arguments. On the day after the poisoning Dr Johnson had informed him that he believed it to be a case of suicide. Smith concurred with the view that Charles Bravo's calling out for hot water showed he was anxious to get rid of something he had ingested. There was nothing in the post-mortem to rule out that he had first taken a large dose of laudanum and then taken tartar emetic to eject it. He conceded, however, that in his 26 years of experience, he had never known this to occur.

Mr Royes Bell stated that Mrs Cox informed the doctors about Bravo's alleged statement of having taken poison after he regained consciousness, although he was not sure Mrs Cox was aware that he was awake when she spoke to them. Bell was Charles Bravo's cousin and said he was "scrupulously truthful to a fault" and outspoken.

Dr Moore, the first doctor on the scene, found the victim lying back against a chair, unconscious, with a pulse so weak that his heart had almost stopped. The doctor's initial opinion was that the patient was under the influence of a narcotic poison. Bravo regained consciousness at about three o'clock in the morning, he believed, and refused to take laudanum when offered to relieve the pain.

George Harrison stated that on his arrival Mrs Cox had told him, "I'm sure he's taken chloroform". The lawyers pressed the doctor about whether Mrs Cox's delay in informing him about Bravo's alleged confessional would have made any difference to the treatment and whether a stomach pump would have saved his life. Harrison insisted the patient was too weak and had one been used it would have killed him instantly.

After the heat of Sir William Gull's appearance, the next witness provided more light. Professor Redwood proved to be the most instructive about the poison that killed Charles Bravo. He first launched into great detail about the chemical tests he had performed, losing everyone in the room, before turning his attention to his findings. We now briefly return to the Bedford Hotel to hear his key points of evidence.

*

"I found, on analysis of the vomited matter, no arsenic or mercury," Redwood said slowly, his hands resting on the edge of the billiard table in front of a medical bag and several small bottles. Sporting an English moustache, a full beard and bushy eyebrows, he was the modern stereotype of a professor.

"But I found lead and antimony. The presence of lead a little obscured the result of the first investigation, but when I had eliminated it I had no difficulty in getting abundant and very conclusive evidence of antimony. The presence of the lead was afterwards explained to me, though I did not know at the time, from the fact that the vomit having been scraped up from the lead gutter."

"What was the result of the analysis?" the Coroner asked.

"The whole of the vomited matter would have yielded a quantity of antimony equal to 10 grains. I also found distinct evidence of antimony in the liver."

"You're quite sure that it was antimony and no other poison in the body of the deceased?"

"I made my examination most carefully, and have not the slightest doubt of the presence of antimony. I did not detect arsenic. I sought for it, but found none."

"Can you tell from analysis whether it was antimony proper, tartar emetic or butter of antimony which you found?"

"Not from analysis, but from the symptoms I conclude that it was tartar emetic. The effect of butter of antimony mixed with water would not be so speedy, it would not pass into and affect the whole system, as tartar emetic does, and there would be violent inflammation of the stomach, which was absent in this case." Having confirmed the antimony was ingested in the form of tartar emetic, the words "antimony" and "tartar emetic" were used interchangeably.

Sir Henry James, who was charging an eye-watering 100 guineas a day to represent Florence, stood. "Could you tell how much tartar emetic was ingested by the deceased?"

"From the evidence, the quantity taken by the deceased could not have been less than 20 grains, and probably ranged between 20 and 40 grains."

"Assuming the deceased absorbed 30 grains taken in the Burgundy, and assuming he drank one third of the bottle, you would come to the conclusion that the bottle contained 90 grains?"

"Yes, at the very least."

James rubbed his whiskers. "Would that amount be readily dissolved in wine?"

"If the person put it in a bottle and shook it, I don't expect that the whole would be dissolved in any reasonable time."

"What would be the effect of drinking back four ounces of water with 40 grains of antimony in it?"

"The first effect would be nausea." The professor paused, pursing his lips as he marshalled his thoughts. "Although there are several cases recorded where quantities of 30 to 40 grains have been taken into the stomach without vomiting, but where they immediately produced depressing effects and killed the patient. In other cases, where there was vomiting within 10 to 15 minutes, the tartar emetic was thrown off the stomach and the patient recovered."

"What is considered the usual dose to produce vomiting?"

"Two grains. In fact, chemists keep it in solution in the proportion of two grains to one ounce of water. Drinking one ounce is supposed to produce its vomiting effect in half an hour – sometimes more, sometimes less."

"And what would be the first symptom following the taking of antimony?"

"I should expect an acute pain in the stomach to follow almost immediately."

"Would the deceased have been able to taste any antimony in water?"

"Antimony in water would be practically tasteless." Redwood picked up a phial from the table and held it up like a magician in the middle of his act. "This bottle contains 40 grains of antimony in four ounces of distilled water." With a pop, he uncorked it. A profound silence of disbelief engulfed the crowded room as he picked up a small wine glass in his other hand. Jurors leaned forward in their seats in rapt attention like eager students. The same thought was held in every mind: he's surely not going to drink any!

The professor carefully poured some of the solution from the phial into the glass. He raised the wine glass to the room as to make a toast but then tipped it back. He washed the liquid around his mouth before spitting into a bowl in front of him. "It can be held in the mouth without any taste being perceived."

"May I?" asked James, motioning for the glass. Like a wine connoisseur, he gently swirled the colourless liquid in the glass and placed his nose above. He cautiously sampled the potentially deadly solution.

"May we try?" a juror asked eagerly. Like a ritual, the glass was solemnly passed to the young man.

"Please do not swallow any," Redwood advised, passing the bowl. "The solution you have tried may be regarded as a strong one." The understatement caused a ripple of nervous laughter.

"I just did!" retorted the juryman, handing the glass to a fellow juror. There was a collective gasp. "But I can feel nothing wrong with my throat!" The tension broken, laughter rang out.

"Is such a solution made quickly with cold water?" James asked.

"If 40 grains of tartar emetic were put into a bottle of distilled water and shaken up, it would all dissolve. It would take a little longer without heat."

"You said distilled water. What about ordinary water?"

"It would dissolve. The taste is likely to be even less noticeable in ordinary water."

"If it were taken in Burgundy and with food, would the action be considerably delayed?" George Lewis asked.

"I should expect that the action would be delayed."

"We have heard from Mr Bravo's father," the young lawyer continued, "that the deceased went to Jamaica several times without being sick. Would antimony take longer to act on a stomach not easily nauseated?"

Redwood nodded. "I should expect it would, but I cannot speak from practical experience of such cases."

"Is it possible to determine whether the antimony was taken all at once?"

"No. Part of it might have been taken at dinner and part after."

"Could the tartar emetic be taken in the Burgundy without being detected?"

"I think it is possible that 30 grains were taken in half a bottle of Burgundy without detection." The professor hesitated before adding, "But I would be surprised to find the emetic effects of such a quantity deferred for an hour and a half."

"Would that be impossible in your opinion?"

"No, it's not impossible."

For the rest of the afternoon, the professor patiently fielded questions from lawyers and jurors. It was a distinguished performance from an eminent scientist.

*

Members of the Cold Case Jury, the juror who swallowed some of Redwood's solution was not sick at the inquest. Yet, by my rough calculation, as little as a couple of teaspoons would have contained two grains of tartar emetic, the standard dose

86

to make someone sick. Presumably he sipped a very small quantity, considerably less than a mouthful, or had been joking.

Redwood also stated that he had been requested at the end of May to test any medicines and wine bottles from The Priory for the presence of antimony. Rowe retrieved over a dozen used bottles of Burgundy, and not surprisingly, all tested negative. It was a futile exercise. If the wine had been poisoned it would have been after it was decanted and left on the sideboard. It was a similar story with the testing of the medicines and bottles retrieved from different rooms in the house. Even if there had been something to find earlier, it was all too late a month after Bravo's death.

The chloroform bottle from Bravo's bedroom was never found. However, despite Mrs Cox's insistence that she smelt its distinctive sweet odour on the stricken man, we can be certain he had not ingested any. A corrosive substance, it would have burnt Bravo's mouth, throat and oesophagus, but all were unaffected according to the post-mortem. Yet the little bottle was empty save for just one drop when it was examined by Mr Harrison that night. Could this seemingly trivial detail be an important clue? We will return to its significance later when we reconstruct the different ways Charles Bravo might have died.

Redwood left little doubt that antimony was ingested as tartar emetic, most likely dissolved in water which would be undetectable to anyone who drank it. It was estimated that Charles Bravo ingested about 30 grains of tartar emetic. A fatal dose is considered to be 10 grains, but this varies considerably with the circumstances. One man survived after taking nearly ten times the amount Bravo ingested.

Before we move on, I think a brief summary of the medical evidence would be helpful.

- The antimony was almost certainly ingested as tartar emetic.
- Bravo ingested approximately 30 grains, about two grams, of tartar emetic.
- If the tartar emetic had been ingested with the wine then most probably Bravo would have been sick at the dinner table or in the morning room.
- Most likely a teaspoon of the powder was dissolved in water.
- After ingestion, the first symptoms are likely to progress from acute stomach pain to nausea and violent vomiting {see *Exhibit 5* for details of the poison and its effects}.

During his controversial ride to The Priory with Sir William Gull, Dr Johnson stated there were two questions to answer: what was the poison and how did Bravo ingest it? Medical science had answered the first. The Priory servants would next find themselves in the crosshairs of the squabbling lawyers, who each sought a different answer to the second question depending on the interests of his client. What was the view of those who worked downstairs? Could the case turn on a trivial detail they had observed? And what would the returning George Griffith say about his remarkable prophecy? All would be revealed as the inquest entered its second week.

Chapter 7

THE VIEW FROM DOWNSTAIRS

The weekend had seen the capital bathed in glorious sunshine and roasting temperatures. The fine weather persisted into the new week and the first servant to be called, the butler Frederick Rowe, gave evidence on one of the hottest days of the summer.

As it had been since the inquest opened, the stuffy billiard room was packed with lawyers, reporters and onlookers. By 10:30 am, when the Coroner resumed the inquest, the outside temperature was already nearly 80°F and conditions inside the hotel were uncomfortable. All the sash windows were wide open in a vain attempt to entice a little breeze inside to reduce the oppressive heat.

Under examination from the Coroner, Rowe described relations between Mr and Mrs Bravo. They appeared to be a happy couple and he had never witnessed them quarrel. The only tension he had observed was when Charles Bravo refused to write cheques to pay bills. The next line of questioning focused on the events surrounding the dinner, especially the wine consumed. This is where we pick up his evidence.

*

Standing straight-backed by the table, Rowe was handed his neatly written cellar book which kept records of the wine bought and consumed at The Priory. Holding it open like a prayer book, he announced, "For the ten days between 9 and 18 April, the quantity was a dozen bottles of Marsala, five of sherry, one bottle of port, one quart of Champagne, seven bottles of Burgundy and one of best Champagne."

Even allowing for entertaining, it was a substantial consumption. Mr Gorst, representing the Crown, inquired further. "Mr Bravo usually drank Burgundy?"

"Yes."

"And if he drank Burgundy he would not drink sherry too?"

"No," the butler replied, closing his book and placing it on the table before him.

"There was a great deal of sherry drunk in the house. Who drank it?"

"Mrs Bravo and Mrs Cox."

"Did they ever drink Burgundy?"

"The ladies stuck to Marsala and sherry." A few eyebrows were raised; the two ladies were quaffing nearly two bottles every day.

"To the best of your belief, was the bottle of Burgundy in the cellaret all afternoon?"

"I don't recollect when I decanted it."

"If you decanted for luncheon it would be there?"

"Yes."

"Did you expect Mr Bravo to luncheon that day?"

"I don't remember whether I did or not."

"Where did you decant the wine?"

"In the pantry."

"When did you decant it for dinner?" Gorst enquired again.

"A quarter of an hour before, if it were needed."

"You thought there was something wrong with Mr Bravo at dinner?"

"Yes."

"It was not from the horse running away?"

"I put it down to the horse."

"But now you think it was not the horse?"

"I do not know what it was."

"Well, to put it plainly, do you think Mr Bravo was poisoned before dinner?"

"I do not know."

"Did you see Mr Bravo return from his horse ride?"

"No. I went to the morning room to look at the fire, and saw him sitting at the side of it. I think this was about half past six or quarter to seven. He was leaning forward in his chair. He looked very pale and his mouth was drawn; he looked ill. Mr Bravo did not seem to notice me. I closed the door so very quietly, thinking Mrs Bravo was asleep on the couch."

"Did Mr Bravo ring the bell later?"

"Yes, he told me to ask the servant to get him a bath. I asked Mr Bravo whether I should light a fire in his bedroom. Mrs Bravo answered for her husband, 'Yes, of course.' And I did so."

Through the open windows, a shriek of a whistle pierced the room. As a train thundered across the arched bridge by the hotel, the floor shook and the top hats danced in unison on the rack. The heat was now almost unbearable; female onlookers fanned themselves while the men dabbed the sweat from their brows with handkerchiefs.

Gorst moved on to Mr Bravo's reaction over dinner when he was shown the photograph of the Worthing house by Mrs Cox. "Was his expression, 'I shall not be there'?"

"Yes," Rowe asserted confidently.

"Did you ever tell anyone that the expression was 'I shall not live to see it'?"

"No, sir. I remember him saying that he should not see it."

"But you did not mention one word of this when you gave your statement in May?"

"I thought I was boring the gentleman. He said to me, 'I suppose you mean that Mr Bravo was agreeable to it?' and I said 'Yes'."

"Now be fair, Rowe, you did not mention it because you did not remember it, did you?"

"I believe I should have thought of it had they given me more time; but they left that point and went on to other things. I first told Mr Campbell after I had given my statement."

"And you did not state then that Mr Bravo said he should not live to see it?"

Rowe was adamant. "No, sir."

As Florence's father never gave evidence, this point was never corroborated. The experienced lawyer now focused on another matter. "Did you go up to town last Friday week to see Mrs Cox?"

"No, sir."

Gorst knew Rowe was being economical with the truth, and rephrased his question to obtain the answer he wanted. "Did you go to town last Friday week?"

"Yes."

"Where did you go to?"

Flustered, Rowe responded, "I did not know where I was going." Perhaps realising the foolishness of his response, he added "I went to Mr Bravo's office."

"Before this enquiry began?"

"Yes."

"And when you came back did you come into this very room, and say anything to Mr Willis, the proprietor of this place?"

"Yes," Rowe responded without volunteering further detail.

"Did you say, 'I am not going to get into trouble, I shall tell the whole truth'?"

"I said that Mrs Cox had been speaking the truth and will get into trouble for it, and perhaps I will too."

"Was that all you said?"

Rowe was agitated and evasive. "It amounts to nothing."

"Was that all you said?"

"I'm trying to remember," Rowe shot back defensively. He hesitated. "I might have said something about a fine mess or something like that."

"That's what we're all getting into," Sir Henry James quipped.

Like the changing of the guard, Gorst sat down and another lawyer rose. George Lewis, Mr Joseph Bravo's representative, again focused on the Burgundy at dinner. "Was the bottle of Burgundy finished?"

"I cleared away the dinner things and my impression is that a portion of the Burgundy must have remained in the bottle."

"Did you ever see the remains of that bottle of Burgundy afterwards?"

"I cannot swear that I did or that I didn't," Rowe answered cagily.

"What usually happened?"

"The Burgundy was decanted into a large bottle similar to that used for the sherry."

"Can you tell me whether the next day that bottle of Burgundy was placed on the table?"

"I believe it was, but I cannot remember."

*

Members of the Cold Case Jury, the fate of the Burgundy was important. Although many of the doctors believed the tartar emetic was most likely dissolved in water, it was not certain, and it remained a possibility that the red wine had been spiked. The effects of the alcohol in conjunction with Bravo's apparently strong constitution could have delayed the onset of symptoms. The bottle needed to be identified, if only to eliminate it as the source. Yet, it appears Rowe could not remember what had happened to it. Perhaps this was understandable given the traumatic events that engulfed the household shortly after dinner, but it was not the butler's only memory failure. As we have seen, he also claimed he could not remember when he had decanted the Burgundy that day. Again, this seems entirely reasonable until we read Chief Inspector Clarke's report dated 11 May:

I wish to particularly call attention to the butler's statement as to his having brought the wine from the cellar and decanting it that afternoon and leaving it on the sideboard where what remained after dinner was again placed, and he is unable to say what became of it. Further, it is his belief that it was consumed by the medical gentlemen during the night. I have questioned each medical gentleman about this point and they state most emphatically that they did not drink any Burgundy on Tuesday night and I am unable to gather what became of it.

Rowe had told the chief inspector that he decanted the wine in the afternoon and the doctors had consumed the remainder. It appears Clarke was open to the possibility that someone might have tampered with the wine before dinner, especially as the doctors had not finished the wine as Rowe initially believed. Had the butler tried to imply the wine was not the source of the poison? Or did he later realise he was mistaken and became more guarded with his statements at the inquest?

The mislaid bottle of Burgundy was not the only curiosity of the butler's evidence. His recollection of Bravo's dismissive reaction to the Worthing photograph at dinner was denied by both Mrs Cox and Florence, who sat next to her husband at dinner and claimed to have heard nothing of the sort. Edward Smith, the footman who assisted Rowe in the dining room that night, was not asked about the incident, and failed to volunteer any information to confirm or deny it.

Rowe believed the women did not appreciate the significance of what Bravo said and further observed that he "appeared out of sorts with everything that night", possibly due to the horse's bolting and his father's admonishing letter. It is difficult to reconcile the different accounts. Did Rowe want to leave the impression that Charles was not in a stable state of mind that night? It seems implausible to believe the butler fabricated this incident because it was obviously deniable by the others present.

Although she did not confirm the specific incident at dinner, Mrs Cox would later testify that Charles was reluctant to travel to Worthing due to the expense. Yet, on the Wednesday morning after his collapse, Charles ruefully told Keeber that they would not be having their "little trip to Worthing", suggesting he had been intending to travel. The dismissal of the trip is probably trivial, but could it be linked to the timing of the poisoning? This is a point to mull over, and we will return to it later.

The most interesting aspect of Rowe's evidence concerned his meeting with Mrs Cox in London on Friday 7 July, just days before the inquest opened. This was not by chance. Ann Campbell, Florence's mother, had invited him, which hints at some level of coordination prior to the second inquest. In his evidence, Charles Willis, the owner of the Bedford Hotel, claimed he spoke to Rowe later the same day and Rowe had told him that he had seen Mrs Cox in London. Willis remembers it because he was surprised, believing Mrs Cox was staying in Birmingham. Rowe then said, "I have seen her, poor old woman, and she has got herself into a great deal of trouble through not telling the truth." Willis confirmed that Rowe had used the phrase "not telling the truth", although Rowe stated the opposite when examined. The publican also remembered Rowe telling him that he was "not going to get himself into trouble hereafter" and he intended to "tell all the truth." I suggest this detail is pivotal in determining who was correct; the conversation makes sense only if Rowe said, in effect, "Mrs Cox has lied but I will tell the truth to avoid her fate."

Strangely, the significance of the proprietor's statement was not widely recognised at the time, perhaps because it was based on a casual remark made in the pub, but it was a bombshell: Rowe was aware that Mrs Cox had lied. We are left wondering about the exact nature of the falsehoods, and her motivation, but the butler certainly knew more than he was prepared to divulge. Never recalled, his apparent evasiveness leaves a vague aftertaste of suspicion.

The next servant to provide evidence was 24-year-old Mary Ann Keeber, who was questioned at length about the events on the night of the poisoning. To hear some of what she said, we now return to the Bedford Hotel on the morning of Tuesday 18 July 1876, when she is recalling events immediately prior to Charles Bravo's collapse.

*

"When I came out of the dining room Mr Bravo came out of the morning room." The petite housemaid spoke in a soft but assured voice. "I knew he was going upstairs, so I let him go before me. I had the wine for Mrs Bravo in my hand then. As he was going up the stairs he turned round and looked at me twice, but did not speak. I thought how queer he looked."

Sitting daintily beside the table, she looked at the male lawyers and court officials across a sea of top hats strewn across the table like tall ships in a harbour. To her left, the all-male jury scrutinised her, some scribbling notes.

"Explain what you mean by 'queer'?" the Coroner probed.

"He looked very strange from what I had ever seen him." She paused. "He was very pale."

"Did he appear in pain?"

"No, I thought perhaps he might be angry because he did not speak to me. He always used to speak with me whenever we met. He went into Mrs Bravo's dressing room and I went into Mrs Bravo's bedroom with the wine."

An older member of the jury raised his hand, and the Coroner nodded. "At the time, did you think Mr Bravo might have been angry because of his horse ride?"

Keeber turned to look at the jury. "I had not heard Mr Bravo had been overriding, and did not think that it might account for his being cross."

After describing her final duties that night, Keeber recalled the moment Charles Bravo raised the alarm. "I went to the bottom of the first flight of stairs and Mr Bravo opened his bedroom door. He was in his nightshirt and called 'Florence' twice and 'Hot water!' very loudly. I rushed into Mrs Bravo's bedroom and said 'Mr Bravo is ill, will you come?' Mrs Cox rose and went into Mr Bravo's bedroom. I stood at the door. Mr Bravo was then standing by the window. I heard him cry out for hot water. Mrs Cox then said to me, 'Fetch hot water' and I went downstairs for it."

George Lewis, counsel for Joseph Bravo, hurriedly scribbled a note: the housemaid had said nothing about Charles speaking to Mrs Cox. Keeber explained to the Coroner she had followed Mrs Cox's instructions, rushing to collect hot water, mustard and spirit of camphor. "Mrs Cox told me to put his feet into mustard and water, and I did so. I said to her, 'What is the matter with him?' She said, 'Rub him as hard as you can.'" The housemaid recalled that she was later instructed to fetch more hot water. "While I was in the kitchen, Mrs Bravo came and said, 'Rowe, fetch someone. Mr Bravo is ill. He is dying!' and he said, 'Mr Harrison is sent for'. She said, 'Get someone nearer! I don't mind who it is.' She was very much distressed."

The perceptive foreman of the jury, Mark Cattley, raised his hand. The Coroner nodded. "Did she assign any reason for giving him the mustard?"

Keeber turned to her left again. "No."

"What was your idea?"

"I know they give people mustard and water to make them sick."

"Did she not tell you why he was to be made sick?"

"No."

The foreman, asking questions like a seasoned lawyer, continued: "And not a word was said about poison?"

"No."

Another member of the jury asked: "When he called out, how far was Mr Bravo from the bedroom in which Mrs Bravo and Mrs Cox were?"

"Quite close. The two rooms adjoin each other."

Mr Gorst continued the examination of the witness. "So someone in that room might have heard him call out?"

"I don't know why they did not hear him."

"When you left the room earlier, did you shut the door?"

"There are two doors. I don't remember shutting more than one. To the best of my belief, the outer baize one was not shut."

"And when Mr Bravo came onto the landing, how did he call out?"

"Loudly and impatiently."

"And what did you find when you returned to Mrs Bravo's bedroom?"

"Mrs Cox was where I left her – sitting by the side of the bed. Neither she or Mrs Bravo had risen to answer Mr Bravo's cry."

"And Mrs Bravo was asleep?"

"I don't know whether she was asleep or awake." Keeber paused, smiling faintly. "I think she was asleep because if she had heard the cry she would have got up."

"Did you or Mrs Cox first come out of Mrs Bravo's bedroom?"

"I let Mrs Cox pass. On entering his room she went right to the opposite side of the bed, and up to the open widow where Mr Bravo was standing. I did not go further than the door. He then cried out again for hot water. I did not actually see him vomit out of the window." Keeber sipped some water from a tumbler as proceedings were temporarily interrupted when another train rattled past the hotel.

"Were you aware that night that Mr Bravo had taken poison?"

"No," she replied, gently replacing the glass on the table. "I talked with Mrs Bravo at Brighton about his being poisoned with antimony."

"What did she say?"

"She said Mr Bravo had died from antimony poisoning but she could not account for it."

"Did she say any more than that?"

"No, sir."

"Did she not say how he got it?"

Irritated, Sir Henry James threw up his hands. "Surely you ought to tell the witness what you mean by 'got it'?"

Gorst's face flushed with priggish indignation. "I must really object, Mr Coroner, to being called to order by my friend Sir

Henry James, who has no position here which enables him to object to my questions."

Henry James, not one for backing down, retorted, "I do have a position here."

Fearing an argument he could not control, the Coroner replied, "I think the question objected to might…" He paused, wishing to steer the most diplomatic course. "…be put in another shape."

The knight of the realm was having none of it. "The phrase 'how he got it' may mean how he bought the poison or how it got into his body." Looking sternly at Gorst, "Will you explain to the witness what you mean?"

The Coroner retreated by making a note. Rather than accepting the validity of the objection, Gorst simply asked the housemaid, "What did Mrs Bravo say to you?"

"She said she did not know how it came into his body and could not account for it in any way. That is what she said to me." It was probably not the exact words, but the intelligent housekeeper had conveyed what she believed Florence meant, to silence the bickering lawyers.

"And did Mrs Bravo not say that he must have taken it himself?"

"Yes."

Sir Henry James asked about Mr Bravo's usual routines. "Mr Bravo was in the habit of cleaning his teeth frequently," Keeber explained, "and I should think he always used a tumblerful of water in doing so. He used to clean his teeth during the day. I had to fill up the water bottle afterwards, and the next morning I always found a considerable portion of the water gone."

"So presumably he drank the water during the night?"

"I don't know if he was in the habit of drinking water at night."

"And did you notice the condition of the water bottle on the night he was taken ill?"

"No, I did not observe it."

"And the next morning?"

"I had a lot to attend to the next morning and did not notice the water bottle."

"So, it could have been emptied or changed?"

"As far as I know nothing was done to the water bottle during the night."

*

Members of the Cold Case Jury, in light of the scientific evidence that the tartar emetic was most likely ingested through contaminated water, the last exchange is important. Mary Ann Keeber knew that Charles almost always used the bottled water at night or first thing in the morning. A jug on the washstand was used for washing and other ablutions, the bottle by the foot of the bed was only for drinking; this is why a tumbler was placed on top. Therefore, she must have known he regularly drank from it, probably at night, and yet her answer was strangely guarded on this point.

Later, another witness confirmed Charles Bravo always drank water at night. John Atkinson was a close friend and colleague who had known Bravo for over 12 years. They had shared a house when they were at Oxford together and also chambers at Essex Court Temple. He stated that, before retiring to bed, Charles "always took a large drink of cold water, very often from the water bottle without pouring it into a tumbler. This was his invariable habit... He very often used my water bottle." On a recent trip to Paris together, about a year before he was married, he noticed Charles had maintained this habit.

The friend's testimony was revealing. If Bravo took a large drink from the water bottle soon after entering his room at 9:30pm on the Tuesday night, it would account for him being violently sick about 20 minutes later. Atkinson also insisted that his high-spirited friend was the "last person in the world" to take his own life. His view was consistent with every friend, relation and colleague. In which case, the mystery still remained: when had the tartar emetic been deposited in the water bottle, by whom, and why?

With respect to the first of these questions, Mary Ann provided a tantalising clue during her examination: "I filled up the bottle on the Tuesday evening after he came down to dinner... I tidied up his room after his bath and when he dressed for dinner... I filled up his water bottle that evening, probably half a pint had gone when I filled it up." From this, it appears that in the evening the housemaid topped up the water rather than completely changing it. This is important: it means the water could have been laced with poison at any time during the day. It should also be emphasised that she was the last known person to have touched the water bottle on the Tuesday evening before Charles Bravo collapsed.

Another important insight of Keeber's testimony regarded the state of the marriage. As housemaid and acting ladies' maid, she was frequently in the presence of both Charles and Florence, and observed no bitterness or arguments between the newlywed couple. On the contrary, she stated that Charles treated his wife with "the greatest of affection", confirming Rowe's evidence.

Despite the clarity of Keeber's testimony, there was one oddity. It concerned the wine she brought to Florence's dressing room on the Tuesday night. Chief Inspector Clarke wrote in his report of 5 June:

Mary Ann Keeber further states that when she saw Mr Bravo on the stairs she was then taking a bottle of sherry to her mistress.

Yet, at both inquests Keeber clearly stated it was a glass of Marsala she fetched for Florence, a detail confirmed by both Florence and Mrs Cox. One might reasonably conclude that Clarke had made an error, but at the second inquest she was pressed on whether she had told the same thing to William Campbell, Florence's elder brother. She did not remember telling him that, she replied. If it was a bottle of sherry, it would certainly explain why Charles went into Florence's bedroom to remonstrate with his wife in French, another point that Keeber declared she did not remember telling William. These trivial details do not affect the fundamentals of the case, yet they might indicate Mary Ann glossed over some details to paint Florence in a better light. Again, one is left wondering whether the servants knew more than they were prepared to say.

In addition to the butler and the housemaid, other servants were called. Ellen Stone, the cook, confirmed the menu of the Tuesday night and that nothing unusual occurred during the preparation of the meal. More significantly, all of the remaining food was eaten by servants the next day with no ill effects. Charles Parton recalled hearing no arguments on the several occasions he drove Mr and Mrs Bravo to London, including on the day of the poisoning. These examinations were cursory, filling in a detail here and there. But there was one servant the inquest was eager to interrogate at length, and that was the seer – former coachman, George Griffith.

Chapter 8

THE PROPHET SPEAKS

George Griffith was a coachman in the service of Dr Gully at Malvern from 1862 until the doctor's retirement in 1871. In that year, on the recommendation of Dr Gully, Griffith was employed by Florence Ricardo. Two years later, after marrying Florence's maid, he and his wife left Florence's service because she was unable to accommodate married staff, a situation that changed when she moved to The Priory. She invited them back, and they returned in May 1875, only for George to be sacked six months later at the instigation of Charles Bravo in his obsessive pursuit of retrenching the household expenditure. Both the coachman and his wife were forced to leave the relative luxury of the lodge nestled in The Priory's beautiful grounds and seek new employment.

Griffith had a grievance, for sure, and he was a person of great interest because of both his prediction and his direct connection to the poison and Florence's former lover. We return to the Bedford Hotel, where he stands before the pack of lawyers hungry for answers.

*

PART ONE

"Mrs Ricardo kept three horses, a brougham horse and a pair of cobs," the 35-year-old horseman stated briskly. His wiry frame, clean-shaven face and working-class accent set him apart from the lawyers and officials huddled around the large table.

"I was in the habit of giving those horses tartar emetic." His eyes darted nervously from one lawyer to the next, until they returned to the stern gaze of Mr Gorst, counsel for the Crown, who stood opposite, one hand on hip, the other holding his monocle. Griffith added hurriedly: "I bought it in a white powder – a quarter of an ounce, that's all they would sell – and I made it into a lotion for sores on the shoulders of the horses. I bought some from a chemist in Streatham and from Mr Smith, the chemist in Balham, next to the station."

"And when did you buy it from Mr Smith?" Gorst enquired.

"I cannot tell when I bought that quarter of an ounce, but it was during the time I was at The Priory. I paid four pence, I think."

"And you turned it into a lotion, you say?"

"I dissolved it all at once, making a pint and a half bottle; enough for 50 treatments."

"How did you learn about it?"

"From a recipe in a book called *The Pocket Farrier*. I don't know the name of the author. It belonged to my father."

"And what was the lotion used for?"

"Treating worms. I used it on the big chestnut – the brougham horse; he used to have boils and things about him."

"And did Mrs Ricardo know about this treatment?"

"I don't know whether my mistress knew that I used it." Griffiths hesitated. "I never told her of it."

"Where did you keep the bottle?"

"In the cupboard in the corner of the stable. It was corked and labelled 'poison'."

Gorst fell silent as he sorted through his papers before him. He placed a small ledger on top of the pile and locked eyes with his quarry. "While you were with Dr Gully, did you give his horses tartar emetic?"

"If they wanted it." His answer made it sound like the animals had requested the treatment.

"Did you?" counsel pressed.

"Yes. Horses want physicking as well as anyone else." His personification of the horses was now met with laughter. Griffith looked around, bemused and clueless, adding to the hilarity.

Gorst managed a gentle smile as he waited patiently for the clamour to subside. "Can you name the Malvern chemist where you bought the quarter of an ounce?"

"No, sir."

Gorst readied his attack. "Did you ever buy more than a quarter of an ounce?"

"No, sir." Without any need, the coachman embellished his answer. "Never in my life."

The wily lawyer pounced. He picked up the ledger, opened it at a bookmarked page and handed it to the hapless witness. "This is a Sales of Poison Register," he boomed, "kept in pursuance with an Act of Parliament by Mr Clark, the chemist at Malvern. Do you recognise your handwriting?"

Griffith returned the book. "Yes, sir," he replied meekly, bracing himself for what was to come.

"It states that on 11 June 1869 you signed for two ounces of tartar emetic. And the name of the purchaser?" Gorst paused for maximum impact. "Dr Gully." A low murmur rippled through the room. "Did Dr Gully know of your buying that?"

"I'm not sure."

"Will you undertake to say that you did not take a note from Dr Gully when you purchased that two ounces of tartar emetic?"

"No, I could not undertake to say because I'm not sure whether I did or not."

"And why did you buy such a very large quantity as two ounces? You told us earlier that a quarter of an ounce would be enough for 50 applications, so that two ounces would be enough for 400. How many horses were you looking after then?"

"Two or three." Even Griffith realised he needed to give some sort of explanation. "I did not want to give it to them all at once. You may keep it for years, and use it when you want."

"So you had a store of tartar emetic to last you for years?"

"Yes, sir."

Gorst sat down, knowing he had left the impression that the tartar emetic could have come from Dr Gully's supply. George Lewis, the ambitious lawyer for the Bravo family, leapt from his seat. "Who dismissed you from Mrs Ricardo's service?"

Sir Henry James leaned forward. "Wait a moment, Mr Lewis, you haven't established whether he was dismissed." After the Coroner shot a glance at the interposer, James leaned back in his chair and muttered, "I suppose it's not worthwhile to discuss the point."

Lewis repeated his question: "Who dismissed you?"

"Mrs Ricardo."

"Not Mr Bravo?"

"I was never in his service. And I never saw him after he was married."

Not satisfied, Lewis asked again: "Who dismissed you?"

"Mrs Ricardo. That is Mrs Bravo now. She gave me a month's notice before she was married."

"Did she tell you why?"

Griffith scratched his nose. "She said it was because Mr Bravo did not wish me to drive her. She told me that, and I believed her. And I would be there now if it hadn't been for him."

"Did she say why he did not wish that?"

"Because I was not careful enough to drive in London."

Lewis now changed tack. "Had you driven Dr Gully?"

"Yes. Mrs Ricardo and Mrs Cox were generally with him."

"How often?"

"Two or three times a week."

"Where was Gully taken up?"

Griffith frowned. "What do you mean, taken up?"

James leaned forward, "I suppose the witness thinks you mean 'taken up' in a different sense." Pleased with his quip, he reclined in his chair and enjoyed the hearty male laughter. The few women in the room looked uncomfortable.

Smiling, Lewis rephrased his question. "Where did you pick him up?"

"Sometimes by the side of the road or at his house."

"And had Dr Gully ever spoken to you about Mrs Ricardo's marriage?"

"No, sir."

"Knowing you were to leave Mrs Bravo's service, did you seek a reference from Dr Gully?"

"Yes, I spoke to him about my character, thinking Mrs Bravo would not give me one."

"And you went to his house?"

"Yes, while Mrs Bravo was away at Brighton."

"And you're saying no reference was made to Mrs Bravo's marriage at all?"

"He might have spoken about it," Griffith replied, blissfully unaware he had contradicted an earlier answer of his. Lewis pressed him on the details of the conversation.

"What did he say?"

"He said it was a great pity that I was going to leave, and that he hoped Mrs Bravo would be happy."

"Was Mr Bravo's name mentioned?"

"No, sir."

"Will you swear that?"

"Yes."

"Do you remember the day that Mr Bravo was to be married?"

"Yes."

"Now be very careful," Lewis warned the witness. "Did you express the opinion that he would not live long?"

"Not that I recollect," Griffith replied, trying to bat away the awkward question.

"Will you swear you did not do so?"

"I cannot swear that I did not."

"Why might you have expressed such an opinion?"

Looking to the floor, the witness responded evasively. "I don't know."

"Just reflect and tell me whether you remember having said to anybody about the period of Mr Bravo's marriage, 'Poor fellow, he will not live long'?"

"No sir, I don't recollect saying so." He paused, still looking at his shoes. "I might have done." He hesitated again before contradicting himself, "I don't remember saying he would not live long."

"That is an expression you would not forget saying," Lewis insisted, his frustration showing in his clipped tone. "Did you use it?"

Griffith looked up sheepishly. "Well, I might have said so."

"What did you mean by it?"

A few jurors leaned forward in their seats and the stuffy room fell silent as a tomb. Griffith shifted his weight from one foot to the other. "I did not mean anything by it at all."

Unimpressed, the jurors leaned back in their seats as exasperated as George Lewis, who asked tersely, "Did you express an opinion that he would not live four months?"

"No."

"You swear by that?"

"Yes."

"Do you know Mr Stringer who is employed in this house?"

"Yes," was the subdued reply.

In a moment of pure theatre that would not be possible in a court of law, Lewis looked directly at the Coroner's officer: "Let Stringer come up!" The manager of the Bedford Hotel was brought to the table and stood next to Griffith, who avoided eye contact.

Lewis pointed at the silent witness. "You know Stringer?"

"Yes." The response was almost inaudible.

"Did you use the phrase 'poor fellow' to Mr Stringer?" Lewis demanded.

Griffith looked nervous, his pointed Adam's apple bobbled in his scrawny neck like a bouncing ball. "I don't think I said those words."

"Did you say that Mr Bravo would not live four months?"

"I do not recollect doing so."

Lewis had the wind in his sails, and his manner was assertive but controlled. "There he is right next to you. Will you swear that you did not say to him, 'Poor fellow, he will not live four months'?"

"I don't recollect I said four months."

"Did you say 'many months'?"

Griffith finally made eye contact with the legal advocate. "I might have said five or six months, something like that." It was obvious that Griffith did not want to admit that his prophecy was exact almost to the week, but in doing so he made a fool of himself, and once again the room was reduced to laughter.

Lewis wanted to tear the truth from his prey. "What did you mean by it?"

"Well, I said it from aggravation, nothing else."

"But you had only seen the poor gentleman on two occasions, I believe?"

"Two or three."

PART ONE

"Now explain to all these gentlemen," the advocate declared, pointing to the 17 jurors seated in the corner, "having seen Mr Bravo on only two or three occasions, and having left his service, what did you mean by saying he would live only four months?"

"I meant that it was his fault that I lost my job." Stung by the amusement that his response again generated, Griffith blurted out, "I didn't think it mattered if he was alive or dead."

His adversary would not let up. "How many months did you say he would live?"

"About five or six. I might have said that."

"Did he seem to be suffering from anything?"

Griffith paused, scratching the point of his nose. His eyes lit up. "He had been bitten by a large dog."

"And you swear that is what you meant?"

"Yes." The weary witness grasped the implausible lifeline he had thrown himself. "I thought he might die of the dog bite."

Not surprisingly, counsel was sceptical. "Did you ever mention the dog bite before coming here?"

"Yes, lots of times."

"Did you mention it to Stringer?" Lewis pointed at the barman still standing next to the witness.

The response was all-too familiar. "I don't recollect mentioning it to him."

"When you read the papers I suppose you were not surprised to see that Mr Bravo had died within four months, as you had prophesised?"

"Well, I was rather surprised, sir."

"That he died from tartar emetic?"

"No, sir."

Rubbing his brow, Lewis sat down vexed. Archibald Smith, the lawyer for Dr Gully, rose to his feet. "What had happened with regard to the dog?"

"The dog had been taken by a stable hand to the pond on Sunday morning, about 11 o'clock, I think. Mr Bravo was walking along the path and the dog rushed upon him and bit him on the arm."

"Were you ordered to kill the dog?"

"Yes, by Mrs Ricardo."

*

Members of the Cold Case Jury, the greater part of George Griffith's testimony was rambling, garbled and incoherent. Let's examine his statements about his wedding-day prophecy. Clearly, when he uttered his casual prediction to Stringer, which the manager later confirmed, Griffith did not believe for a moment that Charles Bravo was going to die from a dog bite. This was an improvised excuse conjured up during the inquest. If it had been genuine he would have said so when first questioned, and should have been surprised to learn that Mr Bravo had died from antimony poisoning rather than an infected bite. Yet he did neither.

Perhaps the prophecy was simply wishful thinking or bravado that proved to be coincidentally correct. It would be easy to dismiss the whole episode as insignificant were it not for a paragraph in the chief inspector's report of 29 May:

George Griffith (the late coachman) who I was informed could make an important statement with reference to a conversation he overheard between Mrs Ricardo and Dr Gully in the lodge at the latter end of last year... He declares most solemnly that he never heard such a conversation, viz. that she only married Mr Bravo for a position and not for love as she cared nothing for him and that Dr Gully replied, "If you do marry him, he won't live long," and he also declares he never said anything to anyone to give rise to this.

We do not know how Chief Inspector Clarke heard of this alleged conversation. It might have been from one of the other servants, or from one of the many rumours rife in Balham at the time, but I suggest the conversation at the lodge could be the source of the prophetic pronouncement. It was possibly overheard by his wife, Fanny, who lived with him at the lodge and, in November 1875, was instructed by Florence to fetch Dr Gully and bring him there for a clandestine meeting. Fanny Griffith told the inquest that the couple met in the parlour while she waited in the adjacent room. We know this was the occasion Florence sought advice about her marriage settlement. Although Fanny denied hearing any of the conversation, what are the chances she pressed an ear to the wall, hoping to discover some scandalous gossip?

The timing of the meeting dovetails with Griffith's prophecy: it occurred about a week before the marriage, and it is reasonable to suppose that Fanny told her husband what she had overheard, which he carelessly repeated at the hotel on the wedding day. Of course, we do not know whether Dr Gully's alleged remark was a throwaway expression or something more sinister. We will return to this point later when we consider the possibility that Charles Bravo was murdered.

If my conjecture is correct, George Griffith was never going to reveal the basis of his casual prophecy. Not only would it have cast a poor light on his wife, it would have implicated his former employer. Indeed, one thing clearly evident from his inquest testimony is that he never uttered a detrimental word about Dr Gully. For example, it is probable that he had a note from Dr Gully when he bought the two ounces of tartar emetic in Malvern; it was such a large quantity to sell over the counter to a labourer. Yet Griffith was evasive on this point. Indeed, why he purchased such a large dose and what happened to it was never satisfactorily explained.

Disappointingly, the incoherent testimony of the prophesising coachman failed to provide any insight into the death of Charles Bravo. Although the servants had found themselves caught in the storm that swept through the household after Bravo's collapse, they were never the central players in the drama. Ever since the inquest had begun, everyone was waiting to hear from the two witnesses most likely to know the truth about what transpired that fateful night. And the crescendo of anticipation and speculation reached fever pitch when Jane Cannon Cox was called to give evidence.

Chapter 9

WHAT THE COMPANION SAID

"Call Mrs Cox!"

The court stirred; a wave of murmured anticipation spread through the room and into the crowd three deep in the adjoining corridor. "Clear the door!" the Coroner's clerk barked. After a scuffle, a passage was cut through the human jungle, and a side door opened. A woman wearing black silk and a bonnet emerged from a waiting room and into the breath of alcohol hanging in the corridor; the lunch break had been treated like a theatre intermission. Holding the arm of an old gentleman friend, Mrs Cox serenely made her way into the tightly packed court. The crowd parted, allowing her to reach the small chair by the table, the only empty space in the entire room. She thanked her companion, who melted into the crowd, leaving her alone to face her inquisitors.

Her counsel, Mr Murphy, rose from his seat, holding several documents in his left hand. With his right, he removed his pince-nez and smiled congenially at his client.

*

Members of the Cold Case Jury, over the next two days Mrs Cox was gently examined on every aspect of the case. Much of what she said about that fatal Tuesday night has been incorporated into the narrative you have read. During the questioning she also disclosed there was a second conversation between her and Charles Bravo. On the afternoon of Wednesday 19 April, sometime after he had made his Will, Charles turned to Mrs Cox when they were alone for a moment, and asked, "Why did you tell them? Does Florence know I've poisoned myself?" Mrs Cox replied, "I was obliged to tell them. I could not let you die. What have you taken, Charlie?" Bravo turned his head away, saying "I don't know." At this point Florence entered the room, and the brief exchange ceased.

This revelation is significant in light of what Mrs Cox would say during her searching cross-examination. And it is for this we now return to the Bedford Hotel. It is Monday 31 July 1876, the 15th day of the inquest, and Sir John Holker, the Attorney General, is finishing reading Mrs Cox's Treasury statement to the court.

*

"'He was a person of sound mind. He and his wife lived on affectionate terms. He had no occasion to commit suicide. I cannot give any opinion why he should have taken poison.'" Holker removed his reading glasses and placed the deposition on the table before him. He stared at the witness, but said nothing.

"That is what I said then," Mrs Cox stated gently.

"Then!" the Attorney General exclaimed, waving his hand. Like a seasoned actor he looked to the members of the jury seated in the corner of the room. "Now you say that there is a good deal in it that is not true?"

Mrs Cox readied herself to reply, her lips parted, but there was no response. She sat motionless, apart from her left hand tracing circles on the table top. An uncomfortable silence lingered in the room.

"Do you now say that there is a good deal in it that is not true?"

Again there was quiet, broken only when a spectator struck a match to light his pipe. All eyes were on Mrs Cox who was deep in thought, recalling what she had said at the first inquest. "I will not say it is not true," she began, her voice quiet but resolute, "but I own I did not use the words 'for Dr Gully'. I did say before the Coroner that the deceased did not explain why he had taken the poison."

"Then you did not tell the truth?"

There was no reply. Rather than pressing, the Attorney General allowed another long silence to answer for her, and changed tack. "Now, Mrs Cox, you saw a good deal of Mrs Ricardo and Dr Gully. What do you suppose was the nature of their acquaintance?"

"I thought he was very much interested in her."

"Did you look upon him merely as a friend or as her lover?"

In the hushed courtroom, Mrs Cox brushed the table top with her gloved hand, as if caressing it. Time transmuted the silence into discomfort, and each tick of the clock on the mantelpiece amplified it, but still Mrs Cox did not reply. Finally, without looking up, she said softly, "I cannot say exactly."

"I put it to you again. Did you know Dr Gully was her lover?"

No answer. "You lived with her for years," the Attorney stated, "and I ask you, did you not know during that time that Dr Gully was her lover?"

Mrs Cox looked away. "Yes, I think I did." Her tone and body language showed an equal measure of resignation and regret.

Having elicited a fact that might be important in establishing a motive for murder, Holker now focused on Charles Bravo's collapse. After taking Mrs Cox through the events following her return from Worthing, he began a forensic examination of what happened when she first went to Bravo's aid. It would lead to arguably the most important exchanges of the entire inquest. It concerned the question that George Lewis had noted almost two weeks earlier: if Mary Ann Keeber was standing at the bedroom door, why had she not witnessed the confessional made by Charles?

"You did not hear any cries for hot water, but Keeber came running to you and then you went immediately to Mr Bravo's room?"

"Yes."

"You rushed as quickly as you could?"

Nodding, she replied quietly, "Yes."

"Do you know if Keeber followed you?"

"I cannot remember."

"When you got there, was Mr Bravo leaning out of the window?"

"No, he was standing by the open window."

"Was it while he was standing by the open window that he made a statement?"

"Yes. He said, 'Mrs Cox, I have taken poison for Dr Gully. Don't tell Florence.'"

"When he made this statement to you, you were quite convinced he had taken poison?"

"Yes."

"You thought he was dying?"

"No, I thought he had taken chloroform and was sick, but I thought it very likely he might recover from the effects of it. I smelt chloroform and found the empty bottle on the chimneypiece. There was no other bottle in the room but the small laudanum bottle."

"Do you know of any reason why you should not tell Florence, or why he should ask you to do so?"

"No, I don't know any reason unless it was to save her pain."

"You understood that Mr Bravo had taken poison because he was jealous of Dr Gully?"

"Yes, that was my idea, but he had no occasion to be jealous."

"Why did you not tell the doctors that he had taken poison for nearly five hours?"

Mrs Cox fell silent, and to the jury it appeared she was thinking through all her answers like moves in a high-stakes game of chess. "I told Mr Harrison directly he came that Mr Bravo had taken chloroform. He said it was not chloroform, and my impression is that I replied, 'It must be chloroform because he says he has taken poison.' Mr Harrison does not remember that, but it is my impression I said so."

The last answer lacked conviction. Holker underlined this point by asking the same question differently: "Why did you not, on the first opportunity, tell the doctors that Mr Bravo had taken poison?"

"Because when Dr Moore came, I expected Mr Harrison in a moment, and as soon as he came, I told him immediately."

Holker missed the opportunity to remind the jury that it was Mrs Cox who sent for Dr Moore, begging the question whether she would have told him anything of the confessional statement had the other doctors not been called. Looking gravely at the witness, he asked, "You told him about chloroform. Did you tell Mr Harrison that Mr Bravo said he had taken poison?"

Mrs Cox sipped some water, replacing the tumbler to the exact same place on the table top. She replied quietly, almost in a whisper, "No, I did not."

"Why did you not tell him?"

"I can't give any reason for omitting it any more than I have done." In fact, she had given no reason. After further questioning, Holker returned to events earlier in the night, when Mrs Cox had first rushed to Mr Bravo's aid in his bedroom.

"He looked dreadfully ill, did he not?"

"Yes, very ill indeed."

"Do you know where Keeber was at the time?"

"No I do not. I never noticed her. It was immediately after I went into the room he made that statement. I then asked him how he could do such a thing, and then he screamed out, "Hot water! Hot water! He was then sick out of the window."

George Lewis, the ardent lawyer representing Joseph Bravo, seized on the last point and fired a salvo of sharp questions at the witness. "Keeber had called you – was she not standing at the side of the open door?"

"I never noticed her."

"When did you notice her?"

"She came with the hot water when I next saw her. She must have heard him calling for hot water, as I do not remember telling her to fetch any. I…" She hesitated. "I may have told her, or she may have heard. I cannot say any more."

If Mrs Cox had instructed Keeber to bring some hot water, the housemaid must have been standing by the bedroom door. Lewis probed further. "Then you think she may have heard what took place in the room when you were there?"

Mrs Cox paused, her head tilted downward. "I don't know that Mr Bravo was shouting loudly for hot water," she stated hesitantly, contradicting her earlier reply that he had screamed out for it. "He did not speak very loudly to me."

The answer was evasive. Lewis pounced like a lynx. "This is what Mary Ann Keeber swore to this court." He picked up a piece of paper. "She said, 'Mrs Cox rose and went into Mr Bravo's bedroom. I stood at the door. Mr Bravo was then standing by the window. I heard him call for hot water, and Mrs Cox asked me to fetch hot water.'" He replaced the paper on the table in front of him, and locked eyes with the witness. "Will you now deny she was standing at the door?"

"I don't know whether she was or not."

Lewis was having none of it. "Was not Keeber in a position to know what took place?" His words thundered around the billiard room as Mrs Cox wavered.

"I don't know how soon she came to the door after me."

Lewis looked at the jurymen. "That is your answer?" he asked with disdain.

"Yes."

"Was not Keeber in a position to hear what was said?"

John Murphy, Mrs Cox's counsel, leapt up. "The witness has already answered this question!"

"I really must protest!" Lewis exclaimed to the Coroner, barely containing his anger. "Please prevent Mr Murphy from interfering at such a grave moment in my cross-examination of the witness."

"Please sit down, Mr Murphy," the Coroner instructed.

"The jurymen will draw their own conclusions at interruptions at such moments," Lewis added, his voice quivering with agitation.

Looking directly at her combative adversary, Mrs Cox took the initiative, stating firmly: "I told you I did not know."

Lewis was in no mood to let up. "My question was whether, if Keeber were standing at the open door, looking at Mr Bravo, she could tell what passed at the window, and whether you would undertake to swear she was not there?"

"I have already answered that I do not know whether she was there or not."

"Assuming she was there, looking at him with the door open," Lewis snapped back, his patience starting to evaporate, "do you, or do you not, believe that she could have heard?"

"I cannot tell whether she could have heard or not," she replied calmly, "because Mr Bravo did not speak in a loud voice."

121

Some of the jurors jotted down some notes. Knowing there was little more to be gained from pursuing the line of questioning further, Lewis moved on. "Did you know that Mr Bravo all through his illness denied that he had taken poison?"

"Well," Cox replied, resetting the spectacles on the bridge of her nose. "He acknowledged that he had taken poison to Sir William Gull."

"Acknowledged taking poison?" the younger lawyer asked, surprised.

"He acknowledged that what he had taken he took himself."

It was not the same thing, of course, but Lewis appeared thrown off course as another train thundered across the adjacent bridge; everything in the room shuddered as if a minor earthquake had struck Balham. Lewis returned to a topic raised earlier by the Attorney General. "At the first inquest, did you swear falsely?"

Unlike her earlier replies on this point, Mrs Cox replied without hesitation, "I don't consider it swearing falsely; I did not repeat all that was said."

"You don't consider that swearing falsely?"

"I withheld some words because I thought they would injure Mrs Bravo's reputation."

"You stated yesterday that on the Wednesday 19 April Mr Bravo made a statement to you. Did you swear at the first inquest, 'I saw him continually until he expired, but he did not explain to me how he came to take poison?'"

"He did not explain to me how he came to take poison. On the Wednesday morning he said, 'Let Florence know I've poisoned myself,' but he gave no reason for it."

This was new information, at odds with the alleged conversation in the afternoon when Florence entered the room, a perfect opportunity for everything to have been discussed. The discrepancy was never challenged; Lewis was more concerned with the continual evolution of her account. "Why didn't you state this at the first inquest?"

"I was about to state it but was interrupted when someone asked another question. I mentioned it to Mr Joseph Bravo on the second morning of the first inquest and he said, 'If you say that, it will be at utter variance with what he said on his deathbed." Indeed, it was contrary to everything Charles Bravo had told everyone during his final days, including Mrs Cox on the night he collapsed.

"Did you also state, 'Why he should have taken poison I cannot give an opinion'?"

"I could not give an opinion because I could not mention Dr Gully's name."

"Was this a false statement?"

"Except for the withholding of that name, it was the truth."

Like a dog with a bone, Lewis would not let go. "Was it false, said in the interests of Mrs Bravo?"

"I withheld those words for Mrs Bravo's reputation's sake. She was not aware of it. I never thought of myself. I only thought of Mrs Bravo."

John Murphy, Mrs Cox's lawyer, needed to show that there were perfectly reasonable explanations for his client's actions. In particular, he was keen to show that Mrs Cox tried everything to save the life of the stricken man. He stood, removing his pince-nez, and smiled reassuringly at his client.

"When you first went to Mr Bravo, did he seem in great pain?"

"I don't know he seemed in pain, but he was very sick. I fancied I smelt chloroform and I think I sent for the doctor immediately when I found the chloroform bottle empty."

"Did he say anything more to you?"

"No, he sank down upon the floor."

"And was Keeber in the room at this time?"

"I didn't notice her. She may have been there."

"When did you give him camphor?"

"After the mustard and water and before or after the coffee. He would not swallow that."

"He took the camphor and water?"

"Oh yes, I gave him two drops in about half a tumbler of water and rubbed his chest with it."

"Why did you give him camphor?"

"Because I thought it might do away with the effect of the chloroform."

"Is it a stimulant?"

"Yes, I should think it is. I have taken a few drops when I have felt faint, and given it often."

*

Members of the Cold Case Jury, you will recall that *The Lancet* remarked that Mrs Cox gave the textbook treatment for poisoning, although Bravo's symptoms were consistent with other illnesses. Now we have Mrs Cox's side of the story. She claimed to have smelt the distinctive odour of chloroform on Bravo's breath and discovered an empty bottle of it standing on the mantelpiece to confirm her belief that he had ingested some. She administered a mustard emetic to induce vomiting followed by the stimulants coffee and camphor to counteract the effects of the sedative. She told Mr Harrison of her suspicion that Charles had taken chloroform the moment he arrived. It is a plausible account, and one that does not rely on Bravo's statement about poison. If Mrs Cox had never mentioned the confessional statement, everyone might have believed her.

Similarly, her drip-feed of information to the doctors is also explicable. The amount of information she provided was proportional to her trust in the respective doctor. To Mr Harrison, a doctor she knew for several years, she mentions chloroform; to Mr Bell, Bravo's close cousin, she speaks of the confessional but without the words "for Dr Gully"; and confidentially to Dr Dill, who knew about Florence's affair, she tells all. Does this suggest the cautious companion, ever faithful to her close friend, was telling the truth?

On the other hand, there are several points that may only increase your suspicions. Mrs Cox claimed that Bravo made his confessional immediately she entered the room. She asked him how he could do such a thing before he vomited and collapsed. This leads us to a troubling issue. When she reached Bravo, who was on the far side of the room, Mary Ann Keeber would have been by the bedroom door, making her a witness to what happened during those first moments. She remembers only Bravo standing by the window shouting for hot water. This apparent contradiction was seized upon by George Lewis and led to the most uncomfortable moment during Mrs Cox's entire testimony. Her response was to say that Bravo had spoken quietly to her, although he had screamed for hot water.

Finally, during her cross-examination, Mrs Cox said that on the Wednesday morning Charles had instructed her to "let Florence know" he had poisoned himself. This is surprising because his confessional statement implored Mrs Cox not to tell Florence. If true, Charles had obviously changed his mind, but a puzzle remains. Why did Mrs Cox wait two weeks *after this conversation* before telling Florence? And, just as perplexing, why did he not tell his wife himself?

Once again, there are no witnesses to this conversation, so we only have Mrs Cox's word. The brief exchange appears convenient, contrived and contradictory. The shadow of suspicion falling on Mrs Cox grows longer and darker. One thing is for certain. By dragging Dr Gully into the case, she had ensured her friend would endure a most unpleasant experience at the hands of lawyers mostly concerned with exposing a scandal. How would Florence react?

The first day of Florence's testimony was conducted by her own legal counsel, Sir Henry James. It covered her family background, her marriage to Alexander Ricardo and its problems, the hiring of Mrs Cox, her family estrangement, her engagement to Charles Bravo and the financial settlement of the marriage. James tackled these highly personal matters as sensitively as he could. He also had no choice but to cover the uncomfortable topic of her intimacy with Dr Gully. Although excruciatingly painful for Florence, it was nothing compared to her cross-examination, which provided a personal trial by ordeal, the like of which had never been witnessed before in an English Coroner's court.

Chapter 10
TRIAL BY ORDEAL

Friday 4 August 1876. The cooler temperature and gusty breezes did not deter the crowds gathering outside the Bedford Hotel for the second day of Florence Bravo's testimony. Inside, the approach to the billiard room, and especially the staircase, was so tightly packed with spectators that court officials and witnesses had to force their way through the scrum to reach the courtroom.

Before the inquest resumed, the lawyers were busy preparing and reading their copious correspondence – up to 30 letters every day – from armchair detectives describing a pet theory or suggesting questions to ask. One in particular had fallen under the monocled eye of John Gorst, the lawyer for the Crown and future Solicitor General. Mr Hudson of Peyton Place, London, had written to the police:

Sir, amongst all the suggested sources of the poison causing the death of Mr Bravo, I have not seen that of the salt cellar mentioned. In many expensively furnished houses each person has one for his or her use at the table. It suggested itself to me because of the remark that "most of the antimony was found in the solid food ejected from the stomach"...

It was an intriguing idea. Who would notice tartar emetic crystals mixed into Bravo's personal salt cellar? Gorst scribbled a note to ask a question about it.

A little after ten o'clock, dressed in black and tightly holding the arm of her elder brother, Florence returned to the lair of legal wolves. As they entered, the hubbub of conversation was immediately silenced like a knife cutting a throat. She saw the moral condemnation in the eyes following her every move as she took her seat at the edge of the large table. She was also aware of something else, something visceral that transcended her immediate senses: testosterone. Save for a few older women sitting underneath the windows like theatre patrons watching from the box seats, she had entered a world of men. It would be male voices asking the questions, male hands writing down her replies and male minds judging her in the jury. And the moral condemnation was not for a widow who might have murdered her husband, but for an adulteress who had an affair with a married man over twice her age.

Her worst fears had been confirmed by the previous day's examination, and she was acutely aware that today she would face more of the same; this is what the crowds had come to hear. The next two days would be the longest of her life.

With a trembling hand she took a sip of water from the tumbler. She felt like a condemned French aristocrat placing her head through the lunette of a guillotine. And it was her legal counsel who had to release the blade.

Solemnly, Sir Henry James rose. "Since you gave evidence yesterday, your attention has been called to your statement that your intimacy with Dr Gully occurred at Kissingen in August 1873?"

"Yes," Florence replied softly.

"All through the years of your acquaintance with Dr Gully, and during your evidence yesterday, you were most anxious not to be regarded as his mistress?"

128

"Yes."

"Mrs Bravo, in begging you to tell us the whole truth, do you wish to correct your statement: was there any intimacy between you and Dr Gully before that visit?" The court appeared frozen as it waited for an answer. "You need only say 'yes' or 'no'."

Tears ran slowly down Florence's face. This moment was the sum of everything she dreaded. The terror at the mere thought of her public humiliation had precipitated her nervous break-down in May; and now it was about to be realised. "Yes," she replied. The few mutters from the audience were delivered with a sense of cold satisfaction.

James paused briefly, but decided it best not to prolong her agony. "Have you any correction to make as to your evidence regarding the period after your Kissingen visit – there was no further improper intimacy?"

"No I have not." A note of defiance rang through her sobs.

"And you now state on your oath there was no such intimacy after that?"

She replied tremulously, "No there was not."

"You were anxious not to appear to Mr Bravo, as everyone else, as Dr Gully's mistress for any length of time?"

"Yes."

"And did you present the same view of your intimacy of Dr Gully to Mrs Cox as Mr Bravo?"

"Yes, I did."

"As far as you can judge, had Mrs Cox any knowledge of your intimacy before the Kissingen visit?"

"None whatever." Again her composure broke, releasing a flood of tears.

Sir Henry James leaned towards Mr Brooks, her solicitor: "Do you wish to retire for a little?"

"No, I will go on," Florence interjected, dabbing her face with her handkerchief. She refused to allow men to decide whether she should rest or not.

"I only have one more question to ask on this portion of the case. Did any intimacy ever occur during the lifetime of your first husband?"

The reply was firm and clear. "No."

James moved on to other matters but soon returned to the subject of Dr Gully and in particular her late husband's view of the man. "In what way did Mr Bravo speak of him?"

"Well, he was always abusing him."

"Did he complain of Dr Gully's residence being so close to your own?"

"Yes, perpetually."

"Did he speak of Dr Gully angrily?"

"He said that he wished him dead, and that it angered him to pass his house every morning on going into the city. I do not know, Sir Henry, whether you have it that I offered to leave The Priory in consequence and forego the remainder of the lease."

"Did you make that offer to your husband?"

"Yes, and I wrote to the landlord, the Right Honourable Mr Byng, who would not allow it."

"When did you make the offer?"

"Soon after we came to The Priory to settle down after our marriage. About the end of January."

"You were willing to go away as Dr Gully had not gone?"

"Quite willing."

After lunch, the Coroner and lawyers had to again force their way through a dense thicket of people on the stairs and in the corridor. Even more people had crammed into the courtroom during the break, and there was barely enough space to breathe, let alone move. After resuming his seat, the Coroner brought the court to order. "This is a most important enquiry and the jury must plainly and distinctly hear the answers of the witness," Carter announced. "I must beg those present to keep strict silence and make no sensational observations."

"They stormed the room while we were away!" Sir Henry James commented airily.

"You will admit no more strangers to the room," Carter instructed his clerk, a farcical request to close the proverbial stable door.

"We were late seven or eight minutes," Mark Cattley, the level-headed jury foreman, reminded him. No doubt everyone had again enjoyed the hospitality of the Bedford Hotel a little too much during lunch. When the afternoon session finally began, James continued to ask Florence about her husband, their relationship and the events surrounding the fatal poisoning. The court adjourned at its usual time of 4:30pm.

Concerned that the Bedford Hotel would be overrun by gawking onlookers on the Bank Holiday Monday, the Coroner deferred the resumption of Florence's testimony to the Tuesday. She knew it was merely postponing the most unpleasant part of her nightmare. And sure enough, when her cross-examination finally began, it did not take long before the young legal Rottweiler had again reduced her to tears.

George Lewis began by reading extracts of at least six letters from Charles Bravo to Florence. They were all dated from earlier in the year when Charles was away from his wife, sometimes due to work. For the most part they spoke of his admiration and affection for his wife. However, in one he wrote of "bitter troubles" and in another that her "weakness distresses me". There was no mention of Dr Gully.

Lewis placed the last letter on the table. "Your husband found fault with your drinking too much wine?"

"My husband did not find fault with me," Florence corrected, "he only said it would be better if I drank Burgundy than sherry, and urged me to drink less."

"After hearing these letters, do you mean to tell the jury that your late husband was talking of Dr Gully 'morning, noon and night' in disparaging terms?"

"I do."

"But you only told Mrs Cox?"

"I told others in his lifetime. My mother was one."

"But, Mrs Bravo," Lewis began with the incredulous tone perfected by a lawyer, "do you remember writing this to his mother, Mrs Joseph Bravo?" He read from another letter written at the end of January 1876. "'Charlie and I are happy as can be, and never have an unkind word. It did hurt me to hear you say that I ruined him, but all is forgotten.'" He paused. "So, when did you tell anybody?"

"We discussed it together – all my own family."

"And it was spoken of after his death?"

"Yes."

"Suggesting it was a reason for his committing suicide?"

"Yes."

"Did you at this time tell anybody, other than Mr Bravo, that you had a criminal intimacy with Dr Gully?"

"No."

Lewis picked up a six-year-old letter written by Florence to her former maid: "'I hope you will not allude in any way to anyone of what passed at Malvern. Let it all be buried in the past and if anybody questions, please refuse to answer any enquiries. I shall remain here until January and then think of having a house at Chiltern. Yours truly, Florence Ricardo.'"

He paused, looking directly at each member of the jury for maximum effect. "There is a postscript. It simply says 'Burn this'." He gently cast the letter onto the table before looking at Florence, asking dramatically, "What was it, Mrs Bravo, that was never to be alluded to by anyone, and to be buried, with no enquiries answered?"

Riled, Florence responded emphatically. "It was my attachment to Dr Gully, which has nothing to do with this case of the death of Charles Bravo! As to that I will answer any question. I have been subjected to sufficient pain and humiliation already and I appeal to the Coroner and to the jury, as men and Britons, to protect me." Her voice quivered and tears rolled silently down her cheeks. It was a tragic sight. Not being able to actually applaud, many in the room tapped their feet to make their feelings known.

Like a latterday Pontius Pilate, the Coroner took the opportunity to gulp water from his tumbler, allowing Lewis to continue his onslaught. Eventually the inquisitor-in-chief took his seat, but Florence's ordeal was far from over.

"Now I want to ask you a few questions about the night of 18 April," John Gorst began. "Did you notice your husband looking ill at dinner?"

"Very ill," Florence asserted. "His face worked during the whole of dinner with a peculiar twitching of his face."

"Was there anything at dinner at which he alone partook?"

"In the way of wine, you mean?"

"Of food."

"We all partook of the food."

"The salt?" he asked casually.

Florence furrowed her brow, not sure what to make of the question. "No, we both used the same salt cellar."

With Mr Hudson's ingenious theory set aside, Gorst asked further questions about the evening's events, soon focusing on the crucial moment when the housemaid raised the alarm. "Do you recollect Keeber coming into the bedroom and talking to Mrs Cox about the little dogs?"

"Yes. I remember Mrs Cox saying, 'Be sure to take the dogs out'."

"You were not asleep?"

"I was nearly asleep."

"Then, when Keeber went away, do you know whether she shut the outer door or not?"

"I was nearly asleep," she repeated, eager to emphasise the point, "and I really don't know."

Without a pause, Gorst changed the line of questioning. "Do you remember the conversation with Dr Johnson and Mrs Cox about your husband saying he had taken poison?"

"Yes."

"Did you ever talk to Mrs Cox more about that?"

"No."

"What did you understand happened?"

"I understood, as I said before, that my husband had accidentally taken a large quantity of laudanum for his neuralgia."

"Did you ever question Mrs Cox about that afterwards?"

"No, I did not."

Gorst arched an eyebrow in surprise. "Were you not much shocked when you first heard that your husband had committed suicide?"

"I was horrified."

"And you first became aware of it from what your husband had said to Sir William Gull?"

"Yes."

"And you say that you did not want to say a word against your husband?" Gorst asked, readying another attack on a personal matter.

"No, most decidedly not, and I would not have given a statement to the Treasury had I known they would be made public."

"Did you make a statement about your late husband to Dr Dill when you were at Brighton?"

"I really forget," Florence responded, a little annoyed. Observing Gorst place his monocle to his right eye to scan the paper he held, she added, "I spoke to Dr Dill."

"I mean did you make a statement to Dr Dill?"

"I told Dr Dill that my husband had been poisoned by antimony and that he must have taken it himself because there was no antimony in the house that I was aware of. When I heard that his father made a statement on the day of the funeral that he kept antimony in his stables, I said, 'Perhaps he got it from there'."

Gorst was not giving an inch. "I do not mean that. Did you not make to Dr Dill a grave charge against your husband?"

"I have told you what I told him. I can say no more."

"When you were at Brighton, did you tell Inspector Clarke to visit Dr Dill and ask him for information?"

"I said if he wanted more information he must go to Dr Dill. I could tell him nothing more. That's all I said to Mr Clarke."

"Did you refer Mr Clarke to Dr Dill for the doctor to tell him particulars about the late Mr Bravo that you could not, but which you had told the doctor?"

"I shall not answer questions on the subject you mean – so there!" Florence replied defiantly.

But Gorst was unrelenting. "Did you not know Mr Clarke would hear a most serious charge against your husband from Dr Dill – a charge made by you?"

"No, I did not."

The puzzled looks on the faces of the jurymen revealed they were in the dark about the nature of the serious charge and its significance to the case. It was clearly a sensitive issue and none followed up with further questions.

*

Members of the Cold Case Jury, what was "the grave charge against her husband" that John Gorst determined to uncover? This is where the shadowy, almost sinister, presence of Dr Charles Dill slides into view. We know that Florence spoke to him in May while she was in Brighton. Although he was never brought to the inquest, presumably respecting patient confidentiality, Chief Inspector Clarke asked the doctor a few questions. He wrote in his report of 5 June:

I also saw Dr Dill who states the communication made to him by Mrs Bravo was after the death of her husband, when she said "he was very persistent in that line of conduct".

In *Murder At The Priory*, Bernard Taylor and Kate Clarke concluded, after several pages of analysis, that this could only refer to anal intercourse, and suggested that Gorst had realised it was a possible motive for murder. Author James Ruddick concurred, adding that "persistent in that line of conduct" was a euphemism used by professionals at the time to describe this particular sex act. He wrote, almost gleefully, that the chief inspector's report was indisputable proof that "Bravo was habitually buggering his wife", and conjectured it was a factor that drove Florence to kill her abusive husband.

According to Ruddick, Florence made the grave charge to Dr Dill in early January 1876, only five weeks into the doomed marriage. However, the chief inspector's report could not be clearer: the communication occurred only after the death of Charles Bravo. If Bravo's sexual proclivity was a motive for murder, Florence would have been absurdly stupid to direct the Chief Inspector to talk to Dr Dill about it.

PART ONE

One can only feel sympathy for Florence Bravo, having to endure three days of intrusive interrogation at the hands of so many male lawyers. Yet, her humiliation was not confined to her testimony. Almost every witness had to answer questions about her relationship with Dr Gully, which was relayed to the nation through a plethora of national and regional newspapers. It is no exaggeration to think the 23-day inquest would have taken half the time had many of these questions been omitted. Nothing probative would have been lost.

Florence's testimony asserted that Charles Bravo was obsessed with her former lover, perpetually disparaging him during angry rants. Yet, no servant corroborated a single instance of this behaviour, apart from Mrs Cox, and he did not commit any such thoughts to paper. But there is a hint of a problem in one letter. On 9 March, Charles wrote to his wife: "Though I long to see you with the longing of intense love, I never wish to see The Priory again!" It appears he was unhappy living at Balham, and when Florence was asked by Sir Henry James what her husband was alluding to, she predictably responded that it was because Dr Gully was living close by.

Although it seems a stretch to believe Florence and her companion fabricated these incidents to lend support to the theory of suicide, they may have exaggerated the situation. In Mrs Cox's statement to the Treasury Solicitor, over half is dedicated to Bravo's ferocious temper regarding Dr Gully. A closer examination, however, reveals it details just two incidents {see *Exhibit 4*}. On the other hand, even if these allegations contained only grains of truth, perhaps they are sufficient to show that Bravo was deeply troubled by Florence's past. The "bitter troubles" letter of 15 February {*see Chapter 2*} might also refer to the offending presence of Dr Gully, but it is just as likely to be about Florence's miscarriage at the end of January, or other marital issues.

A key exchange during Florence's testimony concerned the moments before the alarm was raised by the housemaid. Although "nearly asleep", Florence remembered Mary Ann leaving her bedroom with the terrier. Now imagine starting a stopwatch. The housemaid walks the 10 feet from Florence's bedroom to the stairway door in the corner of the landing; six seconds. She opens the door and, waiting at the bottom of the narrow flight of stairs to the second floor, calls for the other terrier; four seconds. Perhaps she waits to see if the dog will obey; five seconds. According to Mary Ann's testimony, it is now – before she had time to ascend the stairs – that Bravo opens his bedroom door and shouts "loudly and impatiently" for Florence to fetch hot water. Stop the stopwatch: 15 seconds.

In this short space of time, Florence fell into such a deep sleep that she was not disturbed by shouting from the adjacent bedroom, even though the outer baize door to her room had been left open. Mary Ann could not explain why Bravo's cries went unheard and she was unsure if Florence was asleep when she rushed back into the bedroom. She inferred her mistress was sleeping only because she did not get up. Perhaps her large intake of alcohol was a factor. A less charitable construal is that Florence was awake but failed to rush to her husband's side.

At the close of the 21st day of the inquiry, Florence was asked whether she still entertained the same kindly feelings towards Mrs Cox as she had during the years of your acquaintance. She replied, tellingly, "I think she might have spared me a great many of the painful enquiries which have been made."

The following day, on Wednesday 9 August 1876, the last witness was called. Fittingly, it was Dr James Gully, who ruefully admitted the affair. In contrast to Florence's interrogation, Gully's examination was more considerate, as if the lawyers believed the doctor had made an honest mistake in his liaison. No one seemed offended by the double standard.

Gully corroborated much of what Florence had said. He also confirmed that on 8 April he had met Mrs Cox at Balham Station – quite inadvertently – when she informed him that Florence was having difficulty sleeping. Later the same day, Dr Gully prescribed a bottle of laurel water, a sedative, which was delivered via Mrs Cox. Florence stated that she did not use any of the laurel water and Mrs Cox claimed the bottle was later thrown away, unopened. In "a house full of medicines" where bottles of homeopathic remedies could be "found in every cupboard", this last point is surprising. Indeed, some authors have suspected the laurel water and the tartar emetic constituted a deadly, double-barrelled poison {see *Exhibit 7*}.

Dr Gully denied writing a note to allow George Griffith to collect the two ounces of tartar emetic from a Malvern chemist five years previously. It is possible that Griffith merely gave his name, but the Malvern chemist thought it unlikely any would have been sold without a note. Of course, a blind eye might have been turned in the interests of a sale. Gully also denied owning any at the time of the poisoning, but the two ounces were never satisfactorily accounted for. One other fact emerged that might interest us: Dr Gully was godfather to George Griffith's son. This at least explains the latter's protectiveness towards his former employer.

The final day of the inquest began with the Coroner's summing up. In a 40-minute speech, he carefully reminded the jury of the timeline and key evidence. He explained there were three ways in which Charles Bravo might have met his death: he administered the poison himself; he took it inadvertently; or it was administered to him by another person or persons.

For the first possibility, he stated that the confessional statement to Mrs Cox, Bravo's statements to the doctors and his character should all be taken into account. For the second, Bravo either mistook the tartar emetic for another drug, or accidentally overdosed on it. He stated there was no evidence that Bravo acquired or purchased any. For the third option, he said it was equally true that the poison could not be traced to anyone in the household or connected to it.

At 11:30am the jury retired. Nearly three hours later the court reconvened; 13 of the 17 jurors had agreed a verdict. The Coroner was handed a piece of paper, from which he read: "We find the deceased, Charles Bravo, did not commit suicide; that he did not meet his death by misadventure; but he was wilfully murdered by the administration of tartar emetic, but there is not sufficient evidence to fix the guilt on any person or persons."

The court burst into applause, incurring the wrath of the Coroner, who threatened to clear the room. The foreman also asked that the jurymen be compensated for their time. The Coroner said he could only offer 12 shillings in total, meaning each juror received less than a shilling for three weeks' work. By contrast, Sir Henry James earned over 2,000 guineas, a sum that even Charles Bravo could have only dreamt about.

At 3pm on Friday 11 August 1876 the inquest was closed, and the following day's newspaper editorials were quick to dish out sharp criticism. "That such a cross-examination, even in a Coroner's Court, of a crushed and humiliated woman should have been pushed to the length it was at Balham is a disgrace," concluded *The Times*. The moral condemnation was even stronger in *The Saturday Review*: "It is hardly too much to say that the inquiry into the death of Mr Bravo is, in every way, one of the most disgusting public exhibitions which have been witnessed in this generation." Not surprisingly, *The Telegraph* led calls for reform of the inquest system.

The verdict was also seen as flawed. "A more unsatisfactory inquiry never terminated in a more unsatisfactory verdict," decried *The Spectator*. It perfectly summed up the mood. "The result is eminently disappointing and unsatisfactory to those who had hoped that the second inquest would remove the painful uncertainty left by the precipitate closing of the original," wrote *The Standard*. This was echoed by *The Daily News*: "The manner of Mr Bravo's poisoning was so strange and inexplicable that… the matter had the air of a problem in fiction rather than calamity in fact."

The cost of the three-week inquest shocked and enraged *The World*, which calculated that up to £15,000, nearly £2 million in today's money, had been spent on lawyers.

Letters poured into newspaper offices. Many of those who picked up their pens advocated suicide as a more likely manner of death. Were they correct that the jury had been misled by Mrs Cox's suspicious demeanour and distracted by the prying into Florence's affair? Had the inquest overlooked clear signs that no one was responsible for the death of Charles Bravo but himself?

Chapter 11

BY HIS OWN HAND

There were two ways Bravo could have ended his own life. The first was suicide, as claimed by Florence and Mrs Cox. This view was supported by Sir William Gull and several other doctors not connected to the case. One was Edgar Sheppard, a professor of psychological medicine at King's College, London, who wrote to *The Daily News*:

If Bravo committed suicide he did it on the spur of the moment… There is much to support the view of temporary irresponsibility here. It is in evidence that Mr Bravo was a spoiled and wayward child, that his passions were strong, that his anger was of a brief but desperate kind. Fired by an almost fiendish jealously he could strike the dearest object of his affections and then prostrate himself in tears of contrition… He had threatened on several occasions to leave home… He was oppressed also by a morbid conviction of Mrs Bravo's extravagance, and of her alcoholic tendencies…

Dr H. Wigglesworth also wrote to the same paper:

How many people in the same circumstances would not say, "I'm dying and poisoned. Then the poison must have been in that glass of water or that cup of coffee. I was all right until then"? It is most common to refer the symptoms to the last thing taken, however wholesome... Mr Bravo's absolute silence upon his poison cup when strictly and repeatedly questioned is fatal to the verdict of murder.

This argument was repeated in a lengthy letter written by Dr W. Wade published by *The British Medical Journal*. He also pressed the psychological case, pointed out flaws in the murder verdict and cited two reasons to believe it was suicide: Bravo's confessional statement to Mrs Cox and his "I shall not be there" remark about the Worthing trip.

To consider how Charles Bravo might have committed suicide, key events of Tuesday 18 April will be replayed, but this time showing how and why Bravo intentionally took his own life. We first rewind time to the morning. According to Florence's testimony, there was another conversation in the carriage during the journey to London that showed her husband's suicidal state of mind. As the coachman and the footman testified that they did not overhear anything, we only have Florence's word for it.

*

10:20am. The landau gently swayed as it moved along the rutted lane from The Priory. "I told my mother we would take a small house," Bravo said without looking at his wife. "We could really do without the unnecessary expense."

"Janie knows that," Florence replied, a little annoyed. "I'm sure it will not be too dear. I do hope you will come, Charlie."

"I doubt it."

Florence looked hurt. "Why not?"

He paused, before replying tersely, "I think it will be better for your health."

"I would like you to come. I should be unhappy otherwise."

The carriage turned into Bedford Hill Road, soon passing six red-bricked, semi-detached houses. Florence turned her head, pointedly looking the other way. As the carriage trundled by the last, Orwell Lodge, Bravo turned to his wife. "Did you see anybody?" he asked sharply.

Her heart sank. "No, I did not look."

"The old wretch!" he muttered. "It's intolerable."

The houses left behind, the carriage continued its journey under the railway bridge, passing the small station and the Bedford Hotel, but Bravo was in no mood to let it go. "I don't understand it. Why is he still here?" Florence averted her gaze and remained silent, hoping his stormy mood would quickly blow itself out as usual. "Well, why hasn't Gully gone?" He was winding himself up, increasingly agitated by his own dark thoughts. "Well, if he won't go, perhaps I should!"

"What do you mean?" Florence asked softly.

"We should separate."

"You can't mean that!"

"I'm never going to get over it! I'm humiliated every time I leave my own house!"

"But I offered to move away…"

"Yes, but Mr Byng wanted payment in full."

"We could have done it, if it made you happy."

"I'm not prepared to be extorted."

"But you would rather separate!" Florence's lower lipped quivered. "How could you say such a thing, Charlie? I do everything I can to make you happy."

After a calming silence, Charles took her hand and patted it. "Yes, you're right. You are always right, my dearest wife. Please forgive me."

"You've been so unkind."

"Please forget everything I've said. Kiss me."

"I'm not sure I can, Charlie, not after what you've said."

His mood changed again. "If you don't kiss me, just you wait and see what I'll do when we get home!" His face darkened and his eyes became hard and lifeless, as if his soul had been possessed. Frightened, Florence leaned forward and kissed him on the forehead.

9:10pm. In the morning room, Bravo could not get comfortable in his armchair. Every muscle ached and his stomach felt agitated, but worst of all his lower incisors had begun to throb mercilessly. Florence read a volume of Shakespearean sonnets while Mrs Cox pulled a thread through her embroidery frame. Each had a glass of sherry beside them.

"Florence, remember your promise?" Bravo said.

"Yes, Charlie, you're right," his wife replied, getting up.

"The servants will still be having supper," Mrs Cox observed. "Would you like me to assist you?"

"Yes, thank you, Janie."

The two women left the morning room. Moments later, Charles heard Florence ask for a glass of wine from the dining room. She seemed to be drinking more than ever. His attention returned to his stepfather's letter: it's a lazy way to make money and a foolish way to lose it, he read again. It was gambling, his stepfather wrote, something that dishonoured the Bravo name.

He heard Mrs Cox heading back upstairs with the wine. He threw his father's letter to the floor and angrily brushed the others from his lap. He leaned forward in the chair, placing his elbows on his knees and sank his head into his hands. Every part of his body was aching. His mouth was besieged by attacks of sharp pain. His neck, abdomen and thighs ached after the horse ride. The bath had brought temporary relief, but now his body seemed to be rising up in protest.

He felt trapped. His mother continued to plague him over the finances at The Priory. A modest residence like The Priory did not require so many servants, she would tell him. He must retrench the household expenditure and be the master of his own household. Florence was always quick to remind him that it was her money and she could spend it how she wished. His meanness disgusted her, she would tell him. And now his step-father was moaning about his financial affairs.

His dogged, downcast expression was broken only by an occasional wince when a burst of pain surged through the nerves in his mouth. His negative thoughts were drawn to Florence. It was not only the money and her drinking that they argued over. She seemed to be resisting his most intimate needs. No doubt, he thought, she had indulged that old wretch Gully often enough. The thought moved him to anger.

9:35pm. Charles pulled himself out of his armchair and stiffly made his way into the hall, rubbing his aching side. He moved his jaw to try to alleviate the throbbing in his gums. He barely saw the petite servant walking by, only the glass of wine in her hand, a trophy of his wife's defiance. Not another drink. Champagne for lunch, a bottle of sherry in the evening, a nightcap, and still she had not finished. Looking pale and angry, he brushed past Mary Ann without a word. He headed upstairs and straight into his wife's dressing room.

"You have sent downstairs for even more wine, Florence!" he said in French. "You have drunk nearly a bottle of sherry and God knows what else today."

Florence didn't reply. She sat there, back to him, folding a cold water compress. He waited for her to turn to face him and say something. But there was nothing. "Well, goodnight," he said finally. His wife mumbled some reply.

PART ONE

Charles Bravo turned and walked to his bedroom. His body ached like a 60-year-old, but everyone was treating him like a child. He closed the door and headed to the mantelpiece. His teeth felt as though they were on fire. He picked up the bottle of laudanum, poured a little over his lower gums and rubbed it with his index finger. From his jacket pocket he removed a tightly folded square of paper. He sat on the side of his bed opposite the fire and carefully peeled back the flaps to reveal a whitish powder. He had thought of putting a few grains into his wife's drink that evening, but there had been no opportunity – Mrs Cox was drinking the same sherry and almost in the same quantity. A feeling of helplessness overwhelmed him: what's the point? She was never going to change. She was never going to be the dutiful wife he longed for.

As he brooded on his wife's drinking, the thought of her other flaw suddenly returned. In his mind he saw the old doctor entwined with his wife. A rage swelled up and broke the banks of his self-control. In a fit of inexplicable, nihilistic temper he moved to the small table at the foot of his bed and removed the tumbler from the top of the water bottle. He had told her he would do away with himself! She had not believed him. She would now. He poured the powder into the bottle. All of it. After several gulps, he slammed down the bottle and wiped his mouth with the back of his hand. He returned to the side of his bed, screwed up the packet and contemptuously flicked it into the blazing fire. He sat there, watching it blacken and curl in the dancing ribbons of orange.

He did not have to wait long for the poison to have its effect. He started to feel the first stabs of stomach pain. His senses suddenly returned on a surge of panic. What was he thinking! What on earth had he just done! He had to expel the antimony as soon as possible before it was absorbed into his bloodstream. Wide-eyed in terror, he rushed to the door and pulled it open.

9:45pm. "Florence! Florence! Hot water!" He was startled to see Mary Ann appear at his door. He felt a surge of nausea like rising waters from the deep, and spun round, hurrying to the open window on the furthest side of his bed. He felt his stomach twisting, as if it were tying itself in a knot. Seconds later, Mrs Cox rushed into the room. Ashen-faced and covered in pearls of sweat, Bravo leaned forward as she approached. "Mrs Cox, I've taken poison for Dr Gully, don't tell Florence," he whispered.

"Charlie, how could you do such a thing?" she enquired, her voice also hushed.

"Hot water! Hot water!" Bravo shouted impatiently towards the bedroom door where the housemaid was standing.

"Fetch some hot water! Be quick!" Mrs Cox ordered Mary Ann.

Turning away, Bravo vomited out of the window onto the roof below.

*

Members of the Cold Case Jury, this reconstruction assumes that Charles made the "Dr Gully confession" to Mrs Cox. Almost every writer on the case has dismissed it as a fabrication, but none has considered two pieces of circumstantial evidence that may point to its truth. First, the timing of Mrs Cox's revelation of the confessional is remarkable. Under cross-examination, Mrs Cox said: "When I told Dr Johnson of the deceased having said he had taken poison, the deceased was just recovering consciousness." This was confirmed by the testimony of Dr Johnson and Mr Bell. If she invented it, surely she would have made the statement much earlier, when it was believed that the unconscious Charles would never recover. Would the shrewd and cautious Jane Cox really have waited until Charles Bravo had regained consciousness to tell a blatant lie?

PART ONE

Second, the confessional might have been uttered just after Mary Ann left to fetch hot water. According to *The Times*, the housemaid stated: "I did not actually see him vomiting out of the window. He was standing at the open window." So, Mrs Cox and Charles were alone in his bedroom moments before he collapsed. Mrs Cox said he spoke quietly to her immediately as she entered the room, implying the housemaid was not at the door, which is almost certainly mistaken as Mary Ann was following right behind. Yet, mixing up events on a timeline is common, especially in a traumatic situation. Could Mrs Cox have got this detail wrong? Contrary to the last reconstruction, perhaps Mary Ann had actually left the room when the statement was made.

Other facts support the suicide theory. Charles was not only indifferent when told he was poisoned, he was adamant that he was fatally ill on several occasions. When he first regained consciousness he told the doctors: "Nothing is going to make me better." Later, to Mary Ann: "My next trip will be to the Streatham churchyard." And finally to Sir William Gull: "I know I am going to meet my maker." It appears he knew he was doomed.

Most importantly, the reactions of both Mrs Cox and Florence make sense if Charles had taken his own life. Mrs Cox did her best to save him and Florence was genuinely distressed, summoning as much medical assistance as possible.

But despite the evidence for suicide, there are several weighty points against. First, if Charles Bravo wanted to take his own life, why did he not overdose on laudanum? This is an opiate with a powerful anaesthetising effect, which was well known at the time. Published in 1874, *A Toxicology Manual* by John Reese states: "…from experience and recorded cases four or five grains may be regarded as the minimum fatal dose for an adult". Laudanum had long been the poison of choice for suicide and Bravo had some in his room. By contrast, tartar emetic is one of the least suitable substances for the task and no trace of it was ever found.

Second, Bravo's insistence that he took nothing but a little laudanum for his gums struck the doctors as earnest and sincere. More importantly, by denying he had taken anything else, Bravo was unconcerned at the prospect of household members becoming murder suspects. "If you die without telling us more," Dr Johnson had warned him, "someone may be accused of poisoning you." Bravo replied, "I am aware of that," but would not say anything more. Is this the behaviour of an honest man who only wanted to end his own life?

Third, to everyone who knew Charles, the idea of him taking his own life was absurd. No one who testified could think of a sound reason why he would do it. Would a censorious letter from his father, a small loss on the stock market and an attack of neuralgia be an overwhelming burden to an unsentimental lawyer harbouring Parliamentary ambitions who had recently married into money?

Finally, it is undisputed that after taking the poison, Bravo shouted for hot water. To believe that he called out for a benign emetic to eject a poisonous one from his stomach is unintelligible if he wanted to kill himself {see *Exhibit 8*}. We are forced to conclude that, if Charles Bravo deliberately took the tartar emetic, he had quickly changed his mind. Yet, there was no sign of any regret or remorse of his precipitate action when he regained consciousness.

The second way Bravo might have taken his own life was by misadventure. In her 1956 book, *How Charles Bravo Died*, Yseult Bridges claimed that Bravo mistook the tartar emetic for Epsom salts that he kept in his room in a similar container. The strength of the theory is that it provides a convincing answer as to why antimony was ingested rather than some other poison, and why it was such a large dose – it was by accident. Let's return briefly to The Priory to see the how Charles might have mistakenly taken tartar emetic that led to his appalling death.

*

9:35pm. Charles headed up the stairs and straight into Mrs Bravo's dressing room. "You have sent downstairs for even more wine, Florence!" he said in French. "You have drunk nearly a bottle of sherry and God knows what else today."

Florence didn't reply. She sat there, back to him, folding a cold water compress. He waited for her to turn to face him and say something. But there was nothing. "Well, goodnight," he said finally. He turned and headed for his bedroom.

Once inside, he went to the mantelpiece, on which there was a pair of small wooden boxes. One contained the white crystals of Epsom salts, the other the whitish powder of tartar emetic. Even Dr Dill had agreed that Florence was drinking too much alcohol and the occasional few grains of tartar emetic added to her sherry might help cure his wife of her drinking habit.

Distracted by thoughts of his father's comments, routine made his next actions automatic and unthinking. He flipped the lid on one of the boxes, took it to the small table at the foot of his bed and shook some of its contents into the water bottle. A quick stir, then he downed about two thirds of the water in a few gulps. Next, he picked up the bottle of laudanum and poured a little over his index finger and rubbed his lower gum with it.

He undressed, putting on his nightshirt. He was about to turn down the gas lamp when he felt an excruciating pain in his stomach. He doubled over. His mind quickly searched for a cause. What was the last thing he had taken? Laudanum, but he had barely swallowed any. Suddenly, he was seized by nausea – and panic. He now realised his terrible mistake – it was not Epsom salts that he had put in the bottle but deadly tartar emetic.

9:45pm. Charles rushed to the door and threw it open. "Florence! Florence!" he shouted, knowing she was just yards away in the adjacent bedroom. "Hot water!" He was startled to see Mary Ann Keeber appear by his door, but rushed inside his bedroom to the open window adjacent to his bed. He leaned out, thrust two fingers down his throat, and vomited.

He withdrew his head, but his ordeal was far from over; his stomach felt as though it was twisting into a knot. When Mrs Cox reached his side, he looked up and shouted impatiently towards the bedroom door, where Mary Ann Keeber was standing, "Hot water! Hot water!"

"Fetch some hot water! Be quick!" Mrs Cox repeated anxiously to the housemaid. After Mary Ann spun away, Bravo bent forwards. "I've taken some of that poison," he said, pointing to the mantelpiece. "Don't tell Florence. Throw it in the fire."

"Charlie, how could you do such a thing?" asked Mrs Cox softly.

Before he could answer, he leaned out of the window and vomited a second time onto the roof below. As he took a step back, he felt his knees weaken. His eyes rolled upwards and consciousness fled. After propping up his head against the chest of drawers, Mrs Cox headed to the mantelpiece. She quickly saw the wooden box with its lid up and threw it in the fire.

*

Members of the Cold Case Jury, this reconstruction closely follows the theory of Yseult Bridges. Her view has gained some support, most notably from Julian Fellowes, the creator of Downton Abbey, in his TV series *A Most Mysterious Murder.*

What supporting evidence is there for the misadventure theory? A little over two weeks before he died, Charles was prescribed Epsom salts for his rheumatism by Mr Bell. And it appears they were found in his room because Professor Redwood tested them for the presence of antimony – none was detected. Bridges suggests that the salts were to be taken orally rather than put in a bath and, on the Tuesday night, Bravo mistakenly took tartar emetic, a similar looking crystal. It seems plausible that the two could be confused in a dimly lit room and by someone in an agitated state of mind.

But why was the poison in his bedroom? Unlike laudanum, it has no analgesic properties. Bridges suggested Charles Bravo had been administering the poison in small doses to murder his wife, pointing to Florence's bouts of nausea in March 1876 as evidence to support her claim. But Florence was pregnant at this time, and morning sickness is an equally convincing explanation for her symptoms. At first glance, Bridges' theory explains why Charles never mentioned the tartar emetic: he would be forced to reveal his murderous scheme. Yet, if he was lucid enough to make his Will, Bravo could have easily lied: he was using it to cure his wife of her drinking habit. One can only conclude that he did not want to admit even this insidious behaviour, in which case I suggest it is the more likely scenario, and this is what the reconstruction assumed.

Once he realised his fatal mistake, Bravo was determined to keep his secret from his wife and family. Like the suicide theory, this explains his indifferent demeanour and his certainty that he was going to meet his maker.

There are issues that squarely confront this theory, however. First, even if Charles had kept tartar emetic in his room, would he really have stored it near to the Epsom salts and in a similar container? Surely, a reasonable person would have taken precautions precisely for fear of mixing them up. The foreseeable possibility of misadventure counts against its occurrence.

Second, the misadventure theory relies on a variation of the confessional statement that Mrs Cox never uttered. Bridges asserts that Charles Bravo probably said to Mrs Cox: "I have taken some of that poison, don't tell Florence. Throw it in the fire." Compare this to the statement that Mrs Cox actually gave to the Treasury Solicitor and at the second inquest: "I have taken poison for Dr Gully, don't tell Florence." So how did Bridges reconcile this glaring incompatibility with the evidence? She wrote of Mrs Cox: "She juggled the truth, adding or subtracting to suit the occasion." Such an accusation could also be levelled at Mrs Bridges.

One suspects Bridges was forced into this speculation to overcome two further obstacles to her account. If it was an accident, why was no tartar emetic found in the room? One would expect to locate the poison or traces of it somewhere, hence the inference for which there is no evidence: Bravo told Mrs Cox to dispose of it. And even if Charles had instructed Mrs Cox to destroy the container, why would she withhold this vital information?

If you are to accept this theory, you must be comfortable that Mrs Cox supressed the words "throw it in the fire" and fabricated her testimony by adding "for Dr Gully" – words that she knew would bring incalculable harm to Florence and also turn a tragic accident into a felony. Remember, suicide was a criminal offence at the time. Finally, there is a timing problem: as soon as Bravo realised his mistake, he would have taken steps to rid himself of the poison immediately. This is why Bridges supposed he induced vomiting by sticking two fingers down his throat. It occurred moments before Mrs Cox entered the room, yet she never mentioned observing any vomit on his hand or smelling its pungent aroma on his breath. It joins a growing list of convenient conjectures: keeping the tartar emetic next to Epsom salts;

instructions to Mrs Cox to throw the poison in the fire so there is no trace of it; and Mrs Cox withholding this information from everyone.

In both the suicide and misadventure scenarios, Charles laces his water bottle with tartar emetic (there was no other source of drinking water in the room). However, Mr Harrison told the inquest that, at about midnight on the night Charles collapsed, he had poured himself a tumbler of water from the same bottle with no ill effects {*see Chapter 4*}. Mr Harrison's evidence forces us to conclude that the contaminated water was changed before he drank from the bottle. One possibility, however, is that it was deliberately discarded to cover up a murder.

Chapter 12

ONE WOMAN'S POISON

Our focus now turns to murder. The first suspect to consider is Jane Cox, and the possible means, motive and opportunity for her to have acted alone in murdering Charles Bravo. Four writers have thought she was the guilty party. The earliest was William Roughead in 1929. Elizabeth Jenkins in *The Balham Mystery* (1949) agreed that "the murder was certainly done and almost certainly planned by Mrs Cox..." Frederick Veale in *The Bravo Case* (1950) also considered Mrs Cox as "Suspect No. 1... who had lied repeatedly on most material matters". Most recently, Bernard Taylor and Kate Clarke in *Murder at the Priory* (1988) again pointed the finger at Mrs Cox. The motive, they suggested, was fear for her position, the loss of which would have had a ruinous effect on her immediate financial security and the education of her boys.

Let's first take a moment to examine Mrs Cox's financial position at the time of Charles Bravo's death. In the long term, she had few money worries as her eldest son, Leslie, was due to become the sole beneficiary of a large estate in Jamaica. Indeed, Jane was being cajoled by her aunt to travel to Jamaica to sort out issues over the Will. Short-term financial security, however, was a very different matter. Jane feared that in her absence

Charles would elbow her out of the household by demonstrating to Florence that her position was no longer needed.

Taylor and Clarke's view was in stark contrast to another writer, James Ruddick, who eliminated Mrs Cox as the poisoner partly on the basis of no motive. He argued that Mrs Cox had known at the time of Charles Bravo's death that her son was to inherit her aunt's fortune and this "incontrovertibly demolished" her financial motive for murder. But a future inheritance, however likely, does not meet immediate financial needs. And in early 1876, Jane had no idea how long her aunt would live, nor could she be certain that her aunt would not alter her Will.

Mrs Cox's possible motive, I suggest, was more complex than any writer has so far considered. Its rational foundation was self-interest, and particularly concern for her boys' future, but there was an emotional construction. She had observed the devastating effect pregnancy wrought on Florence's health and knew Charles was not about to give up his conjugal rights. Indeed, if Charles was becoming sexually aggressive towards his wife, perhaps rooted in his contempt for her past affair, Mrs Cox could have been riddled with a strong sense of guilt because "she had urged the suit." She would be able to rationalise her motive: she was doing it for the sake of her beloved Florence.

To see how Mrs Cox might have poisoned Charles Bravo, we return to the night of Tuesday 18 April. Mrs Cox is travelling to Balham after her day trip to Worthing.

*

7:10pm. Jane Cox sat primly in the train carriage, her hands folded in her lap, troubled and deep in thought. Although Florence had tried to reassure her about her position, she knew that Charles wanted her out of The Priory. Or more accurately, his mother detested the idea of a costly chaperone in her son's marriage and wanted her out. But she couldn't afford to lose her position. What other job would pay even half as well and have the considerable perks that her current employment offered? Things would be different if Leslie inherited Aunt Margaret's estate, but that could be years away. No, she could not leave. Not yet.

Leslie. She had just met her eldest at Brighton station for an hour or so. She was so proud of him; he was turning into a fine young gentleman. Leaving The Priory would jeopardise his future and that of all her boys. So, what should she do about her trip to Jamaica? The words of Joseph Bravo replayed in her mind, his sombre voice in time with the rhythm of the train on the track: "Your duty is to your boys. You must go at once." This is what he had told her when she visited him in March to ask his opinion on the matter. In truth, her request for advice had been a ruse; she wanted reassurance that her job was safe if she went to Jamaica, some indication that he might moderate Charles. But he had given none. She and her boys were on their own.

And so she made her decision: she would travel to Jamaica after the trip to Worthing. She felt she had no choice – she could not risk losing the inheritance. But it was an uneasy situation and anxiety was gnawing at her. She feared that as soon as she boarded the boat, Bravo would make his move and, in the end, Florence would tire of the fight and succumb to her husband's wish. When she returned to England she would have to pack her bags and have no choice but to remove Leslie, Charles and Henry from their schools. Yes, there was Jamaica but she wanted her boys educated in England. And, in any case, Aunt Margaret had already changed her Will once, cutting out the original beneficiary in favour of Leslie. She could certainly do so again.

As the train entered the sweeping curve near Balham Station, it slowed and let out a shriek from its whistle. Out of the sooty window, Jane saw The Priory, shining in the distance like a white castle, among green trees that waved to her in the gentle breeze. She felt they were welcoming her home. Yes, it was her home. For four years, she had been Florence's closest friend, her nurse when she was at death's door and a chaperone when she needed respectability. Surely she was entitled to live there as long as Florence wanted? Charles was the cuckoo pushing her out of her comfortable nest and making Florence unhappy. Everything came back to him. How she wished she had never introduced them; the faint echo of the marriage bells now tolled her demise at The Priory.

She took out the hipflask from the small bag at her feet and took another sip of sherry. It stiffened her resolve. Her life was not going to be derailed; she had worked too hard to see it dashed on the rocks of misfortune. She had done everything she could to change the situation, but she had run out of options – except one. Charles must be removed from The Priory before she was.

Her mind kept returning to her discovery in the stables three months earlier. It was by chance she had noticed the small packet languishing at the back of an open cupboard after Griffith had left his position. It was stamped 'Antimony Tart.' She knew immediately what it was and had removed it to her medicine chest, not for any nefarious purpose but simply because it might come in useful.

She replaced the hipflask in her bag. The train came to a halt, the steam hissing as she alighted onto the small platform. She nimbly walked down the wide steps and onto a path that ran parallel to the track and emerged opposite the Bedford Hotel. She turned right onto Bedford Hill Road and headed home.

8pm. Half way through the dinner service, Florence motioned to Rowe that she wanted more wine. Mrs Cox observed that Charles glared reprovingly as each woman partook of another glass.

"Charles had a terrible ride this afternoon," Florence remarked. "Cremorne bolted."

"It didn't throw me," Charles interjected.

"You were so exhausted, Charlie. You looked like death."

"I felt like it."

Florence turned to her companion. "In fact, I've never seen him look so ill," she whispered. "I thought he was going to have a heart seizure."

Mrs Cox glanced at Charles, whose pallid face twitched as he ate. A large dose of antimony would likely induce heart failure, she pondered, and might be attributed to the effects of the horse ride. He would be sick first, but who was to say that was not brought on by the exhaustion of the ride too? She took another look at him. He looked decidedly off colour and out of sorts. She would never get a better opportunity.

"Damn Meredith," Charles muttered under his breath as he picked up his letter.

As Mrs Cox knocked back her glass of sherry, she silently formulated her plan. Florence had told her that each night her husband would take a large draught of his water directly from the bottle. She found it most vulgar, she had said. Yes, the water bottle used only by Charles was an ideal poisoned chalice. But how on earth could she get the tartar emetic into it in time?

9:10pm. "Florence, remember your promise?" Bravo said, nursing his pain in his flank.

"Yes, Charlie, you're right." Florence rose from her chair in the morning room.

Mrs Cox knew this might be her opportunity to strike. She thought quickly. "The servants will still be having supper," she said calmly, although her heart was beating like a piston. "Would you like me to assist you?"

"Yes, thank you, Janie." On reaching the bottom of the stairs, Florence turned to her companion. "Janie, you couldn't get me a little wine and water?"

Mrs Cox smiled and turned for the dining room as Florence proceeded upstairs. Once inside the dining room, she went to the sideboard and poured some Marsala into a glass, topping it up with water from a bottle standing on a tray. She took the wine from the dining room and crept as stealthily as a cat up the stairs. She placed the glass on a small table on the landing and paused to check whether the coast was clear. Everything seemed still, as if time had stopped. Her stomach knotted with adrenalin: this was her moment.

Breathing more heavily, she glided silently across the landing, up the servant staircase and into her room. She worked rapidly – every second's delay in returning to Florence might look suspicious later. From her medicine chest she removed the packet stamped 'Antimony Tart.' She descended the stairs and one step took her from the landing into Charles' bedroom. She headed straight for the table at the end of his bed. Removing the upturned tumbler from the bottle, she emptied the entire packet of whitish crystals into the water, and swirled it vigorously. Once dissolved, she replaced the tumbler and threw the empty packet into the fire. Walking hurriedly, she collected the wine from the landing table and stepped into Florence's dressing room. She had done it!

9:50pm. "Florence! Florence! Hot water!"

Inside Florence's bedroom, Mrs Cox froze. She had expected Charles to be sick and then collapse. He should be feeling nauseous, so why was he calling out for hot water? It didn't make any sense. She glanced across at Florence, and was relieved to see she had not stirred; alcohol always produced the same effect. She could wait it out.

Suddenly the bedroom door opened and Mary Ann rushed in. "Mr Bravo is ill!" she exclaimed. "Come quick." What a stroke of bad luck! If he had succumbed a few minutes later the housemaid would have been downstairs and no one would have raised the alarm. As she walked briskly into Bravo's bedroom, her mind was racing. What was she going to do now?

Ashen-faced and covered in pearls of sweat, Charles was standing by the open window on the far side of the bedroom. When she reached him, he screamed: "Hot water! Hot water!"

She needed to take control of the situation – alone. She turned to Mary Ann: "Fetch some hot water! Be quick!" Mary Ann spun round and was gone. "What's wrong, Charlie?"

"I have awful stomach ache." He leaned out and vomited violently onto the roof below. Pulling back from the casement, he turned to face her. His eyes rolled upwards as consciousness fled, he sank to his knees and came down like a felled tree at her feet.

It was a case of damage limitation now. She had no choice but to call a doctor, an action that would cast suspicion away from her, but would most likely lead to the discovery that he had been poisoned. She knelt down by the unconscious body at her feet, slapped Bravo's face several times and shook him as hard as she was able. "Wake up, Charlie." No response. He was not going to recover.

She had to destroy the poisoned chalice. She moved to the small table and grabbed the bottle, pouring the contents into the hip bath, which was still full of water. She took the bottle to the washstand and refilled it using the jug; it was not ordinarily used for drinking, but no one would know. Replacing the bottle, she raced to the mantelpiece, rummaging through several bottles standing there. She peered at the label of the first: laudanum. She could say he overdosed on that. No, on second thoughts, there was a problem: how could *she* know he had used it? She put it back and picked up the blue-fluted bottle of chloroform. She prised out the cork, and the distinctive odour immediately met her nose. Yes, that was it! She could say she smelt chloroform on his breath. The bottle was almost full – that was no good. It had to be emptied to make it appear that he had swallowed a large quantity to take his own life. She could not pour the liquid on the fire because it would vaporise, probably rendering her unconscious almost immediately. She glanced around the room. Of course, the bath! What a godsend it was! When she returned the bottle to the mantelpiece it contained just a single drop.

She managed to prop Charles' head and shoulders against the side of the chest of drawers. She realised that if her cover story was to be believed, she now had to call a doctor and treat Bravo for chloroform poisoning. As she swiftly descended the stairs she considered what she would need: a mustard emetic to induce vomiting and a stimulant like coffee or camphor to counteract the effects of the sedative.

She entered the butler's pantry. "Get Parton to fetch Mr Harrison! Mr Bravo's ill!" she told a startled Rowe. As Harrison lived in Streatham this would buy her some more time. More importantly, as the family doctor, he would not suspect poisoning. She was feeling more confident that she was going to get away with murder…

*

Members of the Cold Case Jury, this reconstruction is based on Taylor and Clarke's theory that Mrs Cox alone murdered Charles Bravo, but includes some original ideas of my own. Let's first explore the confessional statement in the light of her proposed guilt. She had initially tried to cover her crime by suggesting Bravo had taken chloroform and, after being forced to change tactic when that was ruled out, claimed that Charles had told her he had taken poison. She had several hours to mull over what she could say to convince everyone that he had poisoned himself. She could not claim that Bravo had said simply "Mrs Cox, I've taken poison" because of an obvious flaw: why had she not immediately told this to Florence or the doctors? The wily companion realised she could circumvent this problem if she said that Charles had implored her not to tell.

The reaction to the confessional at the first inquest must have alarmed her. No one was buying the story that Charles had committed suicide, and she needed to find a credible reason why Charles had killed himself. By adding the words "for Dr Gully" she had found one. In her own words: "He had taken poison because he was jealous of Dr Gully, although he had no occasion to be." It was also a defence for withholding the full confessional from the doctors: it would have been highly damaging to Florence to have mentioned it. It would also introduce a sensational decoy: a spurned lover with a motive for murder. Hence, if Mrs Cox was the poisoner, her suspicious behaviour regarding the confessional statement is fully explained: it was an act of devious self-preservation which evolved to meet the circumstances.

This murder theory also explains some of the case's puzzling features. Bravo's insistence that he had taken nothing but laudanum was genuine: he was unaware that he had ingested tartar emetic. He felt acute pain in his stomach – its first symptom, according to Professor Redwood – but wrongly attributed it to some laudanum he had swallowed; he urgently called for hot water to eject it. He called out for his wife because he had nothing to hide from her. Florence was

entirely innocent, explaining her distressed reaction on finding her husband seriously ill and her attempts to bring in so
many doctors to help save him.

It also explains a suspicious coincidence. Based on his own
statements and the results of the post-mortem, we know Charles
did not ingest any chloroform, yet Mrs Cox said she smelt it on
his breath *and* the bottle happened to be lying empty on the
mantelpiece. Surely, the two are connected. Otherwise, it seems
strange he would keep an empty bottle in his room.

The theory that Mrs Cox was a lone killer is the simplest of
any murder theory. The vast majority of poisonings are the work
of a single individual and, in this scenario, that person is the one
who indisputably acted the most suspiciously. She also had a
motive: her short-term financial security to enable the education
of her boys. It is said that hell has no fury like a woman scorned,
but such wrath is nothing compared to a mother's protection.
Also, we must not ignore malice generated by resentment. As
Mrs Cox was instrumental in bringing together Charles and
Florence, she may have felt particularly aggrieved at how she
was being treated by him and his family. It was quite obvious that
her future, and that of her boys, had been reduced to an unnecessary expense in the eyes of the Bravos.

The use of tartar emetic is surprising, but explicable if the
murder was opportunistic and this particular poison was all she
had to hand. Most of the remedies at The Priory were homeopathic – far too weak to be lethal – but tartar emetic crystals
would have enabled Mrs Cox to give a fatal dose. Charles being
ill and out of sorts at dinner may have been the trigger to use
antimony to induce sickness and ultimately heart failure.
However, she had not accounted for Mary Ann standing right
outside his door when the poison struck. Her bad luck forced her
into inventing a story of suicide to cover up her crime. It was

improvised, explaining why it was continually embellished to overcome problems as they arose.

But why would Florence endorse suicide if it were not true? It is likely that an innocent Florence would have been in denial that someone close to her could have poisoned her husband. She would believe her trusted companion that Charles had confessed, and any doubts in her mind would have been dispelled when Sir William Gull asserted it was suicide. Florence would have also accepted the "for Dr Gully" embellishment if it sprang from a grain of truth. Florence, refusing to accept her husband's death could have been murder, was unwittingly drawn into her companion's web of deceit. When she finally woke up and saw the truth, the friendship ruptured, but it was too late to change her version of events. The die had been cast.

Some thorny problems confront this theory, however. Why did Mrs Cox give Charles the most effective remedy for poisoning if she was trying to kill him? It makes little sense. The reconstruction suggests she had no choice, but do you find that plausible? She would have been forgiven for attributing Bravo's condition to gastroenteritis, which presents with similar symptoms. She could have made him comfortable and waited for the doctors, hoping he would die before they arrived. No one would have suspected her. She showed her hand by treating Bravo for poisoning, a critical mistake which appears uncharacteristic of Mrs Cox.

Was the fear of losing her job a sufficient motive for murder? Mrs Cox was a resourceful woman who had known adversity in her life. Even if she was thrown out of The Priory, it was likely that Florence would ensure she was well compensated and her benefactor, Joseph Bravo, would have been motivated to help if she fell into difficulties. And this assumes, of course, that Charles wanted to sack her. Rowe did not believe she was due to leave imminently, but testified she had been given a further two years.

And would Mrs Cox really kill her benefactor's stepson who had been generous to her boys?

Did Mrs Cox have the means for the murder? The reconstruction assumes she had originally picked up a packet of tartar emetic from the stables, but was she likely to be snooping around there? She was not an equestrian. If not, where did she get the poison? Also, to lace the water bottle, she must have known about Bravo's nightly drinking habit, something she flatly denied at the second inquest.

Was there sufficient opportunity? It is possible she spiked the water bottle just before dinner, immediately after returning from Worthing, but at this point she had not heard of Bravo's horse ride nor gauged his discomfort and mood at dinner. If these were the triggers to murder – enabling her to suggest his death was suicide – the only chance she had to tamper with the water bottle was when she fetched Florence's wine. It was an extremely narrow window of opportunity and not without risk; she had no business being in Charles Bravo's room.

For nearly 150 years, Mrs Cox has been a prime suspect for the death of Charles Bravo. But was someone else responsible for his murder? Someone who was not centre stage but hiding in the wings?

Chapter 13

JUST WHAT THE DOCTOR ORDERED

In crime fiction, the obvious suspect is rarely the murderer, and the world's greatest crime novelist believed this was also true in the case of Charles Bravo. Agatha Christie believed that Dr Gully was responsible and penned her thoughts in a letter to writer Francis Wyndham during the summer of 1968. This was later printed in *The Times* and, with permission of The Christie Archive Trust, the full text of her letter is reproduced below.

> I think it was Doctor Gully who killed Charles Bravo. I've always felt he was the only person who had an over-whelming motive and who was the right type: exceedingly competent, successful, and always considered above suspicion.
>
> None of the other suspects is in the least credible. Florence Bravo had all the money and could leave her husband any moment she wanted to: she always had the whip-hand. The Yseult Bridges theory doesn't really convince – one just can't believe Charles would go on saying "I only took laudanum" when he could easily say "I was buying antimony to cure my dear wife of her addiction to drink, but must have taken it by mistake myself."

PART ONE

Mrs Cox is an obvious suspect at first glance, but not when you look into it – a timid and prudent character.

Doctor Gully – elderly, highly respected, full of self-esteem – falls violently for a young and beautiful woman. He is obsessed by her. She responds, and they agree tacitly that if Mrs Gully dies they will marry; but Mrs Gully is one of the healthy insane who live well-protected in expensive asylums. Florence is in love with Gully, but not, I think, with anything approaching his passion for her.

Gully retires from his practice, leaves his house and circle of friends and patients, takes a house opposite Florence in Streatham – not a neighbourhood where he seems to have any particular friends or social connections. His liaison with Florence has to be well guarded and highly respectable – that is essential. When Florence goes to The Priory, he moves house to be near at hand. They go abroad, and Mrs Cox plays her obliging, respectable chaperone part. She is careful to know nothing, see nothing, hear nothing. Florence's family don't like it (they hadn't been born yesterday); but most people accept the friendship – as was frequently the case in those days – so long as appearances are kept up...

To go on – I think Gully's whole life revolved round Florence. But she was young, and a fatherly, protective lover – was this really what she craved? She wanted a young and attractive husband.

The miscarriage, or a necessary (for respectability's sake) abortion by Doctor Gully, brought her to the point of wanting to get out of her love affair. She wanted to be free, to find a good-looking and agreeable young husband, to get married and have children she could keep and enjoy.

She was a bad picker of men: after first marrying a man she was in love with but who was a drunkard, she then fell for Charles Bravo and couldn't have chosen worse. Poor Florence – a born victim.

She broke with Gully, as kindly as possible: and after his first anger he had the strength of character to take his dismissal apparently well. But I don't think he ever did accept it. If he had, the first thing he would have done – like any man in his position – was to leave Balham, sell his house and move to some place where he had friends and relationships. To go on living in Balham would have been a humiliating thing to do. He had only come there to be near Florence and had no other ties. She had insisted that they should no longer see each other; there would not even be the contact of friendship. She wanted him to go elsewhere – he refused. Why did he stay, in this humiliating position?

Surely because he hadn't given up. He still meant to have her come back to him. The only explanation of the words about Bravo spoken by the unpleasant coachman Griffith – "I only give him four months" – is that Griffith knew something about Gully. Some rather curious procedure in the past; some knowledge of Gully's having removed tartar emetic from the stables; something that Gully said or threatened.

It's possible, I think, that Gully might have had a hand in Ricardo's death. He was prone to giving 'prescriptions' to people at long range, without being in contact with them – prescriptions against Jamaican Fever to Mrs Cox, and so on. A little homeopathic bottle, correctly labelled 'nux vomica' or 'strychnine', all deadly poisons though taken in minute doses: but one pill might be different, and trusting Ricardo might take it for a bad hangover, as dear old Gully recommended.

I think Griffith suspected things about Gully, though he didn't know anything definite. Funny that he should speak with such certainty of Bravo's departing from this life, unless something about his employer had given him ideas. Griffith could have known things about Gully – he was really the one person who might. Gully and Florence used to use the Lower Lodge as a meeting place, and Griffith or his wife may have overheard something there.

Anyway, Gully insisted on remaining close to Florence. He gently discouraged her hurrying into marriage, but Florence was in love and determined to go through with it. Bravo was also in a hurry; his mistress might come along and mess things up.

Gully bided his time. He made no false moves. Undoubtedly he had influence with Mrs Cox; he had at least four accidental (?) meetings with her. Did she act as in some ways his agent? It could have been so. She took prescriptions for sitz-baths and compresses which Florence found beneficial and accepted.

Could Gully possibly have prescribed something which would be 'beneficial' to Bravo's tempers or his rheumatism? "Give it to him without his knowing it..." She could have done that in good faith. And if it was Mrs Cox who added something to the laurel water, or the chloroform, or the laudanum, or the water bottle, the fact that she had been instrumental would terrify her when poison became suspected. Bravo took it "for Gully": did these words in her statement hint at the truth?

Did Gully expect Bravo's death to be accepted as natural, accidental or suicidal? Antimony is like arsenic;

how very many arsenical deaths have been accepted as natural, as gastric inflammation! Perhaps a little too big a dose was given, so that the symptoms were unexpectedly violent.

Doctor Gully was a person of great ability. If he had decided to remove Bravo, he would have been capable of devising a way. And even if events took a turn that was unexpected – who was aloof from it all, a person of good reputation, no evidence against him, the perfect planner, the man whose personality was so strong as to compel belief? The man who was never found out. But I'm quite sure he did it.

Agatha Christie.

Letter © The Christie Archive Trust. Reprinted under licence.

Members of The Cold Case Jury, this letter provides a fascinating insight into the mind of the world's bestselling author. It's easy to imagine how her ingenious theory might have transpired. Dr Gully schemes to 'accidentally' run into Mrs Cox at Balham station – we know this actually happened several times. After hearing about Florence's sleepless nights, he prescribes laurel water and casually asks after Mr Bravo. Mrs Cox informs him that he is suffering from rheumatism and neuralgia. "I'm sorry to hear that," the doctor replies and prescribes homeopathic pills. "Dissolve one nightly in Mr Bravo's drinking water," he instructs Mrs Cox, "but on no account tell him it's from me. He will never take it if you do." All too aware of Charles' jealously towards him, she readily agrees. Like an insidious game of Russian roulette, one pill is laced with an enormous dose of tartar emetic.

PART ONE

As a master storyteller, it should come as no surprise that Christie laid particular emphasis on motive, the foundation of the plot of any crime novel. She believed Dr Gully was deeply resentful at being replaced by a young usurper – his true feelings were revealed by his angry first letter to Florence after the split. After sacrificing so much for her, he was not going to be pushed aside, and resolved to remove Charles Bravo from the situation – permanently. Yet, it might have struck you that the real obstacle to the marriage of Dr Gully and Florence was his much older and infirm wife. For someone so capable, it would have been easy for him to prescribe "something beneficial" for her without ever falling under suspicion. If the doctor was a callous, cold-blooded murderer who was involved in the death of Captain Ricardo, as Christie believed, why did he not then kill his own wife? Even with Bravo dead, he must have realised that with his own wife still alive there would be no chance of getting back together with Florence. Therefore, did Dr Gully have as strong a motive as Christie believed?

What about means? Clearly, as a doctor, Gully had access to tartar emetic. Indeed, George Griffith bought a mother lode of the poison when he worked for him, and it was bought under the doctor's name, something Gully denied at the inquest. A more pertinent question concerns the poison. For someone knowledgeable about medicine, the choice of tartar emetic is surprising, almost unbelievable. Strychnine or a narcotic poison would have been a more reliable method of murder. One possibility is that Gully wanted his victim to suffer terribly. But this would mean that the urbane and intellectual doctor was actually a cruel psychopath, which is not borne out by what we know of him.

The greatest obstacle is the lack of opportunity. Obviously, Dr Gully did not personally lace Charles Bravo's water bottle and therefore he must have had inside help. Mrs Cox is a plausible candidate, but was she as passive an agent as Christie suggests? Gully could have no idea how Mrs Cox would react when it dawned on her she had been a sacrificial pawn in his murderous plan. Terrified, she could have easily confessed the source of the 'medicine', a loose end that might have sent him to the gallows.

Perhaps Mrs Cox was a co-conspirator? Statistically, this is less likely than Mrs Cox acting alone. Of recorded poisoning cases, nearly nine out of ten were perpetrated by a solitary killer. If you suspect the companion, why does she need to involve anyone else? By contrast, Dr Gully must have worked with another person because he did not have the opportunity to administer the poison himself. So, despite its ingenuity, Christie's theory has its problems.

Could Gully have enlisted a servant as his agent instead? Mary Ann Keeber would seem an ideal surrogate killer because she had access to Bravo's water bottle and was familiar with his habits. But why would the housemaid be in league with the eminent doctor? How often did they even speak? She was more likely to work with another servant, like George Griffith, who also had access to the poison and bore a serious grudge against Charles Bravo.

Let us briefly examine the possibility that Mary Ann was the poisoner. She had the opportunity and probably the means, but what about motive? She told the inquest she was leaving Florence's staff to get married, but she actually married John Hills eight years later. Her husband was a gardener, and it has been conjectured – without any evidence – that he was the one who Charles Bravo sacked in early 1876. Alternatively, she might have been close to Mrs Griffith, Florence's maid, and agreed to put a little something in his water bottle to make him sick as payback. Perhaps, she inadvertently mistook the dose.

Such a theory appears plausible and ticks all the boxes, but the housemaid could not have been the poisoner unless Mrs Cox was directly involved. We can be certain of this because the logic is undeniable. If Charles Bravo did not take his own life, Mrs Cox *faked* his confessional to account for his poisoning. And she could only take this perilous step if *she knew* what had happened. It does not matter who we suspect, or what theory we develop, this reasoning is like a road sign pointing us in the direction of the correct solution.

Would Mrs Cox jeopardise her well-paid position and the future of her boys to help a disaffected servant or jealous paramour settle a score and kill her benefactor's stepson? It seems unlikely. Yet, there was someone the loyal Mrs Cox would have helped. Someone she cared for. Someone she had come to love as a close friend.

And that was Florence Bravo.

Chapter 14

MALICE AND MISCALCULATION

For the final reconstruction, our focus turns to Florence. We will discover the means, motive and opportunity for her to have poisoned her husband, and how her loyal confidante Mrs Cox covered up the crime. This conclusion was originally reached by John Williams in his book *Suddenly at the Priory* in 1957, but based on the testimony given at the inquest, I present a new variation. We now return to The Priory for the final time to see how Charles Bravo might have met his terrible death.

*

4:30pm. Reclining on the chaise longue, nestled among the tasselled cushions, Florence held a small, leather-bound volume of Shakespeare's sonnets. The choice was not accidental. Some of the happiest hours of their young marriage had been spent reading Shakespeare together.

Is it for fear to wet a widow's eye, she read aloud to herself softly, *that thou consumest thyself in single life?* She read each line, savouring the words as if they were a delicacy melting on the tongue. Her voice tailed off as she spoke the final line: *That on himself such murderous shame commits.*

Her mind was absorbed. The romanticism of a man eschewing marriage because it would break the heart of his wife when he died was inimical to a materialistic man like her husband, she thought. His heart was rarely moved by anything but money. She had already been forced to part with a maid and a groom since the marriage – all to cut costs and appease her husband and his interfering mother. Their meanness disgusted her. She should have paid heed to the warning sign: his haggling over the marriage settlement. And recently he had raised the prospect of scaling back on her cherished garden, selling her beloved cobs and relieving Mrs Cox from her duties.

She heard footsteps approaching, the door opened and Charles walked in. Florence looked up. "Charlie! You're back!" Closing her book, she placed it on a small table next to an empty wine glass. "How was your day?"

"The Turkish baths were invigorating and it's always a jolly lunch with your uncle!" he replied cheerfully.

"Go up to your bedroom and see what I have bought for you." He was surprised and intrigued by her excited tone. She smiled, waving him upstairs. He returned holding a box of Cavendish tobacco. "This isn't my normal tobacco," he said, "but thank you." He walked over and kissed Florence on the forehead. "It is just like you to be so considerate, getting all the things I like. I'll smoke this in the garden, I think."

He sank his frame into the plush armchair. "Talking of lunch, your uncle agrees with me." Florence's heart sank as she knew all too well what was coming. "He was shocked when I told him you had spent 20 guineas on each fern for your conservatory garden."

"Yes, but that was before we married, Charlie."

"The garden expenditure is still extravagant. One must not be sentimental about this, Florence. We have to live within our means."

"We do."

Charles had been ready for this. The gardening was an opening gambit, but it was not the real target. "Well, we will have to make savings elsewhere then."

"We really don't need to."

"I've calculated that Mrs Cox is costing £200 a year. That's my entire annual salary!"

"Her salary is £80 a year, you know that."

He paused, repeating slowly "Eighty pounds a year" before adding his *coup de grace*. "And that's just her salary. What about the generous clothes allowance that you insist on providing? What about the meals she has with us every day at our expense? And she's costing me her salary again to replenish my wine cellar with sherry!"

"But you know how useful she is," Florence protested. "You said so yourself when Willoughby came to dinner last week..."

He cut her off sharply. "But that's before I calculated the total cost."

"You're happy to take £500 of my money in the morning and then insist we tighten our belts by the afternoon!"

"My mother says..."

"This has nothing to do with your mother!" Florence retorted angrily. The spectre of his mother interfering in their affairs again was the last straw. "You and your conniving mother have been trying to force out Mrs Cox even before our honeymoon!"

"How dare you speak of my mother like that!" Charles snapped, jumping up.

"She won't stop until I have nothing left in this marriage. She wants to get rid of everything I love!"

"But she doesn't know who you *really* love, does she?" he spat at her, pointing his finger in the vague direction of Dr Gully's house. "She would never have agreed to let me marry a tainted woman had she known!"

PART ONE

"Tainted woman!" Florence shrieked. "How dare you say that! You have a mistress and a child out of wedlock!"

"Don't bring them into this!" Charles strode over to the chaise longue with a thunderous look on his face. "It disgusts me to think of you with that old wretch," he snarled, grabbing her chin with his hand. "Well, it's high time you started giving me every night what you gave him. You don't need a chaperone now you're my wife. No other man would put up with his wife's lap dog sleeping in his bed."

"It's because I'm ill, you brute!" she fired back, her eyes open and filled with fire.

He glowered before pushing her way. As his temper quickly burnt itself out his voice calmed but it retained its strident tone. "After Worthing we will share our bedroom again," he said firmly. "And when Mrs Cox is in Jamaica we will get this marriage on an even keel. A marriage is a union of two, not a congregation of three." Florence could hear his mother speaking. "I will give Mrs Cox her notice on her return, and not a word of it until then."

Florence looked away, trying to hide the welling in her eyes. Exhausted from her illness and now distraught at the possibility of losing her close companion, she felt powerless. Charles turned, swiping the tobacco from the arm of the chair onto the floor. "I'm taking the cobs for a ride."

"They were exercised yesterday," she protested.

"Don't tell me what I can do in my own house!"

From the hall she heard him call out: "Rowe, fetch my riding breeches!"

Florence held her head in her hand. She loathed his miserliness and sexual jealously. Impervious to reason, both were intensifying with each passing week. She was already accustomed to his wilful determination, but there was a menace about him now. And it frightened her.

This was not the first time Charles had talked about Jane leaving, but it was the most vociferous. And she had learned all too quickly that once Charles had set his mind on something he would not be deterred until he had his way, especially if his mother's approval was at stake. She was enraged to think that she had given him £500 and yet he was still obsessed with the expense of her companion.

If Jane left, Florence had realised with growing anxiety, there would be no one to help her fend off Charles in the bedroom. If he shared her bedroom again his sexual demands would be unrelenting. This had not been a problem in her first marriage – most of the time Alexander was incapable due to drink and, when he was able, he was rarely willing, seeking the attention of other women. But now, in the first months of her second marriage, the thought of sex with Charles sickened her. And she could not risk another pregnancy; she feared it might kill her.

There seemed no way out. She could not continue to retreat to her family at Buscot Park whenever there was trouble. Florence wiped the tears from her eyes and glanced down at the open book beside her. Her eye caught the line: *thou consumest thyself in single life*. A life of self-indulgent pleasures unshackled from the need to appease a husband seemed alluring once again. She turned the page, reading the final words of the sonnet: *such murderous shame commits*. She quickly pushed the thought aside – but it was not banished from her mind. Rather, it sank below the waves of her immediate consciousness and lurked danger-ously beneath the surface.

6:20pm. Prostrate on the chaise longue, snoozing off the afternoon's sherry and champagne, Florence heard the door open. Although she was aware Charles had returned, she was in no mood to talk, and lay there with her eyes closed. She heard a shuffling of feet and a body slump in the armchair by the fire.

PART ONE

On his rounds to check the fires were lit for the evening, Rowe opened the door of the morning room. He was surprised to see Florence asleep on the couch and stopped in his tracks. Hunched forward in the chair, his face pale and drawn, Charles did not look up. Rowe noticed the large fire burning in the grate, and discreetly pulled the door to; he would return later.

6:25pm. On hearing Charles moan with the pain, Florence opened her eyes and slowly sat up. She noticed he was still in his riding breeches. "What's the matter, Charlie?" Her tone was more curious than sympathetic.

"Cremorne has got a right temper. He bolted as soon as I got through the gate. As far as Mitcham Common." Charles rubbed his side. "My hat was blown clean off my head but I couldn't dismount – my legs felt like stone. I was so weary I even had trouble getting a shilling out of my pocket to pay the lad that fetched my hat."

Serves you right, Florence thought. "You look dreadful."

"I feel worse. I've never been so stiff in my life."

"Would you like a brandy or some Burgundy?" Bravo shook his head as he leaned further forward in the armchair, as if to be sick. Florence realised how wretched he looked; his face was bleached white and his hands were trembling. He looked like death... In that moment the dark idea surfaced like a monster from the deep. She saw him drinking from his water bottle laced with the tartar emetic from that little packet she had kept. If he collapsed tonight, they would say it had something to do with the horse bolting. No one would suspect the poor wife still recovering from her second miscarriage.

"You should take a bath, Charlie," Florence said, rising from her chair. "Let me arrange one for you." As she left the room, she told herself that providence had delivered this opportunity and she must not squander it. She closed the door, turned left and headed upstairs.

181

6:30pm. On the landing she paused, steeling herself for her task, and listened for any servants busy with their duties. There was a deathly silence, punctuated only by the ticking of the clock in the hall downstairs. She moved stealthily into her room and from the medicine chest retrieved a brown paper packet stamped 'Antimony Tart.' From her bedroom it was just a few steps to her husband's room. She slipped inside and closed the door behind her, slowly and quietly.

She moved to the small table at the foot of his bed – the water bottle was only half full but she knew Mary Ann would top it up before bedtime. She emptied the packet of whitish powder into the water and swirled the bottle until all the small crystals had vanished like melting snow. Crouching down by the dormant fire, she shredded the packet and hid the ribbons of paper underneath the blackened coals; they would be burned without trace when the fire was next lit. Finally, she washed the soot off her hands in the wash basin in the corner of the room.

6:35pm. In the morning room, Charles stiffly craned his neck as his wife returned. "I cannot find Mary Ann," she said, kneeling down beside him.

"I'll ring for someone." Like an elderly man, he slowly rotated his body in the armchair and pulled the tasselled cord next to the fireplace. "I'm so exhausted. I should have smoked that tobacco instead." Florence picked up the discarded box from the floor and placed it on the arm of the chair. You'll never smoke again, she thought. She felt no emotion; it was no different to putting down an aggressive dog.

Moments later, Rowe appeared. "You rang, sir?"

"Could you get a servant to run me a bath, Rowe?"

"Yes, sir. Shall I light the fire in your room, as well?"

"Yes, of course," Florence replied keenly.

PART ONE

6:45pm. Rowe helped his master to his feet. Leaning heavily against his loyal servant, Charles ponderously made his way to the hipbath in his bedroom with Florence following behind. Rowe lowered him to the side of his bed, where Charles perched for a few moments, still in discomfort, but enjoying the warmth of the young fire. Rowe knelt down and pulled off Bravo's boots.

As he got up, Bravo winced and placed his hand on his side. He shuffled towards the bath. "Tell Mary Ann this water will do me very well in the morning."

"Yes, sir."

9:30pm. "He's being very selfish," Mrs Cox declared, leaning against the mantelpiece in Florence's dressing room. "Worthing is for your recuperation, it's not a holiday." Florence was sitting at her dressing room table putting up her hair.

There was a knock at the door. "Come in!" Florence called out.

"Mrs Bravo, I have your hot water." Mary Ann placed a small can by the wash basin for the nightly ablutions.

Florence decided she needed as much alcohol as possible to get through the night. "Mary Ann, fetch me a little Marsala will you?" She handed her housemaid the tumbler containing the dregs of the wine Mrs Cox had fetched minutes earlier. Mary Ann took the glass and descended the stairs.

9:45pm. In her bedroom, Florence knocked back the Marsala and placed the tumbler on the bedside table. She slipped into bed.

"You've had rather a lot tonight, Florence," Mrs Cox said, sitting on a small stool nearest the door. Beside her, a terrier was lying in front of the flickering fire.

"It's Dutch courage, Janie," Florence blurted out.

Mrs Cox frowned. "What do you mean?"

There was a knock. Florence lay down, turning her back to the door. "Yes?" Mrs Cox called out.

Mary Ann entered. "Is that all for tonight?"

"Have you brought up the little tray?"

"Yes, it's over there."

"I think that'll be all, Mary Ann. Remember to take the dogs downstairs, won't you?"

The housemaid ushered the terrier out of the room, closing the inner door. Florence sat up. "I've done it, Janie. I've had enough and I've done it!"

Mrs Cox knew at once what Florence was alluding to: she had been threatening to poison her husband with one scheme or another for the past month, usually after drinking too much. "He wants to get rid of you, Janie. I can't let that happen! I won't!" Florence sobbed. "He really means it this time."

"Tell me exactly what you have done."

"It's in his drinking water."

"Oh, dear Lord, no!" Mrs Cox's mind was drowning in its own thoughts. What pretext could she conjure up to enter Charles' room and retrieve the bottle? Was it already too late? What would she do if he collapsed?

Then they heard the haunted shouting from the next room: "Florence! Florence!" Raw, visceral fear tore through Charles' voice. "Hot water!"

Terrified, Florence looked at her companion. "Oh Janie!" she sobbed. "Please help me."

"Roll over," Mrs Cox instructed. "Pretend to be asleep." She was at a loss what to do. How on earth could she save the life of Charles without revealing what Florence had done?

Mary Ann rushed into the bedroom. "Mr Bravo is ill! Come quick!"

Shaking, Mrs Cox rose from her stool. As she rushed across into Charles' bedroom she noticed a bottle of laudanum and one of chloroform on the mantelpiece. The idea immediately formed in her mind: she had to make it look like a suicide. There was no time to think of anything else.

PART ONE

She sped around the bed to the casement window on the far side of the room. As she reached him, Bravo shouted again: "Hot water! Hot water!"

*

Members of the Cold Case Jury, after Charles collapsed, Mrs Cox needed to rapidly assess the terrible situation she now faced. In covering up Florence's crime, the loyal companion had to act as if she were herself the poisoner: empty the laced water bottle into the bath, refill it, deal with the chloroform bottle and send for the family doctor. And when his symptoms revealed that Charles had not been poisoned by chloroform, she desperately invented Charles' confessional statement to avert suspicion from falling on anyone in the household.

This reconstruction suggests Florence laced the water bottle soon after Charles had returned from his horse ride. I derived this timing from an inconsistency in the inquest testimony. When Florence was asked whether she remained in the morning room with her husband, she stated: "I advised him to have a warm bath, and went out of the room to order it." Yet, Rowe stated that "Mr Bravo rang the bell and told me to ask the servant to get him a bath." The bath was filled up and he helped his master to his room.

Clearly, Florence did not order a bath because Charles had to ask for it himself. It begs the question why Florence did not ring for a servant, but the main point is this: she left the room and we do not know where she went or how long she was away. It would only require a few minutes to lace the water bottle. And if she had, it would also explain why she consumed an excessive amount of alcohol that night, even by her standards: she was bracing herself for what was to come.

There was another window of opportunity. Author John Williams believed Florence laced the water immediately after she asked Mrs Cox to fetch a glass of wine on leaving the morning room after dinner. Although possible, it is extremely tight – a couple of minutes at most – if Florence wanted to be in her dressing room before Mrs Cox returned with the wine.

Another detail emerged in the reconstruction. That morning Florence had handed Charles a £500 cheque (nearly £60,000 in today's money) to pay into his personal account; it was the purpose of the trip to London. At the inquest, Florence said it was because she wanted Charles to have his own money, independent of her. Although there is unlikely to be a direct connection, it is striking that he was poisoned on the same day he paid the money into his account. I conjectured that Florence was absolutely furious that he still wanted to evict Mrs Cox from her position to reduce cost, despite being bank-rolled himself.

Let's examine this theory using the categorical trinity of motive, means and opportunity. It seems reasonable to believe that Florence might have regretted her marriage. In just a few months, she had suffered a loss of independence, interference from her mother-in-law and ill health due to two miscarriages. And there might have been problems in the bedroom, exacerbating Bravo's alleged jealousy. Although it is true that Florence was financially secure, divorce was not easy and would have caused intractable differences with her family just when she had reconciled. Considering the marriage was intended to give Florence social respectability, the stigmatism of separation would have been the last thing she wanted; she needed another way to extricate herself from her recent vows.

It has long been suggested that Mrs Cox had the stronger motive – the prospect of losing her well-paid position at The

Priory. Yet, was her possible departure actually feared more by Florence? She would be losing her confidante and friend. Mrs Cox appeared resourceful in the face of adversity, but how would the privileged and entitled Florence respond when faced with problems seemingly out of her control? Although she had no hand in her first husband's death, it cannot be denied that widowhood worked out well for her. Perhaps she believed it was the solution this time, too. All things considered, did Florence have the strongest motive to kill her husband?

The choice of poison is an important consideration in this case. Because tartar emetic has an unpredictable, self-antidote effect – a victim might expel all the poison before it can be absorbed into the body – it is more likely to be used by someone who already possessed some. Having been married to an alcoholic for many years, Florence must have known about it as a drinking deterrent. Further, she was often in the stables where Griffith kept two bottles for treating the horses. The resentful coachman testified he destroyed all the tartar emetic when he left The Priory, but did he overlook a packet? Although the poison could not be traced to Florence, there are grounds for suspecting she had access to it. In which case, she had the means.

An opportunistic poison connected to both alcoholism and The Priory stables makes Florence a prime suspect, yet it is possible that someone else stumbled upon the poison, or it was acquired elsewhere. It is undeniable that Mrs Cox, who had expertise in sickroom nursing, would have at least known about tartar emetic and its properties.

Finally, opportunity. If the water bottle was the poisoned chalice, as seems most likely, then a poisoner needed to know about Charles' nocturnal habits. At the inquest, Florence denied knowing that her husband drank straight from the water bottle before retiring to bed. But having shared a bedroom for at least three months of the marriage, it is inconceivable that she had not noticed him do this.

Apart from the three hours she was away in London, Florence had ample time to lace the water bottle. She was at The Priory for the early morning, almost all of the afternoon and the entire evening. Crucially, she also learned of the cob's bolting immediately after Charles returned and observed its effect on him.

According to the reconstruction, Florence lost her nerve and confessed to Mrs Cox when they retired to her bedroom. With no option but to rush to his aid when the alarm was raised, Mrs Cox was placed in an impossible position: she had to save Bravo and cover up the fact that he had been poisoned by his own wife. The confessional and many of her statements were lies told to spare Florence. Recall she had told the inquest: "I never thought of myself. I only thought of Mrs Bravo." This appears consistent with Rowe's comment: "I have seen her, poor woman, and she has got herself into a great deal of trouble through not telling the truth."

But did she think only of Florence when she introduced Dr Gully into the confessional? Clearly not, but by this time Mrs Cox had become a prime suspect. During the first inquest she was left to face the music alone while the cause of all her trouble languished upstairs. She might have realised that to save her own skin, and her family, she had little choice but to introduce the all-important motive for his suicide.

One of the striking features of the case is that after Bravo's death Florence and Mrs Cox appeared to work together. As long ago as 1926, John Hall suggested in *The Bravo Mystery* that "it is impossible to dissociate the two women" and other writers have agreed, citing the obvious collusion in the women's Treasury statements as evidence of their joint complicity. It is possible they conspired to kill Charles, perhaps on the spur of moment, while they were upstairs and Charles remained downstairs in the morning room. Florence testified that they were in her dressing room for 15 minutes before Mary Ann Keeber knocked on the door, plenty of time to have laced the water bottle. However, a premeditated conspiracy theory changes little from the one we have discussed; Florence was involved and Mrs Cox covered it up.

Like the Mrs Cox theory, this one also explains many of the case's puzzling features: Bravo's insistence that he had taken nothing but laudanum; his calling out for Florence to fetch hot water; and why Florence showed no surprise on being told that her husband had been poisoned. Indeed, this theory makes sense of Florence's reaction to the confessional statement in front of Dr Johnson. "He *said* that?" Florence knew all too well that her husband could never have admitted to taking poison. Mrs Cox was improvising and it was the first Florence had heard of it. No wonder Florence was quickly ushered to bed in case she started to give the game away.

Puzzles remain, however. Florence's behaviour is not typical of poisoners, who frequently shield their victims from outsiders, especially doctors, fearing their crime might be discovered. Yet Florence called no fewer than three separate doctors over two days – Dr Harrison, Mr Bell and Sir William Gull – and indirectly requested the medical opinion of Dr Gully. All the doctors and servants agreed that Florence's distress at her husband's plight appeared genuine. In addition, we should not forget that Florence bought her husband gifts and gave him £500. These would seem to be the actions of a wife who wanted her marriage to work rather than see her husband dead.

Similarly, the reaction of Charles appears inconsistent with a fatal relationship. If there had been arguments and fights prior to the poisoning, would he not have revealed this over the three days on his deathbed? In fact, the opposite is true. He was affectionate and generous to his wife, leaving everything to her in his Will and even asking his mother to be pleasant to her. Surely, if there had been as much acrimony as shown in the reconstruction, he would have suspected something. He might not have confronted Florence directly but hinted of the "bitter troubles" to his cousin or mother.

Does this theory satisfactorily explain why Charles was poisoned on this particular night? Florence was looking forward to her trip to Worthing and Mrs Cox was not leaving The Priory imminently, if at all. The only trigger for the crime appears to be the bolting horse. But would the sight of her husband stiff and in pain really induce her to poison him with tartar emetic? If she did, it was a terrible miscalculation.

We have now explored the four main theories of how Charles Bravo might have died. It's time to sum up.

Chapter 15

SUMMING UP

Members of the Cold Case Jury, the inquest jury believed that Charles Bravo was wilfully killed. So the question before you is, who was most likely responsible for his death? There are four choices:

- **Charles Bravo** took his own life.
- **Mrs Cox** poisoned Charles Bravo.
- **Dr Gully** used Mrs Cox to poison Charles Bravo.
- **Florence Bravo** poisoned her husband and Mrs Cox was an accessory.

An important first question to answer concerns the poisoned chalice: was it the water bottle or the Burgundy at dinner? Most medical opinion favoured the former with a notable exception – Dr Abrath, the author of the first book on the case. If it was the Burgundy, it effectively rules out Mrs Cox, who arrived back too late to have tampered with it, and Charles Bravo, who could not plausibly have laced his own wine before dinner, mistakenly or intentionally. If it was the water bottle, all the suspects remain in the frame.

Was **Charles Bravo** responsible for his own death? The key evidence in favour of this verdict is the deathbed demeanour and behaviour of Bravo himself. His indifference to his plight indicated he knew what he had taken and his morbid pessimism suggested he was aware it was lethal. If so, Mrs Cox told the truth about his confessional statement, and her suspicious drip feeding of information was due to her anxiety around avoiding a scandal. Her waiting until Charles regained consciousness to tell the doctors about it indicates she had nothing to hide. Florence's distressed reaction on seeing her husband's plight and repeatedly seeking medical assistance are consistent with this verdict.

Bravo's quick temper and excitable nature may have triggered a "temporary irresponsibility" (to quote Professor Sheppard), leading him to swallow the poison. If Mrs Cox is to be believed, the precipitating cause was his jealously of Dr Gully, but it might also be due to complications in his own life and specifically problems that night. It must be stressed, however, that Bravo called out for hot water, suggesting he had changed his mind, yet none of his subsequent actions demonstrated any regret.

If intentional, it is, however, extraordinary that Charles did not simply pick up the bottle of laudanum on his mantelpiece – a more effective and suitable drug for his sad task. One explanation is that he ingested the massive dose of tartar emetic by mistake, perhaps confusing it for Epsom salts. Yet, if it was a tragic accident, how do we explain the fact that no trace of the poison was ever found in his room? To manoeuvre around this difficulty, it has been suggested that Mrs Cox threw the remainder in the fire and concocted a suicide story that she knew would cause incalculable harm to Florence. Do you consider this a satisfactory explanation?

Whether deliberate or accidental, Charles did not tell anyone what had happened, not even a member of his own family. Rather, if Mrs Cox is to be believed, he confided in his wife's loyal companion, arguably the last person he would have told if he wished his wife not to know. How plausible do you find this?

PART ONE

Despite the problems with this verdict, it might be your decision if you believe it is more probable than any of the murder theories. The simplest of these is that **Mrs Cox** was the poisoner, which accounts for her unusual behaviour. Although she told both Dr Moore and Mr Harrison that she heard Bravo's shouts for hot water and rushed to his aid, this is not strictly true. She helped only after Mary Ann Keeber raised the alarm.

Charles' confessional statement seems too convenient to be true, and her massaging of it in the weeks following his death only deepens suspicions. She had a motive: to keep her job at The Priory to pay for the education of her sons. It appears she had decided to take a two-month trip to Jamaica to visit her aunt, but could she trust Charles to retain her when she returned, especially with his interfering mother pulling the strings behind the scenes? Was it her desperate need to remove this problem that made her strike that night?

Indeed, the choice of poison and the timing of the poisoning both suggest the killing was opportunistic. Perhaps Mrs Cox possessed only one poison – tartar emetic – and was waiting for the correct moment to lace his water bottle with it. The moment arrived when she saw the physical and mental state of Charles that evening.

On the other hand, was the prospect of losing her job a sufficient motive for murder? Harry Poland, a junior legal counsel for the Crown at the second inquest, believed it was scarcely adequate. After all, how many people today kill their bosses after being made redundant? Motive is closely allied to character and Mrs Cox was a resourceful and self-reliant woman, one capable of supporting her family. Further, it was an opportunistic murder, which appears at odds with Mrs Cox's cautious and prudent personality. Also, did she really have sufficient time to lace the water bottle when she fetched the wine for Florence?

The second possible poisoner is **Dr Gully**, the prime suspect of Agatha Christie, who suggested he had the strongest motive of all: the humiliation of being usurped by Charles and the desire to return to Florence. As a doctor, he certainly had access to the poison, and Christie ingenuously suggested that he used an unsuspecting Mrs Cox to administer it. But would Dr Gully really endanger the life of an innocent courier to execute his devious plan? Could he really bank on the silence of an enraged Mrs Cox when she found out what he had done?

The third murder theory is **Florence, with Mrs Cox covering up the crime**. Florence may have had one of many motives, including the fear of losing her loyal companion to the pecuniary obsession of Charles and his mother. She might have simply regretted the marriage. Remember, it was almost impossible for her to obtain a divorce without her husband's agreement, and legal separation would have also been difficult without a male trustee like Dr Gully, who was hardly going to help her a second time. However, her distress at her husband's collapse appeared genuine and she called multiple doctors to his bedside.

If you look at all of Mrs Cox's actions after Charles called out for hot water, each one can be explained in the context of her being an accessory after the fact, as well as a premeditated poisoner. In fact, some of them become more explicable. For example, her textbook treatment for poisoning makes sense if she was actually trying to save Charles, which would be the case if Florence had poisoned him. On the other hand, some of Florence's actions, such as her grief and summoning several doctors, fit less comfortably if she was the poisoner.

How can you differentiate between the three theories of murder? I suggest it boils down to your view of Mrs Cox. She could have been an unwitting dupe of Dr Gully, but would the responsible Mrs Cox really give Charles 'medicine' without his knowledge? Alternatively, she might have actively conspired with Dr Gully, but how does the addition of Dr Gully explain any more than the simpler theory that the cautious and shrewd Mrs Cox acted alone? And, most importantly, would Dr Gully have played Russian roulette with his murderous scheme by selecting tartar emetic as the poison?

To differentiate between Mrs Cox and Florence, I suggest several questions need to be answered. Who was more likely to have access to the poison? Who had the greater opportunity to lace the water bottle or the wine? Who was more likely to have poisoned Charles on that particular night? And, finally, who was more likely to resort to poison to solve their problems?

Keeping all this in mind, it is now time to turn to the evidence. In Part Two, you will find important documents to help you make your decision. You will discover more about the poison and how it could have been used in conjunction with another lethal drug. You will read the full statements of Florence Bravo and Jane Cox and extracts taken from the reports of Chief Inspector Clarke. Almost all of this information has never been published before. These exhibits are not mere footnotes to the story. They allow us to hear witnesses in their own words and place events in their full context. Only then will you be in a position to decide what really happened that fateful night at The Priory.

In Part Three, I provide my view of the case and the verdicts of other authors. You will also read what happened to the principal characters after the inquest. I hope you will then deliver your verdict. Visit the Cold Case Jury website (**coldcasejury.com**) and simply click on 'Your Verdict' for *Poisoned at The Priory* and follow the simple instructions. After you have cast your vote, you can view the collective verdict of the Cold Case Jury.

It is now up to you, the jury, to decide who was responsible for the death of Charles Bravo.

PART TWO

THE EVIDENCE

Our story is not yet finished.

It can only be completed by listening
to the narrator of every crime.

The evidence.

There are deeper mysteries underlying
the ordinary current of daily human existence
than the most fertile brain could imagine.

The London Journal,
2 September 1876.

LIST OF ONLINE EXHIBITS

Exhibit A   Persons of Interest

Exhibit B   Plans of The Priory

Exhibit C   Photographic Plates

Exhibit D   Picture Album

The Photographic Plates includes images of Florence Bravo, Charles Bravo, Jane Cox, Dr James Gully and Sir William Gull. The Picture Album includes drawings of The Priory and scenes from the second inquest.

To access online, visit **coldcasejury.com** and click on the Evidence File for *Poisoned at The Priory*.

Number 1. ONE PENNY.

THE
BALHAM MYSTERY:
OR,
THE "BRAVO" POISONING CASE.

MR. CHARLES BRAVO ON HIS COB "CREMORNE."

POISONING IN MODERN TIMES.

Almost every one has either read or heard of the wholesale poisonings perpetrated in Italy by Tofana and the Borgias, and in France by the Marchioness de Brinvilliers and La Voisin, whose "Powder of Succession" was in such request amongst expectant heirs. In England, under James I., Mrs. Turner, whose execution in a starched ruff had the effect of sending that much-prized article of dress out of fashion, poisoned the same notorious ending, although secretly on the same extensive scale. In those times, owing to the dearth of medical knowledge and the difficulty of procuring drugs, such crimes were confined almost exclusively to the upper classes, who, by means of their supplements and wealth, were enabled to accomplish their culpable designs. To-day, however, the spread of general information, combined with the great facilities which, in spite of legislative impediments, still exist for purchasing poisons, have caused these crimes to become comparatively common in all grades of society. We all know how prevalent they were a few years ago among the labouring classes in certain agricultural districts, where in more than one solitary instance all the members of a family were successively sacrificed for the sake of the money allowed by the burial clubs for their funeral expenses.

One of our most eminent writers on medical jurisprudence has asserted that some two-thirds of people in England are unsuspectingly put off annually by slow poisoning; and it is a significant fact that particular insurance offices make it a rule never to insure the lives of the wives of medical men. The crime of poisoning, from its dastardly character, is properly held in the utmost horror in this country, and in all cases of grave suspicion great efforts are invariably made to bring the presumed perpetrators to justice. We need only cite the cases of William Palmer, Madeleine Smith, Dr. Smethurst, and Mary Ann Cotton, whose prolonged trials excited the most intense interest. During the past few weeks what is generally known as the Balham Mystery has attracted a large amount of public attention, and whether the death in question proves to have been the result of a skilfully contrived crime, or if it is made evident that it arose from accident—for in the face of the dying declarations of the deceased, and the character the latter is known to have borne among his friends, all idea of suicide seems to be out of the question—there can be no difference of opinion as to the necessity existing for holding the new inquiry directed by the Court of Queen's Bench into the various unexplained surrounding circumstances. This inquiry it is our intention to report with the fullest detail, prefacing it with a narrative of the former inquest, of the after-circumstances of the sudden and mysterious connected with the case, and the friends of the deceased, of the protest on the part of the Coroner's jury, and the proceedings in the Court of Queen's Bench, illustrating the whole with portraits, views, and representations of the more interesting incidents, in every case either from photographs supplied to us, or from sketches taken for the especial purpose.

RIGHT: THE VICTIM. Charles Bravo, aged 30, a barrister with burning ambition. Did his acute temper and jealously of Dr Gully provoke him to take his own life?

RIGHT: HIS WIFE. Florence Bravo, aged 30, a wealthy widow who married in haste. Did she regret the rushed nuptials and, trapped by draconian divorce laws, decided that murder was her only escape?

LEFT: THE LOYAL COMPANION. Jane Cox, aged 48, resourceful and discreet. Did Charles threaten her position at The Priory and the future of her three boys?

LEFT: THE JILTED LOVER. Dr James Gully, aged 68, urbane and charismatic. Did he dupe Mrs Cox into giving Charles a lethal 'medicine' so he could rekindle his affair with Florence, as Agatha Christie supposed?

ABOVE: THE BEDFORD HOTEL. Crowds flocked to Balham to hear the verdict of the sensational second inquest. It was also here that George Griffith made his startling prophecy and the butler Rowe told the proprietor that Mrs Cox had lied.
BELOW: On the left is the Bedford Hotel. Bedford Hill Road passes under the railway bridge. A = Balham Priory; B = Orwell Lodge, Dr Gully's residence; C = Streatham Church.

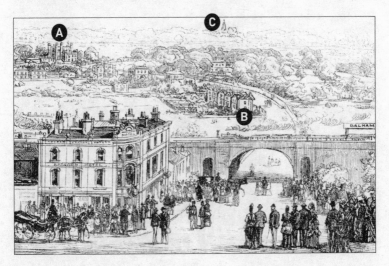

The Jury testing and tasting a solution of Antimony

ABOVE: Professor Redwood allowed the jury to taste a strong solution of tartar emetic from a wine glass. He believed the water bottle in Charles Bravo's bedroom was likely to be the source of the poison.
BELOW: Sir William Gull gave his evidence during a fractious examination. Notice the train through the open window. The Bedford Hotel was not the ideal venue for an inquest, not least because plenty of liquor was enjoyed during the lunch break.

ABOVE LEFT: George Johnson, the senior physician who attended to Charles Bravo. Johnson initially suspected suicide but was guarded as to the manner of death at the second inquest. **ABOVE RIGHT:** Royes Bell, cousin of Charles Bravo, stayed by his relative's side throughout his ordeal and was told of Charles' alleged confessional statement by Mrs Cox.

ABOVE LEFT George Harrison, the second doctor at the scene and the one Mrs Cox initially summoned. Mrs Cox never informed him that Charles had said he had taken poison. **ABOVE RIGHT** Joseph Moore, the first doctor to arrive, concluded that Charles Bravo had suffered heart failure and feared he would not last another hour.

ABOVE LEFT: Frederick Rowe, the butler, holding his cellar book while giving evidence. He told Inspector Clarke he had decanted the Burgundy in the afternoon, something he failed to remember at the inquest. **ABOVE RIGHT:** Mary Ann Keeber proved a competent witness. While standing at Charles' bedroom door, she never witnessed him speaking to Mrs Cox.

ABOVE LEFT: George Griffith, the former coachman, was examined more than any witness apart from Mrs Cox and Florence Bravo. He failed to explain how he was able to make a startlingly accurate prophecy about Bravo's death. **ABOVE RIGHT:** Attorney General Sir John Holker (left) and Sir Henry James (right). All the lawyers gained from the second inquest, financially and professionally.

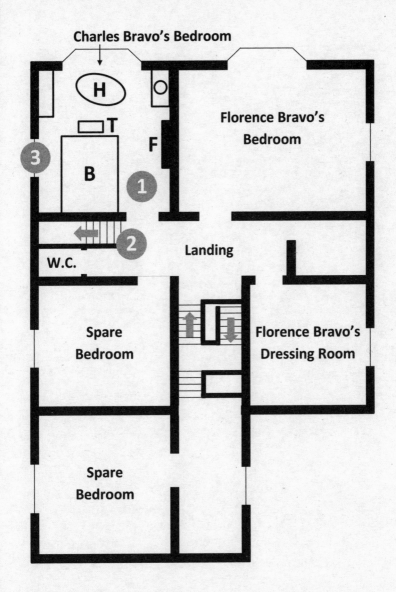

Charles Bravo's Bedroom

H

T

F

B

3

1

2

Florence Bravo's Bedroom

Landing

W.C.

Spare Bedroom

Florence Bravo's Dressing Room

Spare Bedroom

ABOVE: FIRST FLOOR OF THE PRIORY (doors not shown). Charles calls out for Florence (1) as Mary Ann Keeber stands at the foot of the second floor stairs (2). Moments later Charles is sick out of the window (3). Key: B = bed; T = small table; H = hip bath; F = fireplace. Also in his room are a washstand and a chest of drawers.

LIST OF EXHIBITS
DOCUMENTS

Exhibit 1: Annual Timeline

The following timeline provides a wide-angled view of events connected to the poisoning of Charles Bravo. Estimated dates are marked with an asterisk.

1808

March 14. James Gully born in Kingston, Jamaica

1827

Jane Cannon Edwards (possibly Edouard) born [1] *

1840

James Gully marries Frances Kibble [2]

1843

April 28. Alexander Louis Ricardo, son of John Ricardo MP, born

1845

May 30. Charles Turner born; he later takes the surname Bravo from his stepfather

September 5. Florence Campbell born in Sydney, Australia

1858

December 28. Jane Edwards marries Philip Cox

1861

Jane and Philip Cox leave for Jamaica, where Philip has a government post

1864

September 21. Florence Campbell marries Lieutenant Alexander Ricardo

1867

Captain Ricardo leaves army; Philip Cox dies and Jane Cox returns to England with three young boys

1870

April. Florence stays at Malvern

May. Captain Ricardo joins Florence at Malvern

June. Captain Ricardo abruptly returns to London

1871

March 31. Florence and Alexander Ricardo legally separate

PART TWO

April 19. Captain Ricardo dies in Cologne aged 27; his wife Florence inherits his fortune

June. Florence and Dr Gully start affair *

December. Dr Gully retires from his Malvern practice and relocates to Streatham, near Florence

1872

January. Florence and Dr Gully holiday for six weeks in Italy

July. Mrs Jane Cannon Cox joins Florence's staff

1873

August. Florence and Dr Gully holiday together in Bavaria, Germany

November. Florence has an abortion (performed by Dr Gully) and falls dangerously ill

1874

March. Florence moves her household to Balham Priory

April. Dr Gully moves into Orwell Lodge, close to Balham Priory

December. Mrs Cox engineers the first meeting between Florence and Charles Bravo

1875

March. Florence, Mrs Cox and Dr Gully vacation in Italy

April. Mrs Cox receives letter from her aunt in Jamaica about possible inheritance

September. Florence takes vacation in Brighton and meets Charles Bravo again

October 21. In a letter to Charles Florence says she has severed all relations with Dr Gully

November 2. Florence and Charles are engaged *

November 12. Charles Bravo meets with Mr Brookes, Florence's solicitor, to discuss the financial terms of marriage

December 3. George Griffith, Florence's coachman, is given his notice

December 7. Florence Ricardo marries Charles Bravo; Griffith tells the barman at the Bedford Hotel that Charles Bravo will not live four months

December 20. Charles receives anonymous letter sent to his chambers accusing him of marrying for money *

211

1876

January 3. Griffith leaves the service of Mrs Bravo

January 5. Honeymoon ends; Florence and Charles return to The Priory

January 9. Florence telegrams her family saying she is pregnant

January 28. Florence miscarries for the first time *

February 14. First major quarrel. Florence and Charles leave The Priory and live apart for several days

February 15. Charles writes to Florence about their "bitter trouble" and urges her to return to him

March 7. Second major quarrel. Florence and Charles leave The Priory and are apart for nine days

March 8. Jane Cox receives a letter saying she must decide quickly about going to Jamaica

March 13. Florence returns to The Priory

March 14. Jane Cox visits Charles' stepfather, Joseph Bravo, to discuss Jamaica trip

March 15. Charles writes to Florence that giving up Mrs Cox and the cobs would save £400 per year

March 16. Charles returns to The Priory

March 31. Mr Bell prescribes Epsom salts for Charles Bravo's rheumatism

April 6. Florence miscarries for a second time and is confined to bed for 11 days

April 11. Charles tells a colleague that Mrs Cox is costing £300 per year; he tells Mrs Cox her arrangements at The Priory would be decided after her trip to Jamaica

April 18. Charles is poisoned

April 21. Charles Bravo dies; Redwood performs chemical analysis on Bravo's vomit and discovers the presence of antimony {see *Exhibit 5*}

April 22. Post-mortem conducted by Mr Payne in the presence of Dr Moore, Mr Harrison and Mr Royes Bell

April 25. First inquest opens at The Priory {see *Exhibit 9*}

April 26. Mrs Cox tells Dr Dill in Brighton that Charles took poison "for Dr Gully"

April 28. First inquest ends with open verdict

PART TWO

April 29. Charles Bravo buried

May 1. Police informed of suspicious death by Edward Willoughby and Joseph Bravo; Chief Inspector Clarke begins his investigation

May 3. Florence Bravo goes to Brighton to recuperate

May 7. Mrs Cox tells Florence that Charles took poison "for Dr Gully" *

May 8. Clarke interviews Florence and Mrs Cox in Brighton

May 10. The *Daily Telegraph* and *Daily Echo* run stories on the mysterious death of Charles Bravo

May 11. Clarke submits his first and most comprehensive report {see *Exhibit 2*}

May 16. Advertisement placed offering £500 reward for information regarding the poison

May 18. Questions raised in Parliament about the inquest

May 20. *The Lancet* publishes Dr Johnson's medical history of 'The Balham Mystery'; the *British Medical Journal* also publishes an article on the case

May 22. Professor Redwood removes dozens of bottles of wine and medicine from The Priory for chemical analysis

May 27. *Daily Telegraph* notes that Florence and Mrs Cox have not given statements to the Treasury Solicitor

June 1. Mrs Cox tells Florence's solicitor that Charles took poison "for Dr Gully"

June 2. Florence and Mrs Cox give statements to Treasury Solicitor {see *Exhibits 3* and *4*}

June 3. Chief Inspector Clarke interviews Mrs Cox in Brighton; shortly after, Mrs Cox abruptly leaves Florence's service and stays with a friend in the Midlands

June 19. Attorney General applies for a writ to quash first inquest

June 26. Coroner's inquest is quashed and a second one is ordered

July 7. Mrs Cox attends meeting with Florence and her lawyers in London; Rowe sees Mrs Cox (possibly at the same meeting)

July 11. Second inquest opens at the Bedford Hotel, Balham {see *Exhibit 9*}

August 11. Inquest ends with verdict of murder by person(s) unknown

August 14. Police offer £250 reward for information leading to a conviction in the case

August 17. *The Daily News* publishes Professor Sheppard's letter supporting suicide theory

August 19. *The Lancet* publishes detailed medical account of Bravo's death; the *British Medical Journal* publishes article on 'The Balham Case' {see *Exhibit 6*}

August 22. Dr Gustav Abrath lectures on the case, which becomes the first book published on 'The Balham Mystery' {see *Exhibit 7*}

August 26. *The Lancet* continues its account of Bravo's death; the *British Medical Journal* publishes article supporting suicide theory

September 2. A letter to the *British Medical Journal* is sharply critical of suicide theory

1878

September 17. Florence Bravo dies from alcoholic poisoning, aged 33.

1879

October 21. Dr Gully's wife dies, aged 87.

1883

March 27. Dr James Gully dies, aged 75.

Note:

[1] Based on her return for the 1871 census (taken on 2 April), which stated she was 43 years old. Source: Taylor and Clarke (1988, p. 260). Of course, if her date of birth fell in the first quarter, she would have been born in 1828. Mrs Cox was almost certainly 48 years old when Charles Bravo died.

[2] Dr Gully married Fanny Court (b. 1805) in June 1831. She died in 1838, aged 33. Frances Beresford Kibble (b. 1792) was his second wife.

Exhibit 2: The Chief Inspector's Reports

Chief Inspector George Clarke's enquiry into the death of Charles Bravo began on Monday 1 May 1876 and lasted approximately a month. He wrote four official reports during this time and these provide useful insights and thoughts on the case. I have edited and abridged the reports to provide the Cold Case Jury with the most probative and interesting information. Minor changes have been made, mostly grammatical, to make it easier to read. My comments are italicised in square brackets.

Thursday 11 May 1876

I was shown Charles Bravo's diary and cheque book but they throw no light on the matter. I might add that from subsequent enquiries I find there is no foundation to Mrs Bravo's statement as to his being pressed for money or that there was anything in his father's letter to cause him any uneasiness, and there is nothing to account for his being in a state of mind to commit suicide.

I would draw attention to the fact that Dr Gully's statement as to the visit of Mrs Cox on Wednesday morning is a direct contradiction of Mrs Bravo's and Mrs Cox's statements that it did not take place until Thursday evening after the medical gentleman had said there was no hope of his getting any better [*At Florence's request, Mrs Cox visited Dr Gully to seek another medical opinion*].

I have to add that during the enquiry I find that Mrs Bravo and her family hold very strong opinions that Mr Bravo committed suicide and appear most anxious that this should be heard but can give no facts to support their opinions other than those already stated. Should he have committed suicide he must have taken the poison after Mrs Bravo and Mrs Cox left the morning room at about 9pm but nothing has been found in the morning room or his bedroom containing poison. The fact may be accounted for by the confusion which prevailed during the early part of Tuesday night when glasses would be used probably several times and no particular search was made until after the communication made by Mrs Cox.

On the other hand, Mr Bravo's friends and acquaintances entertain equally strong opinions that he did not commit suicide and support their opinion by saying he had nothing to cause uneasiness; he was of a cheerful disposition; in no way pressed for money; he was a most truthful and honourable gentleman and certainly would not have denied or equivocated in any way had he taken the poison himself; and they strongly suspect that the poison was administered in the wine he had for dinner.

Wednesday 24 May 1876

I also saw George Griffith who I was informed could make some important statement with reference to a conversation he overhead between Mrs Ricardo and Dr Gully in the lodge at the latter end of last year. He states that he lived in Mrs Ricardo's service about four or five years ago at Malvern and married Mrs Ricardo's maid, Fanny Plascot. He again entered her service at The Priory Balham in May 1875 and resided in the lodge until 3 January last when he left. He declares most solemnly that he never heard such a conversation, viz. that she only married Mr Bravo for a position and not for love as she cared nothing about him and that Dr Gully replied "If you do marry him he won't live long" and he also declared that he has never said anything to anyone to give rise to this.

I would mention that the wildest rumours are afloat in the neighbourhood of Balham respecting this matter, which in no doubt arise from the mysterious nature of the occurrence. I have made enquiries respecting most of them but they have afforded no information.

A number of letters have been received (mostly anonymous) suggesting that the poison was administered to Mr Bravo by Mrs Bravo, Mrs Cox or both, and supplied by Dr Gully for the purpose of getting rid of him to enable Mrs Bravo and Dr Gully to get married. After careful enquiry I can find no evidence to support these suggestions. Dr Gully is a married man but living apart from his wife. These suggestions are proffered through the close relationship known to exist between Dr Gully and Mrs Bravo during her widowhood, they have travelled together on the continent where they stayed in the same hotels and when at Streatham and Balham he had a key of her premises, and their conduct altogether was the cause of a deal of scandal and they were treated very coolly by the other residents.

I cannot ascertain that Mr Bravo took anything after dinner until he entered his bedroom, from 9:15 to 9:30pm – indeed the evidence of the servants shows that he did not – and if this can be relied upon (and I believe it) he must have taken the poison after he returned to his room, but whether it was with his own knowledge or whether placed there secretly by some other person, I refrain from giving an opinion. The poison could only have been placed there by some other person, in the water bottle or glass upon the chance of his drinking it.

And I would here remark upon the behaviour of Mr Bravo after he was seized with illness. He first calls for hot water, which would indicate a knowledge that he had taken poison, and during his two days' illness I cannot find that he expressed any surprise as to it, or asked any question how it could have been brought about. He said he had taken laudanum, but I cannot find that he had done so – it could have only been a very small quantity – and I cannot but believe that he knew laudanum was not causing his illness. His friends are still strongly of the opinion that he did not commit suicide, and that he had no cause to induce him to do so, but in making these enquiries it appears to me that his marriage was not altogether a happy one, although it does not appear he complained.

Both Mrs Bravo and Mrs Cox are much given to drink, and Mrs Bravo admits to me on several occasions when he attempted to make any change in their domestic arrangements she reminded him that she found the money, and does not appear to have had the sympathy and love for him that he might have expected, and she certainly shows no grief at his death [*a pointed observation, but it was a young marriage of mutual benefit rather than love*].

Monday 5 June 1876

I beg further to report that that I again saw Mrs Cox at Brighton on Saturday last [*3 June*], she states the photograph she showed at dinner on 18 April last was of the Marine Parade, Worthing, and she pointed out the position of the house (No. 46) which she had on that day taken for them, but she had no photograph of that particular house.

Mrs Ede of Gladstone Villa, Worthing, the owner of No. 46 Marine Parade, Worthing, states that on the day in question Mrs Cox called upon her and took that house for a fortnight at £4 10s per week. On Thursday 20 April she received a telegram from Mrs Cox to say that the house would not be wanted on account of illness.

Mrs Cox also states that on the night of 18 April before Mr Bravo retired to his room, he came into his wife's room and said in French "You have drank a bottle of wine today. I hoped that would have been sufficient but you have sent for another." Mrs Bravo made no answer and he seemed pretty much annoyed, and went to his room. He had passed the housemaid (Keeber) on the stairs with a bottle of wine and which she had fetched from the cellaret in the dining room by the direction of Mrs Bravo.

Mary Ann Keeber further states that when she saw Mr Bravo on the stairs (as mentioned in her previous statement) she was then taking a bottle of sherry to her mistress.

Mrs Cox also states that on their way to London that morning Mr and Mrs Bravo had some unpleasant words and Mr Bravo ordered the coachman to turn back, but in a few minutes was prevailed on by his wife to continue the journey but he said, "You will see what I will do when I get home." She only knows this from what Mrs Bravo told her.

Charles Smith (footman) states that the carriage was turned around and went a short distance towards home – when they were a little on the London side of Clapham Common – but he thought it was owing to the weather as it came on to snow: the carriage was open when they started but at this time he closed it.

Mrs Cox further states that on Good Friday Mr and Mrs Bravo had a desperate quarrel; he said he despised himself for having married her, and would not live with her but leave the house at once. Mrs Cox followed him to his room and begged of him to consider his wife's feelings when he said, "She can go to Dr Gully."

PART TWO

Mrs Cox has an aunt in Jamaica in ill health and shortly before the death of Mrs Bravo it was arranged that she should go there to see her (taking a return ticket) and that during her absence Mr Bravo would see to her children and that on her return he would consider what arrangements could be made respecting her. He always treated her most kindly and never said an angry word to her.

I also again saw Dr Dill [*Florence's doctor in Brighton*] who states the communication made to him by Mrs Bravo was after the death of her husband, when she said he was very persistent in that line of conduct. He further states that Mr Bravo called upon him after the marriage and bitterly complained of his wife's drinking propensity and begged that he would see her and endeavour to persuade her to refrain from it, as he knew he had great influence over her. Dr Dill promised to do this and said he knew she drank a great deal, too much to be good to her and should be stopped. He says he had spoken to her about this and her behaviour with Dr Gully at the request of Mr Campbell, her father, last autumn before her marriage, and that on Saturday last [*3 June*] she was in a mad, excited state and for the time had lost her reason, partly arising from drink and excitement consequent upon this enquiry.

Saturday 12 August 1876

I would respectfully draw the Commissioner's attention to the fact that during this long enquiry nothing has been elicited to show by what means the deceased met with his death other than is contained in my other reports (see those of 11 May, 24 May and 5 June last).

Exhibit 3: Florence Bravo's Statement

Below is the complete statement Florence Bravo made to the Treasury Solicitor, Mr Stephenson. My comments are italicised in square brackets.

I am the widow of the late Charles Augustus Delaney Turner Bravo, who died at The Priory, Balham, on the 21 April last. When I was 19 years old I married Captain Alexander Louis Ricardo, of the Grenadier Guards, who died at Cologne on 19 April 1871. In the spring of the previous year, at the insistence of my mother, I went to Malvern with my husband, to be under the care of Dr Gully, who had attended us all previously. I accordingly went to Malvern House with two maidservants and was there attended professionally by Dr Fernie and Dr Gully. I continued at Malvern, at my mother's request – first at Orwell Lodge, then Stokefield and afterwards another house, of which I forget the name.

After leaving Malvern I left my husband and I never saw him again. I went home with my mother to Buscot and then remained abroad for three months… At the suggestion of Mrs Brooks [*who she had met at Malvern*] I came to stay with her at Brooklands, Streatham. I there remained for nine months and then took a house of my own at Leigham Court Road, Streatham, taking with me a Mrs Cox, who was then daily governess to Mrs Brooks' children. I remained two years and then took lease of my present residence, The Priory, Balham.

From the time of my being placed by my parents under Dr Gully he took a great and increasing interest in me and my welfare and I became attached to him and grateful for his care of me. He resided near me at the above houses, he having given up his practice in or about the year 1871. In the autumn of 1875 I casually met Mr Charles Bravo, having been introduced to him some months before by Mrs Cox, an old friend of his father's family. In about a couple of months afterwards he proposed marriage, and I ultimately accepted him, and we were married on the 7 December, 1875.

My income then was about £3,000 a year [*over £300,000 in today's money*] and the house, horses, carriages and everything at Balham were mine. He had nothing but a very small income of his own and casual allowances from his father. He was pressing me to put down my garden and my cobs – my two great hobbies – and turn away Mrs Cox to save. I was paying her a salary of only £100; but he thus hoped, as he said, from all these sources to save £400 a year.

I used to ask him, why was there the necessity of this retrenchment, as I had always been accustomed to live largely within my income. He told me that he had kept a woman before marriage at Maidenhead for years and I believe he continued her an annual payment after marriage, and owed her or her sister £500, which he had borrowed, of which last fact I was ignorant until after his death.

He was a very passionate man and short-tempered to the last degree. He once struck me because his mother was interfering in my household arrangements, requiring me even to put down my maid. This was three or four weeks before the fatal Tuesday, as far as I can recollect. He had on that day received a letter from his mother. He always met the postman himself, and took and read my letters. This letter made us both very angry.

Mr Royes Bell, who attended me in my miscarriage, had recommended me a change of air, and my husband said it was a useless expense. When we got to bed that night he continued to be very angry and at last jumped out of bed and threatened to cut his throat. He rushed into the dressing-room and I went after him to get him back. His words were "Now I will go and cut my throat!" and actually left the room for the purpose.

On Good Friday last I had just recovered from my second miscarriage. He was very restless. He got into an awful passion because I was weak and had only left my bed that day for ten days and he still did not like me asking to be left alone to rest, which was my habit after luncheon. He was always reading Shakespeare and we had a happy three weeks before then and I got quite to like him [*not a marriage blessed with love*] and forgot his meanness, which had previously disgusted me.

A compact between us before marriage was that Dr Gully's name should never be mentioned, as I had told him, and requested him to tell his family, of my attachment to him. The attachment was quite innocent and nothing improper had ever passed between us [*this was a blatant lie but Florence was hardly going to admit the truth*]. But although I never saw, heard or spoke of Dr Gully after our marriage he was continually – morning, noon and night – speaking of him, always abusing him, calling him "that wretch", and upbraiding me for my former acquaintance with him.

On Saturday, Sunday and Monday [*the three days prior to the poisoning*] I observed nothing unusual in him. On Tuesday Mrs Cox went to Worthing to choose a house for me, as recommended by Dr Bell. I accompanied my husband to London, at his request, to pay bills. Passing Dr Gully's house, which is near mine [*on Bedford Hill Road*], he said: "Do you see anybody?" I said "No, I did not look." He went on quarrelling about him and said he thought I had better go to Worthing for a few days without him, which I refused to do. I then said I thought it was a very cruel thing his always bringing up that name. "I am not always talking to you about that woman." And he admitted his error and asked me to make it up and kiss him. I said in a pet: "No I won't!" And then he said: "You will see what I will do when we get home!" He looked at me in a very determined way and I became frightened, and I then kissed him, and he said it was very wrong of him.

PART TWO

We paid bills together [*no mention of the £500 she had given her husband*] and I left him in Jermyn Street and drove home, getting him some tobacco and hair wash, unknown to him, on the way. He was delighted when he came home, between 3:30pm and 4pm, and I said "Go and see what I have got for you," alluding to the tobacco, which he then said he would go out into the garden to smoke. I was astonished in a few minutes, however, to see him come down dressed for riding. He had not told me he was going out. He went out and was absent nearly two hours. He said the pony had bolted with him twice and he was quite exhausted. I helped him out of his chair, he was so weak, and I recommended a hot bath and, I think, a glass of Burgundy. I think he took the wine and I went up to him in the bath, being anxious about him. I never saw him look so ill.

After his bath he said, "I'm all right now; I feel much better." He then wanted me, seeing I was so tired, to go to bed – about 6pm to 6:30pm. I said: "Oh, do let me stay up and give you your dinner." He said: "Well, I will, if you promise to go to bed immediately after." I said: "Well then, I will."

We then both went to dress for dinner. Mrs Cox had not come back from Worthing. I had been occupying for ten days a separate bedroom but we were constantly in and out of each other's rooms. We both came down to the drawing room until dinner was announced, waiting a little for Mrs Cox. At dinner he got a letter from his father which made him furious. It was about money – the sale of Caledonian Railway shares which he had bought a few days previously – and his father said he did not like stock exchange transactions. A sale note of this transaction enclosed in the letter was not found after his death. He said, "I will write him a shirty letter, I won't be interfered with in this way." His face worked the whole dinner, such a strange yellow look. I thought he would go mad every minute and if I tried to turn the subject he always returned to it.

223

We all went into the morning room for a few minutes after dinner and he said, "Well, you know what you promised?" (about going to bed) and I said, "Yes, I will" and I went to my dressing room. He came in and wished me good night as I was going to my bedroom. Being so exhausted with my first long day in town, I fell asleep almost directly. The next thing I remember was being awoken by the housemaid, I having discharged my maid [*at the insistence of Charles*] whom I had been accustomed to from a child. She said he was ill. I got up immediately and went to my husband. He was lying by the window unconscious in the spare room. Mrs Cox was with him rubbing him and she told me she had sent for Dr Harrison. I was so frightened I ran downstairs and ordered Dr Moore to be fetched at once. He came first. Then I sent immediately for Mr Royes Bell from London. I was then in and out [*of the sickroom*] all night.

Not a word was said about poison by anyone until Sir William Gull came, but then not to me, or in my hearing [*she must have forgotten the conversation between Mrs Cox and Dr Johnson in her presence*]; but I said loudly to Mary Ann and Mrs Cox "I am afraid he has been poisoned." He was so sick. I thought he had been poisoned by the copper kitchen utensils or other vessels used at St James' Hall, where he lunched, being improperly tinned (I said this during the night as I had known of such a thing happening to a gentlemen who lived at Epsom) [*a surprising statement because Bravo's symptoms were consistent with gastroenteritis or any number of other illnesses*]. He recovered consciousness, as far as I can recollect, about three or four o'clock on Wednesday morning; I was by his side, Mrs Cox and four doctors being also present. He looked up to me in the most piteous manner and said "Kiss me, my wife. Oh, Christ Lord have mercy upon me," and being in such agony begged me to read the Burial Service to him. He had no religion and had only been to church three times at my wish.

On the same day he said: "You must marry again but not a word of the past." I thought he might get well. I had never heard of poison. It never occurred to me to ask what he had taken at luncheon, as he said he had a good one and had a pint of Burgundy. He did not tell me he had killed himself, nor did he charge anyone with having killed him. He kissed me several times and repeatedly asked his mother to be kind to his "darling wife".

When we first married he thought I took too much sherry and I gave it up to please him [*this is untrue*], for which he thanked me. He was sensible on the Wednesday and Thursday. On Wednesday he said: "You will take care of Katie", meaning a child of his former mistress. He made no inquiry as to what caused his illness.

Florence Bravo, 2 June 1876

Exhibit 4: Jane Cox's Statement

Below is the complete statement Jane Cox made to the Treasury Solicitor, Mr Stephenson. My comments are italicised in square brackets.

I was examined as a witness at the inquest on the late Mr Bravo, but from confusion and a mistaken idea of shielding, as I thought, the character of Mrs Bravo, I did not state the full particulars, which I am now anxious to state. There was no cause whatsoever or the slightest reason for his committing suicide for Dr Gully, and therefore there was no reason for why I should not have stated this before. "Mrs Cox, I have taken poison for Dr Gully. Don't tell Florence." Beseechingly were the words he used when he first told me he had taken poison. The words, "Don't tell Florence" were used emphatically in a most imploring way. I said, "How could you do such a thing?" He only screamed as loud as he could three times for hot water [*Charles screamed loudly for hot water but, according to her testimony at the second inquest, spoke quietly to Mrs Cox*]. Before the hot water arrived he was sick out of the window, and detecting the smell of chloroform when he vomited, I rushed to look at the bottle of chloroform, which I found nearly empty. Of course, I thought that it was the poison which he said he had taken [*Mrs Cox never asks Charles whether he has taken chloroform but rushes to the chloroform bottle*]. There was a good fire burning in the room.

About a quarter of an hour before I was called, I was in Mrs Bravo's dressing room with her, and Mr Bravo came into the room and said, "You have sent for more wine. You have drunk nearly a bottle today." He said this in French to prevent the servant Keeber who was following him with a glass of Marsala, understanding. He said nothing else that night.

I put his feet and hands in hot mustard and water and gave him an emetic, but he kicked his feet out of the basin, and I then put mustard poultices to his feet and, with help, raised him up into a chair. I gave him strong coffee to keep him awake, but he could not keep it down. He was too weak to swallow. He could not get it down his throat. His nightgown was so saturated with mustard and water we had to change it. I rubbed about his chest with camphor.

This was while Mr Harrison, whom I sent for, was coming. Dr Moore came previously. I did not tell him about Dr Gully. I thought it would cause such a scandal. I told Mr Harrison, who was his regular attendant, directly he arrived that he had taken chloroform. Here is a copy of Mr Harrison's letter to me. I have the original, it is at Brighton, and I will send it to you. I did not like to tell Dr Moore, thinking suicide would cause such a scandal. Mr Bravo's temper was so violent. Had he recovered, as I thought he would, if it was only chloroform, he would have been so angry [*yet Mrs Cox had been told it was not chloroform and Charles Bravo was so dangerously ill he might not live another hour*].

He had no reason to poison as she, I know, had no communication with Dr Gully since her marriage, and their acquaintance before marriage was, although imprudent, I conscientiously believed, entirely of an innocent character [*Mrs Cox must have known before the marriage the nature of Florence's relationship with Dr Gully*].

On Good Friday, the first day she had come down after her illness, he was annoyed with her for lying down after luncheon and not wishing him to remain in the room. He was so restless she could not rest. He got very angry and went out of the room, and I put a match to his library fire, and he went and sat there. In the evening he said he despised himself for marrying her, and said she was a "selfish pig", that he had quite made up his mind not to live with her, and that he was going away and that he wished he was dead. He was in a temper. I remained with him for some time, and I said, "What do you think will become of Florence if you go away?"

He said, "Let her go to Dr Gully" or "go back to Dr Gully". I can't remember exactly what he said. I told him it was very wrong of him; there was no reason. "You know her every thought is for you. You know she does everything she can to make you happy." He was quite determined, however, he would go, and when he said he wished he was dead, I said it was wrong of him to say such wicked things, as God had given him life to do good in. "Pray go in to Florence and make it up with her." He said, "Good night," but would not promise he would not go away.

He seemed so determined I followed him upstairs. He went up and locked his door. He would not open it for some little time. I knocked again two or three times. He then opened it and I begged him not to leave the house. He said that he had quite made up his mind to go; that he would not live with her any longer. I again reasoned with him for a long time but he seemed quite determined, and shook hands, saying "You are a good little woman. I will always do what I can for you. Good night!" He turned and kissed me on the cheek and said "Good night" again. He thanked me again, saying "You love Florence, and you do the best you can for me; I thank you for it."

I then went and told his wife she had better go to him as he was going to leave the house. She went, and I understood he was still very angry. He was determined to go. I could not rest all night; I thought he would go.

The next morning he came up to my room and asked me if Florence had acknowledged she was sorry. I said she had done nothing wrong, only wanting to rest in the afternoon, and I begged him to go down to her. About 10 minutes afterwards he told me he had seen her and made it all right.

Three or four weeks before that there was a quarrel between them, I believe through a letter from his home, and he was very violent, and said he would go. This was about 10 or 11 at night, they usually going to bed early, and he went, unbarred the front door, and went down the drive to leave the house. I followed him, and entreated him to come back. He would not for some time, and I said "Just fancy what a scandal it would be, and what will your mother say?" He said, "Oh, mother will be only too glad to have me back at any price." He seemed determined to go. I said, "Do you think you are doing your duty as Florence's husband to leave her?" and he repeated, "My duty!" and he then consented and returned to the house. He went upstairs to his wife and I rebolted the door myself for fear the servants should know anything about it.

He often said he hated Dr Gully and how he wanted him dead. I always tried to make peace between them. These sudden passions seemed to overtake him because at other times he was quite pleasant.

The Coroner interrupted me when I was about to say, "Why did you tell them? Does Florence know I have poisoned myself? Don't tell her," imploringly. I said I had not. "What have you taken, Charlie?" He turned his head round, away from me, and said, "I do not know". I never said he took it medicinally. He was jealous of Dr Gully, though he knew everything before marriage.

He did not want to go to Worthing, and asked at dinner, "Have you taken a house there?" He had a letter from his mother that morning objecting to Florence going, and he asked me whether he should show Florence.

I told Mr Royes Bell that he told me he had taken poison, and I repeated it to Dr Johnson. That is all.

Jane Cannon Cox, 2 June 1876

Comment: The statement is approximately 1,300 words in length, and half of it concerns just two incidents when Charles Bravo threatened to walk out. If Mrs Cox is to be believed, despite his burning anger on both occasions, he only once said he wished he was dead. Taken in context of his desire to leave the house, it appears to be a figure of speech. Mrs Cox states that Charles often said how he hated Dr Gully, yet apparently none of the servants heard any similar comment on any occasion, or refused to say so, if they had. She also reports that Charles did not want to go to Worthing. This is consistent with Rowe's observations at the dinner table.

Exhibit 5: About Tartar Emetic

Common Name: Tartar Emetic
Scientific Name: Antimony Potassium Tartrate
Appearance: Fine, pale yellowish crystals
Solubility: Highly soluble in water (83g per litre), insoluble in alcohol [1]
Taste: A faint, metallic tang (easily masked)
Flammable: No
Uses: Industrial chemical, pesticide
Former uses: Anti-parasitic drug
Fatal dose: Varies; as little as 3 grains (or 200mg) may be fatal.
Moderate ingestion: Nausea, vomiting, abdominal pain and diarrhoea; may be mistaken for gastroenteritis. Onset typically within 30 minutes to two hours.
Severe ingestion: Severe vomiting and bloody diarrhoea. Haemorrhagic gastritis (inflammation of stomach lining), myocardial depression (weakening of heart function), vasodilation (dilation of blood vessels leading to reduced blood pressure), fluid loss and renal failure may ensue. Cerebral oedema (fluid on the brain), coma and death are possible.

Notes:
[1] Wine is approximately 85% water, 13% alcohol and 2% sugars and acids. Tartar emetic will dissolve in the water but its solubility in wine is likely to be reduced by the alcohol.

Sources:
Murder with Venom (1993) by Brian Mariner; *The Elements of Murder* (2005) by John Emsley; National Poisons Information Service, UK.

Exhibit 6: What The Medical Journals Said

After the initial inquest, *The Lancet* published an article by Dr George Johnson, 'The Balham Mystery', on 20 May 1876. This article is the most comprehensive medical account of Charles Bravo's death. Below are some points from Dr Johnson's paper.

Dr Johnson, accompanied by Mr Bell, entered the patient's room at 2:30am on Wednesday 19 April. Charles Bravo was unconscious, lying on his back, breathing deeply with a weak pulse of about 100. The actions of the heart sounded normal, Johnson observed, and the pupils were of natural size. By 2:45am there were signs of returning consciousness. A little later Bravo recognised Mr Bell and replied to his questions. Soon after 3:00am, Mr Bell called Dr Johnson out of the room to hear Mrs Cox repeat a statement which she had just made to Mr Bell. According to Dr Johnson, Mrs Cox said that when Mr Bravo was taken ill in his bedroom he said to her 'I've taken *some of that* poison, but don't tell Florence' [my emphasis]. Dr Johnson concluded that the symptoms of thirst, severe abdominal pain and tenderness, a rapid but feeble pulse, and cold and clammy skin, were the result of some powerfully irritant poison. Johnson also observed that Bravo's "intellect was clear".

In its next edition, *The Lancet* considered – and then dismissed – the hypothesis that Bravo took laudanum to end his life and, after changing his mind, took tartar emetic to eject the laudanum. It held that Bravo's lack of reference to the *cause* of his illness, and his denial of knowing how it was caused, was far more consistent with genuine ignorance than anything else. If Bravo had *knowingly* taken tartar emetic to produce vomiting, and when sickness became his most obvious symptom, he would have felt that the tartar emetic was the cause.

PART TWO

The *British Medical Journal* also published an editorial on 'The Balham Mystery' on 20 May 1876. It was exasperated at the failures of the Coroner, who appeared to have already decided that Bravo's death was an act of suicide. It was scathing that Florence Bravo was not called as a witness, and that much evidence was passed over in a perfunctory manner. As ten grains of tartar emetic were found in the undigested food when he first vomited, it was reasonable to infer that Bravo had ingested a much larger dose. It also claimed that, for such a dose of the poison, it was likely that nausea and vomiting would have followed in a few minutes to a quarter of an hour. If the poison had been taken during dinner, the journal argued, it would most probably have produced some symptoms before Bravo left the dinner table; this indicated that the tartar emetic had been taken by the deceased after he had retired to his bedroom.

In an article published on 19 August 1876, after the second inquest, the journal was more definite on the last point. It also commented that in most cases of murder by poisoning, proof rests upon establishing the means, opportunity and motive of the murderer. The first is all-important. In this case, however, it noted that there was no evidence of any suspect purchasing, or possessing, the poison at or about the time of the alleged murder. It added that the case would remain unsolved until the possession of tartar emetic had been traced to a member of Mr Bravo's household when he first collapsed.

The following points are taken from 'The Balham Mystery', an article written by Dr Wade and published in the *British Medical Journal* on 26 August 1876. Wade argued for suicide, claiming that Mrs Cox's immediate treatment of Bravo after his collapse, and Mrs Bravo's reactions, were inconsistent with the view that they were involved in murder. When Charles Bravo was first told of Mrs Cox's statement that he had confessed to having taken

233

poison, Dr Wade found it inconceivable that Bravo should have replied "I do not remember having spoken of taking poison", rather than "I did no such thing!" or something similar.

Dr Wade noted that Bravo had a quick temper and had been suffering with facial neuralgia. On the afternoon of Tuesday 18 April, Bravo had been shaken by the horse bolting. At dinner, he had a facial twitch, appeared generally ill, and was distressed on receiving a letter from his father about a financial loss. On retiring to bed, he had been agitated by his wife's excessive drinking. Under such circumstances, Dr Wade concluded, "an insane impulse" to commit suicide that night was unsurprising.

Whether it is surprising or not is surely relative to Bravo's general character and his overall circumstances – for instance, the fact he had recently married into wealth, which would aid his Parliamentary ambitions. Wade fails to consider either.

Exhibit 7: The Two Poison Theory

In August 1876, *The Lancet* ran two substantial opinion pieces regarding the Bravo case. A major observation was the unlikely rapidity at which the tartar emetic acted if it was in the drinking water. Although we do not have a precise time-line of events, Mary Ann Keeber initially estimated that as little as five or six minutes elapsed from Bravo retiring to his bedroom until he called out for hot water. The journal floated the idea that Bravo ingested tartar emetic and another poison:

It is scarcely probable that a dose of the emetic would have acted so quickly... The symptoms described by the medical men first in attendance, coupled with the statement of Mrs Cox, suggest the operation of another agent... [possibly the tartar emetic] was combined with a drug capable of causing the sudden and complete collapse, which actually occurred, and during which the metallic poison was undoubtedly absorbed.

This theory was developed and expounded by Dr Gustav Abrath, who gave a lecture on the poisoning days after the second inquest finished. It was later published as the 'The Balham Mystery', the first-ever book on the case. He suggested the Burgundy at dinner had been laced with both tartar emetic and a small dose of laurel water. The latter would produce unconsciousness, allowing some of the antimony to be absorbed before it could be expelled through sickness. Naturally, Abrath concluded that Bravo had been wilfully poisoned. The following excerpts from his book are published for the first time. The subtitles are mine. My comments are italicised in square brackets.

THE BALHAM MYSTERY
A Lecture On Tartar Emetic & Laurel Water
Delivered on 22 August 1876 at Sunderland
By Gustav Abrath, MD.

On tartar emetic. Generally speaking, in the case of an adult, a dose of from 10 to 20 grains, if taken at once, proves fatal; but there are cases on record where recovery has taken place after as much as one ounce [*over 400 grains*] has been swallowed. The latter fact is accounted for by the immediate severe vomiting, or by the profuse purging, which follows... A person may take a fatal dose of tartar emetic in wine or water without ever tasting the poison – in Burgundy wine an immense dose would be required before poison could be tasted... Its potency or otherwise as a fatal poison depends, in the first place, upon the dose taken, and whether it was quickly eliminated; next, on the frequency of the repetition of the dose; and thirdly, on the constitution of the individual who receives the poison, whether it will be readily absorbed into his system, or otherwise.

On laurel water. Laurel water is made from cherry laurel leaves and its poisonous ingredient is Prussic acid [*contains cyanide*]. One man poisoned by laurel water in 1781 showed symptoms of dying in ten minutes; and in five minutes more he was found quite insensible, with eyes fixed, froth running from the mouth, teeth clenched, and there was a gurgling in the throat and a heaving at the stomach. Within half an hour the unfortunate man was dead...

There is another case in which a man, after taking one and a half ounces of laurel water, felt quite well for three hours. Then there followed, first, numbness of the hands and legs, severe headache and involuntary stools. The arms and legs became cold; the patient had no power over them, but had feeling in them. The man was conscious, but had a small pulse. He became weaker and died during the same night...

A man of 60 years of age who, tired of his life, swallowed two ounces of laurel water... vomited... his face was pale, the whole body was cold, the pupil of the eye was dilated, and the pulse was slow, soft and irregular. The most striking feature of the case was a general paralysis of the nerves of motion, so the man could not move a muscle...

Now let me instance a person who takes a small dose, which produces faintness and insensibility, loss of breathing, interruption of muscular power, with involuntary purging, accompanied by convulsions and sometimes temporary paralysis.

On what happened. A servant said as he went up to his room he appeared queer. Undoubtedly he did. At that time he must have felt the premonitory symptoms of the poisoned wine he took at the dinner table... He feels unwell before he goes upstairs; the feeling of illness, in addition to the pain in his gums, increases every moment after he gets there... He took laudanum, and very likely a little more than usual, for his gums. The sickly feeling increased, nature wanting to get rid of the deadly enemy, tartar emetic. Very likely he thought at the time his stomach was disordered, owing to having eaten a splendid meal, and he could not vomit... Mr Bravo shouted to his wife for hot water.

On cause of death. Did Mr Bravo die from tartar emetic alone? It may be so, but judging from the symptoms he exhibited, I do not believe it was the only poison. Did laudanum contribute to his death? No. Then what was the poisonous agent combined with the tartar emetic? Laurel water, I believe. The marked symptoms lead me to think so. Before the Vivisection Act came into force, I poisoned several rabbits with laurel water and tartar emetic combined, and considering the effect on them in conjunction with the cases I have already quoted, I can come to no other conclusion than that Mr Bravo died from the effects of tartar emetic and laurel water combined... I suggest Mr Bravo received the poison in the wine he drank at dinner, and probably also in the water, if he drank any... The antimony was put into a bottle of wine and three drachms [*5 grams*] of laurel water added. Such a combination would not alter the taste of a strong bottle of Burgundy; indeed the laurel water would cause it to have a nice flavour.

*

As you will recall, Mrs Cox acquired a bottle of laurel water from Dr Gully two weeks before the poisoning. It was prescribed for Florence to help her sleep. However, she did not take any, and Mrs Cox kept it in the medicine chest in her room until it was thrown away after Charles died. It is undeniable that the presence of the laurel water is suspicious, and Abrath interpreted Bravo's symptoms in light of this fact.

Abrath stated that rabbits poisoned with the laurel water and tartar emetic exhibited the same symptoms as Bravo. Even if this is accurate, it is not sufficient to suspect both poisons were used. He needed to establish a symptomatic difference between the two poisons taken together compared with taking tartar emetic alone. For example, if he had been able to show that taken together the two poisons led rapidly to sickness and unconsciousness, whereas only tartar emetic produced sickness, we might conclude that both poisons had been administered to the water. But he did not. It was a pointless experiment and several rabbits were needlessly tortured for bad science.

Laurel water has a distinctive taste and odour of bitter almonds. Notice that, on the one hand, Abrath claimed a strong Burgundy would disguise its taste, yet on the other, he said it would add a nice flavour. This is a classic example of trying to hedge your bets. If there was a residual smell or taste, Bravo would have most likely noticed; he was a connoisseur and sent wines back if they were unsatisfactory, according to Rowe. Its presence would have been even more noticeable in water. Therefore, I suggest it is unlikely that laurel water was the second poison, but this does not preclude some other toxin being used in conjunction with the tartar emetic.

If a double-barrelled poison was used, Bravo was murdered by someone with an organised mind and medical knowledge. The prime suspect would be Dr Gully, but it remains unclear why he would not have simply used the second poison by itself. It is worth repeating: a large dose of tartar emetic points away from a well-planned poisoning because its effects are too variable.

Exhibit 8. A Strange Coincidence

In August 1876, two days after the second inquest ended, a 50-year-old Field Officer wrote to *The Times* recounting his experience as a subaltern in the British army. He believed it had a striking parallel to the Bravo case. In the early 1850s, the officer was stationed in India and was in ill health. On being told by the regimental doctor that he would not be returning to England, he became suicidal and swallowed a wine glass of laudanum. Minutes later he received word that the doctor had been joking and he was to prepare for the journey home. He continued:

I then swallowed three or four glasses of water, with, I believe, the intention of making myself vomit, or at least delay the action of the laudanum... but I also caught sight of a bottle of tartar emetic. It was white stuff, I remember. I only knew it would make me sick, and I at once took two large table spoonfuls of it to make me vomit out the laudanum... The consequence was that I, in about four minutes, felt pain, then violent sickness and subsequent stupor, but I had, I know, vomited most freely... Then came the doctor with a stomach pump.

Pray mark this... I never, until 1876, knew that I had in reality poisoned myself with tartar emetic as well as laudanum... Not one of those present, nor did the doctor, know that I had swallowed a monstrous dose of tartar emetic... Had I been dying, I declare on my honour that I should have solemnly stated that I had only taken laudanum (as poison), for I did not know that tartar emetic was poison; I only know it by the recent inquest... I can declare on oath that I should have died convinced that I had not taken no poison but laudanum...

The writer, named only as "Field Officer", did not wish his real name to be published in connection with the scandal of an attempted suicide. I wish to highlight one point: vomiting occurred within minutes of ingesting tartar emetic, suggesting onset might be far quicker than the medical profession generally assumed. This has implications for the two poison theory {see *Exhibit 7*}.

Field Officer's view that Charles Bravo unintentionally over-dosed on tartar emetic while using it as a remedy to eject laudanum was supported by a doctor, who also wrote to *The Times*. He stated that he was one of the physicians who attended to Charles Bravo, but his name was published only as "F. R. C. P." This happens to be the acronym for Fellow of the Royal College of Physicians. Almost certainly the writer was none other than Sir William Gull, elected as a fellow in 1848 and the only doctor called to The Priory who supported a suicide verdict. He wrote:

The theory as to the cause of Mr Bravo's death, written by me some weeks ago, coincides exactly with the statement of facts so graphically told in your columns in a letter by Field Officer. It was proved that Mr Bravo had suffered, in Jamaica, sunstroke. In many cases, the injury to the brain caused by sunstroke is followed, often years afterwards, by sudden fits of violent anger and outbursts of insanity… Mr Bravo, under an insane impulse, took laudanum, and, immediately repenting, unwit-tingly drank, as Field Officer did, a dangerous dose of a poison which in a less quantity would have been a proper and harmless remedy.

Another correspondent in the same paper disagreed with the 'remedy overdose' theory, pointing out that no trace of tartar emetic was found in Bravo's bedroom. Like the misadventure theory, if an overdose was taken accidentally, there was no reason for the tartar emetic container to be missing.

What do we make of Field Officer's account? Could Bravo have overdosed on laudanum and then used the tartar emetic to eject the narcotic poison from his stomach? Such a possibility was widely discussed at the time. An editorial in *The Lancet* dismantled the theory, emphasising that Bravo was sick almost immediately after calling for hot water but that tartar emetic does not act instantly. If this theory is to be believed, he must have patiently waited for at least several minutes, possibly more, and then impatiently called for hot water. It reveals a major difference compared with the Field Officer, who took the more powerful emetic after the water to hasten his vomiting. By contrast, there was no reason for Bravo to call for hot water once he had taken the tartar emetic.

Additionally, on being told that laudanum would not account for his symptoms, and having knowingly taken tartar emetic, *The Lancet* asserted that Bravo would have explained the whole story to someone. The Field Officer's main contention that Bravo might not have recognised tartar emetic as a poison, and hence did not think to tell anyone, was similarly dismissed. When sickness was the most agonising feature of his condition, the medically aware Bravo would have realised tartar emetic was the cause. Claims that he was confused or depressed do not stack up: he was lucid enough to draw up his Will and summon back Sir William Gull to impress on him that he was telling the truth.

Although interesting, the Field Officer's situation has significant dissimilarities to the Bravo case and does not adequately explain it. I suggest the most plausible account of suicide is the one shown in Chapter 11.

Exhibit 9: The Inquest Minutes

The following provides a succinct account of both inquests. For most witnesses, I provide only a brief excerpt of their testimony, highlighting an interesting fact that adds to our knowledge of the case. A number in a brace {} refers to the chapter where greater detail of the witness' testimony is presented.

THE FIRST INQUEST

Venue: The Priory, Balham
Date: Tuesday 25 April 1876
Duration: 2 days
Coroner: William Carter

Day 1 – Tuesday 25 April 1876

Joseph Bravo, father of the deceased, stated that his son did not complain of being in pain when he saw him on the Wednesday.

Jane Cox, companion, said she saw Bravo in his bedroom at about 9:30pm, when he told her he had taken poison.

Amelia Bushell, maid to Mrs Joseph Bravo, Charles' mother, stated that Bravo was in great pain on the Wednesday and Thursday but did not account for his condition to anyone in her presence.

Mr George Harrison, surgeon, testified that Bravo was treated for a complete collapse, and his initial symptoms were consistent with chloroform poisoning, but no effluvia of chloroform was detected.

Day 2 – Friday 28 April 1876

Mary Ann Keeber, housemaid, stated that at about 10pm she was requested by Mrs Cox to fetch hot water. When she returned Bravo was collapsed on the floor, insensible with difficulty breathing.

Joseph Payne, physician, testified that he conducted the post-mortem on the deceased but found no signs of disease that could account for his death.

Royes Bell, surgeon, confirmed that Bravo had not made any admission of having taken anything apart from laudanum for his neuralgia.

Theophilus Redwood, analytical chemist, reported that he found antimony in the vomited food, a sample of urine and in the lower intestine. It was most likely ingested as tartar emetic.

Jane Cox (recalled) stated that the same food was consumed by everyone at dinner but only Bravo became ill.

Frederick McCalmont, barrister, testified that Bravo was most unlikely to commit suicide.

The jury's verdict: **The manner of death was undecided.**

THE SECOND INQUEST
Venue: The Bedford Hotel, Balham
Date: Tuesday 11 July 1876
Duration: 23 days
Coroner: William Carter, assisted by Mr Muir
Lawyers:
For the Crown – Sir John Holker QC, John Gorst QC, Harry Poland
For Florence Bravo – Sir Henry James QC
For Jane Cox – John Murphy QC
For Joseph Bravo – George Lewis
For Dr Gully – Serjeant Parry

Day 1 – Tuesday 11 July 1876
Coroner's statement. Carter reminded the jury to remain impartial, ignoring anything that they may have heard about the case.

Viewing of body at Norwood Cemetery.

John Mold, undertaker, stated that he performed the interment of Charles Bravo and confirmed the identity of the body viewed by the jury.

Mr Joseph Bravo, father of the deceased, testified that he agreed it was not wise to expose his household to the charge of about £300 for Mrs Cox. About two months after his son's marriage, he advised Mrs Cox to return to Jamaica, but she declined.

Day 2 – Wednesday 12 July 1876

George Brooks, solicitor, confirmed that he placed an advertisement with a reward of £500 for any information regarding purchase of the poison.

Dr Joseph Moore, physician, stated that no cause of Bravo's condition was provided, apart from Florence Bravo mentioning that her husband had been out riding and the horse had bolted. {6}

George Harrison, surgeon, remembered that, not long after his arrival, he told Mrs Cox that Bravo would not live an hour. Mrs Cox never told him anything that Charles had said to her, only that she believed he had taken chloroform. {6}

Day 3 – Thursday 13 July 1876

Royes Bell, surgeon, stated that Bravo was conscious when Mrs Cox spoke of his taking poison, but she might not have been aware of the fact (the conversation took place in the dressing room). {6}

Dr George Johnson, physician, testified that he had never known a case of suicide by antimony poisoning. Bravo died when it was absorbed and acted on his lower bowel. {6}.

Frederick McCalmont, barrister, stated that Bravo was in excellent health and high spirits when he met him in London on the afternoon of Tuesday 18 April.

Day 4 – Friday 14 July 1876

Sir William Gull, physician, stated he was only at The Priory for 40 minutes, and was much surprised that Bravo appeared indifferent when told he had been poisoned. {6}

Theophilus Rewood, analytical chemist, stated that, based on his experiments, tartar emetic made Burgundy turn cloudy after an hour. He also said that he received a quantity of Epsom salts in a paper packet, which also tested negative for the presence of antimony. {6}

Day 5 – Monday 17 July 1876

Frederick Rowe, butler, testified that he was alone on several occasions with Charles Bravo during his illness. His mind was clear, and he never expressed suspicion of anyone. {7}

Day 6 – Tuesday 18 July 1876

Charles Willis, proprietor of the Bedford Hotel, stated that Frederick Rowe told him he visited London, where he had met Mrs Cox, and made a comment that her lies had landed her in trouble.

Mary Ann Keeber, housemaid, believed she fetched Mrs Bravo within 10 minutes of her husband calling for hot water. {7}

George Brooks (recalled), submitted some letters of Charles Bravo into evidence.

Day 7 – Wednesday 19 July 1876

Mary Ann Keeber (resumed), testified that both Florence and Mrs Cox appeared distressed at Bravo's condition, and that Mrs Cox appeared to give him every assistance she could. {7}

Charles Parton, coachman, said that when Bravo returned from his horse ride he appeared very pale and unnerved.

Edward Smith, footman, noticed no sediment in the wine glasses used for dinner on the Tuesday night.

George Younger, groom, recalled telling Bravo not to ride the cobs because they had been to Streatham the day before.

Day 8 – Thursday 20 July 1876

Amelia Bushell, maid to Mrs Joseph Bravo, said that Florence told her, "What a dreadful thing, Amelia! I cannot account for it, unless he had lunch cooked in a coppery pan that was not clean."

Ann Bell, wife of Royes Bell, said that Florence had remarked that the death of her husband was a mystery.

George Griffith, coachman, testified that when Florence gave him a month's notice it was because Mr Bravo did not want him driving her. {8}

Day 9 – Friday 21 July 1876

George Griffith (resumed), could not recollect if Dr Gully had ever asked him to buy tartar emetic. {8}

Charles Stringer, hotel manager, confirmed that Griffith had said that Charles Bravo would not live four months. {8}

Henry Clarke, Malvern chemist, thought it unlikely that two ounces of tartar emetic would have been sold to Griffith without a note from a medical man.

Charles Robinson, Streatham chemist, stated that his records showed he had not sold any tartar emetic to Griffith.

Percy Smith, Balham chemist, stated that there was no record of him supplying tartar emetic to Griffith.

Day 10 – Monday 24 July 1876

Frederick Payne, physician, confirmed that two hours after a large dinner, the stomach would be particularly active and any antimony would have been absorbed more rapidly. {6}

John Meredith, assistant to Henry Clarke, said he had no recollection of selling two ounces of tartar emetic to Griffith and did not remember Dr Gully [*the register for June 1869 showed Dr Gully as the purchaser*].

Charles Maddox, assistant to Percy Smith, stated that he had never sold any tartar emetic to Griffith.

George Griffith (resumed) was questioned about the book "The Pocket Farrier" and was surprised to learn it did not contain a recipe involving tartar emetic. {8}

John Pritchard, butler to Dr Gully, stated that Mrs Cox had visited Dr Gully, on Wednesday 19 April or Thursday 20 April, to ask advice on how to treat Charles Bravo.

Day 11 – Tuesday 25 July 1876

George Griffith (recalled) was shown his record book from The Priory and agreed that tartar emetic might have been purchased on either 31 July or 16 August 1875. {8}

Dr George Johnson (recalled) described the conversation he had with Sir William Gull on the journey to The Priory. {6}

Frederick McCalmont (recalled) said that he had asked Bravo why Mrs Cox had been kept on, and he replied that she was useful and he owed her something because she had "urged his suit" [recommended him to Florence].

Edward Hope, barrister, recalled Bravo calculating the cost of Mrs Cox's service at £300 per annum, and Hope joked that Bravo could keep an extra pair of horses for that amount of money.

Edward Willoughby, barrister, stated that he last saw the deceased on 6 April 1876 and Bravo had told him he would be at Worthing during the Easter week.

Ann Campbell, mother of Florence Bravo, confirmed that the estrangement between the family and Florence ceased when she "entirely and completely" gave up seeing Dr Gully.

Day 12 – Wednesday 26 July 1876

Ann Campbell (resumed) stated that Mrs Cox was going to Jamaica immediately after the inquest ended and that she had been intending to go before the death of Mr Bravo. She believed that Bravo was anxious to reduce the expense of Mrs Cox's salary.

Day 13 – Thursday 27 July 1876

Joseph Bravo (recalled) testified that he had never kept any antimony at his stables and reported that his son had made a £20 loss on selling his Caledonian Railway shares.

William Hemming, coachman to Joseph Bravo, stated that he had never applied antimony to Mr Bravo's horses.

Jepson Atkinson, barrister, said that Bravo always took a large draught of water before bed and he had done so the last time they were together in Paris in about 1874. {6}

Meredith Brown, stockbroker, reported that 1876 had not been a good year for stocks, but Bravo had not lost money and had not shown any financial concerns.

Jane Cox, companion, stated that Charles was formally introduced to Florence in December 1874. {9}

Day 14 – Friday 28 July 1876

Jane Cox (resumed) testified that she spoke to Joseph Bravo in March regarding her trip to Jamaica and it was agreed that she should go soon [*a point disputed by Joseph Bravo in his testimony*]. {9}

Day 15 – Monday 31 July 1876

Jane Cox (resumed) confirmed that on 11 April 1876 she received another letter from her aunt (dated 26 March) asking her to travel to Jamaica. {9}

Day 16 – Tuesday 1 August 1876

Jane Cox (resumed) stated that, on a traumatic night, it was possible for Mr Harrison to have forgotten that she had told him about Bravo's confessional statement. {9}

Day 17 – Wednesday 2 August 1876

Jane Cox (resumed) said that Florence was extremely anxious about her affair with Dr Gully being made public. On the night before giving the Treasury Statement, Florence was "very ill". {9}

Day 18 – Thursday 3 August 1876

Florence Bravo, wife of the deceased, stated that she met Charles Bravo in Brighton at the end of September 1875, and that within three weeks marriage had been discussed and she had written to Dr Gully breaking off their friendship. {10}

Day 19 – Friday 4 August 1876

Florence Bravo (resumed) testified that she and Mrs Cox were alone in her dressing room for 15 minutes before Mary Ann Keeber arrived with a hot water can [*I suspect it was nearer 20 minutes, between 9:10 and 9:30pm*]. {10}

Day 20 – Monday 7 August 1876

Ellen Harford, close friend of Mrs Cox, confirmed that in March Mrs Cox had asked her advice about visiting her aunt in Jamaica, and she had urged her to go and offered to look after her boys while she was absent.

Charles Maddox (recalled) stated that on 8 April Dr Gully had purchased a bottle of laurel water, which is primarily used externally as a lotion but can be taken orally as a sedative.

PART TWO

Dr Joseph Moore (recalled) testified that he ordered hot water but not cold water, and remembered Mr Harrison taking a drink from the water bottle. {5}

Dr George Harrison (recalled) stated that when he poured himself a glass of water, there was only one tumbler and it was unused. {5}

Ellen Stone, cook, stated that the whiting and the lamb from dinner were eaten by servants in the kitchen after service with no ill effects.

George Brooks (recalled) testified that a very angry Mr Bravo had told him that he would not marry Florence unless he owned the furniture.

Henry Smith, surgeon, said that on Thursday 20 April, Dr Johnson had told him that he believed Bravo had committed suicide. {5}

Day 21 – Tuesday 8 August 1876

Florence Bravo (resumed) reported that Mrs Cox had decided to travel to Jamaica but she did not like leaving her. {10}

Day 22 – Wednesday 9 August 1876

Elizabeth Evans, under-housemaid, stated that she helped lift the unconscious Mr Bravo from the floor onto a chair before the arrival of Dr Moore.

Fanny Griffith, wife of George Griffith (coachman), remembered that her husband had some tartar emetic powder wrapped in a chemist's paper before they left The Priory. {8}

James Gully, hydrotherapist, stated that, although he was curious to see Charles Bravo, he had never done so. {10}

The inquest was adjourned for one day to enable the coroner to prepare his address to the jury.

Day 23 – Friday 11 August 1876

Coroner's summing up. William Carter fixed the time that Keeber went upstairs with the hot water can at 9:30pm, or a little after.

The jury's verdict. **Charles Bravo was wilfully murdered.**

Exhibit 10: Letters

Many letters were submitted as evidence at the second inquest. The selection below provides insight into three central characters – Charles, Florence and Mrs Cox.

FLORENCE BRAVO

This letter, written about two weeks after Charles' death, provides a revealing glimpse into Florence's emotional state.

6 May 1876

A letter received this morning from Royes Bell fully confirms my suspicions as to poor Charlie's committing suicide. Hence his motive for reducing our expenditure, as he could not tell me how hard he had been pressed by that dreadful woman. I wish he had, poor fellow, for I should not have been hard on him; but it is a most sad reflection upon his memory for me, and I intend to sift this matter. We have Sir William Gull's evidence, and I shall not allow the living to lie under any imputation such as is cast upon them by such a wicked verdict. I leave it all in my father's hands, and shall abide by his decision.

Yours sincerely,

Florence Bravo

This is a remarkable letter when you consider it is written by a supposedly grieving widow to her father-in-law. With hardly a trace of emotion, it defiantly asserts her husband's death was a suicide and even his reason: he had been harassed by his former mistress over his debts. Even if this were true, how can it be reconciled with his alleged confessional statement, "I have taken poison for Dr Gully"? Surely, he would have said something similar to "I have taken poison because of that woman." However, it is likely that Mrs Cox had not told Florence of her bombshell when this letter was written. In which case, how closely were the women working together? It appears both were independently seeking an explanation – any explanation – as to why Charles would have taken his own life. For the record, a letter submitted into evidence at the second inquest shows that Charles was not being pressed for money; he was talking about paying back the £500 he owed with more interest the following year.

MRS COX

The first two letters below were written by her aunt in Jamaica and shed some light on whether Jane Cox had decided to visit there. The third is written by Jane to Mr Harrison about the treatment she gave to Charles.

1) From Margaret Cox

Margaret Cox was the wife of Henry Cox (d. 1855), a slave owner and Member of the Jamaica House of Assembly. She was actually the aunt of Philip Cox, Jane's husband. She died on 24 September 1878.

26 March 1874

My Dear Jane, I think it right to let you know that I have left in my Will all I have to John [*Leslie's first name*] – Carlton, Content, cattle, horses, carriages, furniture and land; and should I die before he comes of age you will not allow these properties to be sold, but carried on for his benefit... Some years ago I wrote to the Rev. John Cox [*Jane's father-in-law*] when he was living at Walgrave, saying that I would leave these properties to his sons by his first wife, W. A. Woodward, but have long since revoked this, and I do not wish any of his family to have anything belonging to me. I never got anything from them. My own money paid for these properties and I can leave them to whom I please. You had better keep this to yourself; say nothing about it to anyone, not even John, while I am alive.

Margaret Cox

Jane Cox knew about the possible inheritance months before Florence first met Charles Bravo. Is it possible that Jane encouraged the marriage of Florence and Charles because she knew that she would be leaving for Jamaica at some point in the future? Note that two years later, in March 1876, she received a letter telling her to come as soon as possible. This is when she visited Joseph Bravo to discuss the matter.

2) From Margaret Cox

This letter, written by a friend of Margaret Cox on her behalf, was dated after the death of Charles Bravo, although it seems the news had not yet reached her aunt in Jamaica.

8 May 1876

[*Margaret*] bids me to tell you that she notes all you have said in your letter about coming out, and she hopes most earnestly that you will try to come out as soon as you can. It is very kind of Mrs Charles [*Bravo*] to promise to take care of the boys while you are away. I suppose it will make your mind more easy to think that they are with her while you are away. If you have not already left when you receive this, try and hasten out, for I know poor Mrs Cox [*Margaret*] wishes to see you.

It appears that Jane had written sometime in April 1876, after she and Charles Bravo discussed taking care of her boys in her absence. This note implies she had decided to travel to Jamaica, but we do not know if this was before or after his death.

3) To Mr Harrison

This letter was written sometime in May 1876, probably near the end of the month.

Dear Mr Harrison,

...I wanted you to tell me about the stomach pump. Mrs C. Bravo has told me several times that she thought had the stomach pump been used Mr Bravo's life might have been saved. I told her you told me afterwards it was impossible to use it; and I know long before Dr Moore arrived we could not get the strong coffee down – his teeth were clenched. Mrs Bravo said that Sir William Gull said it might have been used, but I told her Sir William Gull could not know the state Mr Bravo was in. Of course this has grieved me dreadfully, and I should be much obliged if you would kindly write me on this subject, and give me your own opinion.

Jane Cox

By mentioning the stomach pump to Mrs Cox, is Florence showing genuine distress, or guilt? Similarly, is Mrs Cox writing the letter out of anguish, or is she already thinking about her defence? One thing is clear: Sir William Gull was far too eager to offer his opinion before establishing the facts. He was not at The Priory immediately after Bravo's collapse. Both Mr Harrison and Dr Moore were, and agreed that Charles Bravo was so weak a stomach pump would have killed him.

CHARLES BRAVO

The following snippets are relevant to the misadventure theory. The first is from a letter to his father, the second, to his mother.

26 March 1876

…With the exception of a slight twinge of rheumatism, which I alleviated by the Turkish bath, I have been unusually well all week. Florence is not strong…

31 March 1876

…Royes came down on Wednesday to dinner. He prescribed for my rheumatism, and ordered me to stay at home, which I have been glad enough to do. I am now almost well…

Charles was taking hot baths to treat his rheumatism. Indeed, he took another Turkish bath on the afternoon he was poisoned. It appears the Epsom salts prescribed by Mr Bell were for this purpose; an Epsom salt bath was a well-known remedy for rheumatism. It is unlikely that Charles was taking them orally, in which case he would not have put the salts in his drinking water and could not have mixed them up with tartar emetic.

Interestingly, Charles writes of being "unusually well" and then "almost well". We do not know his symptoms, but there were no reports – by doctors, servants or friends – that Charles was suffering nausea and sickness, symptoms of slow antimony poisoning.

PART THREE

THE VERDICT

You have read the story. You have sifted the evidence.

Here is my view on what happened at The Priory.

The case began in mystery, and has ended in mystery.

British Medical Journal, 19 August 1876.

The Verdict

MY JUDGEMENT

Who was responsible for the death of Charles Bravo? It is time for me to offer my opinion. There are four potential verdicts:

- **Charles Bravo** took his own life.
- **Mrs Cox** poisoned Charles Bravo.
- **Dr Gully** used Mrs Cox to poison Charles Bravo.
- **Florence Bravo** poisoned her husband and Mrs Cox was an accessory.

A key question to be answered is: what was the poisoned chalice? I believe all the evidence suggests it was Bravo's water bottle. The only other plausible contender is the Burgundy, but how could the poisoner know that only Charles would drink it? After all, any remaining wine would be left in the dining room and drunk the next day, possibly by guests. Also, according to the experiments of Professor Redwood, the tartar emetic would form a precipitate in wine after an hour or so, and nothing unusual about the wine was observed.

The long delay between dinner and Bravo's illness also counts against the Burgundy. The use of an additional poison might have delayed the action of tartar emetic, but a large dose of antimony entirely accounts for Bravo's sickness and collapse. There is no need to postulate a second poison in the Burgundy when it explains no more than a single poison in the water bottle.

Finally, there is evidence to suggest the tartar emetic acted rapidly. The Field Officer's experience showed it was possible in just a few minutes. Additionally, Frederick Payne, the doctor who performed the post-mortem, believed an active stomach after a large meal would speed up the action of antimony. There appears no reason to reject the view that the tartar emetic acted within minutes of Bravo ingesting it from his water bottle.

With that question decided, let's look at the four theories. Agatha Christie was certain that **Dr Gully** was the poisoner, or at least behind the poisoning. It is well known that the Queen of Crime was partial to pointing an accusing finger at a dodgy doctor in her novels. In fact, a disproportionate number of her major characters are connected to the medical profession. This is unsurprising when you consider that homicidal doctors are ideal characters for devising ingenious murders, and Christie's pharmacist background provided a good knowledge of poisons. We can agree that a sinister Dr Gully poisoning his romantic usurper makes the most interesting story, but does fact mirror fiction in this case?

I am certain it does not. First, there is simply no evidence that Dr Gully was involved. It is true that prior to Bravo's death he gave laurel water to Mrs Cox as a prescription for Florence, but I do not believe it was used in the crime. Second, Dr Gully had no opportunity. Not even Christie proposed he waltzed into The Priory and laced Bravo's water bottle. In which case, he must have had an accessory and the only plausible candidate is Mrs Cox. I find it unlikely that she would kill Charles at the behest of Gully or cover up for him; she had sufficient motive, means and opportunity to kill Bravo by herself. And remember that a poisoning is more likely to be perpetrated by a single person.

Finally, even if he had duped Mrs Cox into secretly slipping Charles a lethal 'medicine', I find it difficult to believe Dr Gully would have chosen a notoriously unreliable poison. If this once-only attempt failed, his chance was blown.

If Dr Gully is eliminated, how can we make sense of George Griffith's prophecy? In my opinion, there was no conspiracy or anything sinister behind the remark. The most likely explanation is that his wife overheard something when Florence and Dr Gully spoke at the lodge. Perhaps, Gully said, "I wish you well, but I won't give the marriage four months," and this was misheard or misinterpreted to mean Gully would actively put an end to it after four months. By a process of Chinese whispers, it is not implausible to believe this was eventually summarised by Chief Inspector Clarke as "If you marry him, he won't live long." In my view, Agatha Christie's theory can safely be rejected.

Was **Charles Bravo** responsible for his own death? He might have unintentionally killed himself, as adduced by Yseult Bridges, although I am surprised how this theory has garnered support over the years. Genuine accidents are honest events with everything left in plain sight. To my mind, if it were true, a container of tartar emetic would have been found in his bedroom alongside the Epsom salts. It was not, and this makes me sceptical. After all, if you discovered a dead body with a bullet wound to the head, would you accept a theory of misadventure if the gun was never found and its absence from the scene never satisfactorily explained? The only way Bridges extricates her theory from this insurmountable difficulty is to conjecture that Bravo instructed Mrs Cox to throw the tartar emetic in the fire, a secret that Mrs Cox supposedly took to her grave.

Moreover, it would mean Mrs Cox covered up an accident by concocting a suicide story that involved Florence's scandalous past, which she knew would devastate her friend if it became public knowledge. And, in any case, if there was something nefarious to hide from his wife, the last person he would tell would be his wife's well-paid, live-in drinking companion. There are other problems with the misadventure theory, but this is enough for me to eliminate it without further consideration.

This does not mean I have rejected the theory that Charles Bravo was responsible for his own death – he might have taken his own life intentionally. What can we say about the suicide theory? It would explain why he knew he was doomed, did not enquire about his condition and the reactions of both Mrs Cox and Florence. Mrs Cox was trying to save his life and delayed revealing his confessional statement to protect Florence, who was genuinely distressed and called as much medical assistance as possible. Yet, I have a massive problem with the choice of poison. All Charles had to do was knock back some of the laudanum and lie down on his bed to die peacefully. Instead, he chooses to mercilessly torture himself by using tartar emetic. Unsurprisingly, there is not a single case on record of someone taking their own life using this poison.

The possibility that he took laudanum followed by an accidental overdose of tartar emetic runs into even greater problems. Because tartar emetic does not act instantly, Bravo must have waited for several minutes before it took effect and, just when he began to feel nauseous, called for hot water. It makes no sense. And clearly he would have known that tartar emetic was the cause of his dreadful symptoms. Described as someone who was truthful and demonstrative, I find it implausible that he said nothing to the doctors or his family.

In my opinion, there is no coherent case for believing that Charles Bravo took his own life. I reject this theory, and suspect he was murdered. The two theories remaining are Mrs Cox alone or Florence with her companion covering up the crime. Which one is the more plausible? This is a difficult question.

PART THREE

Mrs Cox is the obvious suspect and there is a compelling case against her. I believe her motive was concern for Florence's wellbeing as well as her own financial security in the short term. Her actions on the night are totally suspicious. The truth does not change, but liars often alter and embellish their stories, and this is what Mrs Cox did with important aspects of her account. However, you can interpret most of her actions just as easily if she was covering up for Florence. Indeed, you could argue that if the organised **Mrs Cox** was the poisoner she would have had her story worked out in advance. The haphazard nature of her cover indicates she was taken by surprise.

Another point against this verdict is that Mrs Cox administered the textbook treatment for poisoning. If she wanted Bravo dead, she had the option of doing little until the doctors arrived. To me, her actions make more sense if she had only just been made aware of what had happened to Charles and was genuinely trying to save his life.

If **Florence** was the poisoner, she had as equally a compelling motive as Mrs Cox, perhaps more so. To differentiate between the two remaining verdicts, I suggest several questions need to be answered. Who was more likely to have access to the poison? Who had the greater opportunity to lace the water bottle? Who was more likely to have poisoned Charles on that particular night? Who was more likely to resort to poison to solve their problems?

I believe the tartar emetic came from Florence's stables, and the probability that she knew of its existence is higher than Mrs Cox finding out about it. Similarly, although Mrs Cox was possibly aware of Bravo's nightly drinking habit, and would have known only if Florence had told her of it, Florence must have known, yet denied it.

Florence had a greater opportunity to lace the water bottle than Mrs Cox. She was at The Priory all afternoon but Mrs Cox only arrived a few minutes before dinner, and her only window of opportunity was extremely narrow: when she fetched the glass of wine for Florence.

I believe the bolting horse was used by the poisoner as a smoke-screen, and this explains why the poisoning occurred on this particular night. Florence knew about the horse ride whereas Mrs Cox only learned of it over dinner. This was an opportunistic murder using an opportunistic poison. I believe this also points to Florence more than the cautious and circumspect Mrs Cox.

Mrs Cox was resourceful and had learned to live by her own wits; she would face any adversity stoically. In particular, if she lost her job I believe she would have coped, perhaps relying on help from Florence and Joseph Bravo. By contrast, Florence was privileged and entitled, and not accustomed to finding obstacles in her way. Recall, she even sued her father and abruptly broke off with Dr Gully when it suited her needs.

Finally, I believe that Rowe's statement points to the truth: "I have seen her, poor old woman, and she has got herself into a great deal of trouble through not telling the truth." This express-es sympathy toward Mrs Cox. In my view, the servants knew more than they were prepared to divulge.

When I look at the arguments against the possibility that Florence was the poisoner, I find only one: her grief and distress appeared genuine. Yet, it is not implausible to believe she faked it. Florence broke down over a dozen times at the second inquest, but on all but three occasions this was in relation to her affair with Dr Gully and her humiliation. Fewer tears were shed over her husband. Although her actions are untypical for poisoners, they are not unprecedented. Mary Ann Cotton, a Victorian serial killer who killed at least four people with arsenic, nursed her victims carefully, exhibited sympathy for them and sent for medical men.

PART THREE

Another explanation is that her grief was genuine, but born of fear and remorse. When she saw her husband suffering on his death bed, perhaps the gravity of the situation now hit her and she realised the best way to extricate herself from her predicament was his recovery. Whether faked or genuine, her reaction can be explained in the context of her guilt.

Taken together, I believe these factors point to Florence Bravo as the poisoner. She never had the whip hand, as Agatha Christie believed. She married for respectability, but quickly realised it had been bought at far too high a price. A divorce or separation, even if either were actually possible, would not help; she would be ostracised once again, especially by her family. She was trapped with only one option: the removal of her husband. Mrs Cox was involved, of course: not as her sinister black-dressed companion, but as a loyal friend taken by surprise and doing her best for Florence. Once Mrs Cox had invented the confessional, she had to stick with it. In the end, desperately seeking a motive for Charles' suicide to alleviate the growing suspicion that she was the killer, she reluctantly introduced Dr Gully. It led to the splintering of her relationship with Florence, but it saved both their necks.

If we travelled back in time together and discovered Mrs Cox was the poisoner, I would not be shocked. But in the absence of a time machine, we are left to evaluate the evidence left to us, and it points elsewhere. Therefore, my verdict is:

Florence Bravo poisoned her husband and Mrs Cox was an accessory.

I am not the only author to arrive at this verdict. Hat tip to John Williams, who was the first to realise this was the most likely solution to the case. But the purpose of this book is not to convince you of my favoured theory but to seek your opinion.

Members of the Cold Case Jury, as you ponder your verdict, you will be interested to know the conclusions of other writers.

OTHER VERDICTS

The following provides brief overviews of the major books and articles on the case and a succinct summary of the author's conclusion. All were used as secondary research sources in writing this book.

Abrath, Gustav. The Balham Mystery (1876)

This book is exceptionally hard to find (to my knowledge, the Bodleian Library in Oxford is the only library in the UK that has a copy). Abrath's theory is that a combination of laurel water and tartar emetic killed Charles Bravo. Laurel water (prussic acid) was prescribed by Dr Gully for Florence, but no other writer believes it was involved in Bravo's death.

Conclusion: Charles Bravo was murdered.

Hall, Sir John. The Bravo Mystery and Other Cases (1923)

Hard to find, and the most measured and insightful analysis of the case. About a third of the book is dedicated to the Bravo Mystery, while other cases include The Northumberland Street Tragedy, The Duke of Cumberland's Valet, An Affair of Honour, and George IV and the Jockey Club. Hall's account was the first to be published after all the main characters in the case had died. He claimed it was impossible to dissociate Florence and Mrs Cox – they were innocent or guilty together – and was suspicious of them both, although he thought their motives for murder were insufficient. However, he firmly rejected suicide and misadventure.

Conclusion: Charles Bravo was not responsible for his own death.

Roughead, William. Malice Domestic (1929)

Published in The Murderer's Companion (1941), this book is quite hard to find in the UK. Roughead was an accomplished crime writer who became heavily involved in the case of Oscar Slater. This account of the Bravo case is a good overview, but lacks the insight of Hall and some of the details given by Jenkins in similarly abbreviated accounts. He believed that Florence Bravo was innocent of the poisoning and that she should share the exculpatory epitaph of Hero, Leonato's daughter in *Much Ado About Nothing*. Someday, he wistfully conjectured, among the papers of Mrs Cox, we would find the true account of the Bravo tragedy. He would have been disappointed.

Conclusion: Mrs Cox played the lead in murdering Charles Bravo.

Jenkins, Elizabeth. The Balham Mystery (1949)

The Balham Mystery is the last chapter in Six Criminal Women. It is a good overview with some well-researched details. The author claimed that "Mrs Cox was the evil spirit" whose influence dominated the "self-indulgent, greedy and pleasure-loving" Florence.

Conclusion: Mrs Cox poisoned Charles Bravo to maintain the security for her family.

Veale, Frederick. The Verdict In Doubt: The Bravo Case (1950)

A very hard-to-find book. A brief (48 pages) but well-reasoned account. It is unusual in that its emphasis is more on the rational argument than on the story and the detail. This appears to be true of the other books in Veale's series: The Wallace Case, The Trial of Lizzie Borden and The Case of Oscar Slater. All are very difficult to acquire and, if you do locate a copy, it is likely to cost in excess of £100.

Conclusion: Mrs Cox was the number one suspect in the murder of Charles Bravo.

Williams, John. Suddenly At The Priory (1953)

In my view, this is the best book on the Bravo case but with one important caveat. First, the positives. It provides fine detail on the characters, the antecedent events to the poisoning and the three days during Bravo's terminal illness. It is less detailed on the inquests than Bridges' book (see below), although these are still covered admirably, but it is better argued. It was Williams who saw the possibility that Florence did the poisoning but Mrs Cox told the lies; an unusual situation that would explain some of the mysteries in the case. He also saw that motives may be more complex than simply Florence wanting to go back to Dr Gully. He believed that Florence had the opportunity to poison the water bottle when she was alone upstairs for a few minutes after leaving the morning room. The one flaw is that Williams, in his desire to provide the strongest support for his theory, accepts the questionable view that Alexander Ricardo, Florence's first husband, also died of antimony poisoning. Clearly if both husbands were poisoned in the same way, it would be extremely likely that Florence was culpable. However, there is no evidence that this was the case and the theory is given short shrift by Taylor and Clarke (see below).

Conclusion: Florence poisoned Charles Bravo and Mrs Cox covered up the crime.

Bridges, Yseult. How Charles Bravo Died (1956)

Bridges provides the most comprehensive background to the case of any book I have read, complete with many letters. However, one criticism is that the author does not spend enough time evaluating her own solution to the case and has a propensity to fit the evidence to her theory using conjecture. For example, Charles telling Mrs Cox to throw the tartar emetic in the fire blatantly flies in the face of Mrs Cox's testimony and leads to enormous problems of why she introduced the words "for Dr Gully". Overall, this book

provides the reader with a wealth of detail about the antecedents and the inquests, and is recommended for those wanting a deeper background to the case.
Conclusion: Charles Bravo died from misadventure.

Christie, Agatha. Personal Correspondence (1968)
The Queen of Crime turned her attention to true crime in a letter written to a friend in the summer of 1968. She was quite certain that Dr Gully was the devious killer. He duped Mrs Cox into administering the poison to Charles Bravo disguised as medicine. He had the strongest motive of any suspect, she believed, and Griffith either knew or suspected something.
Conclusion: Dr Gully murdered Charles Bravo.

Jenkins, Elizabeth. Dr Gully (1971)
In her historical novel, Jenkins changed her mind and presented a different conclusion from her 1949 book. Jenkins viewed Florence's character and motive more critically, portraying her as the poisoner, with Mrs Cox as the accomplice who created a "monstrous fabrication... most skilfully woven from deceptive fragments of the truth".
Conclusion: Florence poisoned her husband and Mrs Cox was an accessory.

Taylor and Clarke. Murder At The Priory (1988)
The most recent and comprehensive account to find that Mrs Cox acted alone in killing Charles Bravo is an excellent addition to the canon. Previous writers had arrived at this conclusion but provided scant detail on how and when Mrs Cox executed her deed. Bernard Taylor and Kate Clarke also provide a sophisticated motive: Mrs Cox's short-term security, and especially the English education of her boys, was being jeopardised by Charles and his

insistence to relieve her of her position at The Priory. The hard-back also provides the best photographic plates of any book.

Conclusion: Mrs Cox poisoned Charles Bravo.

Ruddick, James. Death at the Priory (2001)

The most recent analysis published on the case, Ruddick's book is skilfully written, intertwining the personal story of his search for a solution, which took him to the West Indies and New Zealand, with the Bravo story itself. On several occasions he claims to have discovered something that sheds new light on the case but in truth it was either already in the public domain or does not materially affect what was already known. Indeed, much hype appears to have surrounded the book launch – the case was solved, no less. However, Ruddick's verdict is identical in virtually every respect to the one proposed by John Williams nearly 50 years earlier (see above) but this fact is disingenuously airbrushed from the book.

Conclusion: Florence poisoned Charles Bravo and Mrs Cox was an accessory.

Fellowes, Julian. A Most Mysterious Murder (2004).

This excellent historical crime docudrama series, first broadcast by ITV, examines five unsolved murder cases, including Charles Bravo, Rose Harsent and Earl Erroll. Each episode combines quality period drama with Fellowes appearing in scenes as the narrator, breaking the 'fourth wall'. The series is recommended viewing. For the Bravo episode, Fellowes closely follows Yseult Bridges' account, believing that Charles was administering tartar emetic in small doses to kill Florence but ended up killing himself accidentally.

Conclusion: Charles Bravo took his own life.

EPILOGUE

THE IRREPRESSIBLE TIDE

Charles Bravo's dreadful death has given him a place in criminal history, but what happened to the other protagonists in our drama?

The poisoner of Charles Bravo also poisoned the last years of Dr Gully's life, bringing him professional and social ruin. To the calloused eye of Victorian morals, his extra-marital affair with a woman less than half his age was as great a sin as murder. He was expelled from the medical societies of which he had been an eminent member, and the whispers of puritanical condemnation continuously stalked him. The stigma even dogged his only son, William, a Liberal MP and Speaker of the House of Commons. On taking his seat, unruly members greeted him by shouting "Bravo, Gully!" Dr James Gully died in 1883.

Florence fared the worst. She left The Priory, finally settling in Southsea on the south coast of England. There she escaped the long shadow cast by the death of her second husband by conjuring up the same demons that had killed her first. A reclusive alcoholic, she suffered a lonely, pitiful end for someone born with beauty and wealth. She died just two years after Charles, in September 1878, aged only 33. Some romantic writers have suggested she died of a broken heart, but I suggest her health followed her reputation; neither survived the ordeal of the inquest. For her, it was a fate worse than death.

If she was the killer, a natural and cruel retribution had followed, but the roots of her terrible crime were firmly planted in the misogynistic soil of Victorian England; an England in which women were denied professional careers, the vote and even possessions in marriage. Regardless of class, women had fewer choices and opportunities, including the chance to escape an unhappy marriage. This is not to condone murder in any way, if that is what transpired, but it explains why it might have occurred. Equally, Charles Bravo was not a monster; he did not deserve his appalling death. He was a gentleman living in a world of smoke-filled gentlemen's clubs, able to keep a mistress and father an illegitimate child.

The sad truth is this. If Florence had lived a century later she could have led the life she yearned for. Instead, she was a subjugated spirit, born out of time, swimming against the irre-pressible tide of fate she could never overcome.

In her Will she left some money to each of Mrs Cox's three sons. To Mrs Cox, her former companion and close friend, she left nothing. It was an empty epitaph for a broken friendship. What Jane Cannon Cox thought of this when she heard the news, no one knows. Unlike Florence, she appears to have been a resilient survivor. She left for Jamaica with her three sons soon after the second inquest but, many years later, returned to England with her youngest leaving her two eldest sons to manage the estate they had inherited in 1879. When and why she came back we do not know, but it appears she was in Brighton at the time of the outbreak of the First World War. If so, she must have lived to a ripe old age, possibly into her nineties.

Mrs Cox was tight-lipped to the end about the events of April 1876. There was no writing desk, to echo the erstwhile hopes of

EPILOGUE

William Roughead, in which there was found "among the papers of that ambiguous widow... the true version of the Bravo mystery". Rather, the ambiguous widow was lost over the distant horizon of history, and lived the rest of her days in the obscurity she would no doubt have enjoyed had Charles Bravo never been poisoned at The Priory.

NOTES
RESEARCH SOURCES

In researching this book I have relied almost exclusively on primary sources – police reports held at the National Archive (ref: MEPO 3/2860) and newspaper accounts of the second inquest, most notably *The Daily News*, *The Times* and *The Morning Post*.

NOTES

Chapters 1 – 2. Much of the back story was gleaned from the inquest testimony, particularly from Florence Bravo, Ann Campbell and Jane Cox, and also *How Charles Bravo Died* by Yseult Bridges. Details of the wedding to Captain Ricardo are from The Farringdon Advertiser, 24 September 1964. In the late 1850s, Balham Station was part of the West End of London and Crystal Palace Railway, which was soon absorbed by the London, Brighton and South Coast Railway Company. However, contemporaneous maps name the line as "West London and Crystal Palace". Mrs Cox's eldest son was named John Leslie. According to Taylor and Clarke (1988, p.15), he was known as Leslie.

Chapter 3. The stated times are estimates but based on a thorough assessment of all relevant testimony. The details are gleaned from the testimony of Florence, Mrs Cox, Rowe and Keeber.

Most authors have Keeber heading downstairs when Charles opens his bedroom door, but this is incorrect. She called at the foot of the stairs to the servant's quarters adjacent to Bravo's bedroom. Similarly, the visit to the bank to pay in a £500 cheque – the same amount Charles Bravo owed his former mistress – is another detail that has escaped most authors.

Chapter 4. Again, the times are my estimates. Witnesses differed as to when Charles collapsed. Mrs Cox believed this occurred at 9:30pm, according to her testimony at the first inquest, but Mary Ann identifies this as the time she was fetching a glass of wine for Florence. Another important detail is Mr Harrison drinking from the water bottle at about midnight; this is based on his testimony and that of Dr Moore.

Chapter 5. The reconstruction of Mrs Cox's appearance at the first inquest was based on notes published by *The British Medical Journal* on 20 May 1876.

Chapters 6-10. I present extracts of key testimony, closely following the relevant exchanges at the second inquest. Obviously, these are heavily abridged – a complete transcript of the inquest would fill five paperbacks. Incidental facts, such as passing trains and the crowds, are culled from newspaper reports. Other details, such as Mr Hudson's letter, were found in the police file. The weather descriptions are based on meteorological records held at the Met Office archives. Most of the servants gave statements to the Treasury Solicitor, but these are not included in the file at the National Archive, and I was not able to locate them. References to them are made in Chief Inspector Clarke's reports.

NOTES

Chapter 12. According to Mrs Cox, she saw her son at Brighton station on the journey home from Worthing. I presumed this was Leslie, her eldest, although she never explicitly identifies which son she met. Her meeting is a trivial detail, but it might have significance in assessing her state of mind, as suggested in my text.

Chapter 13. Agatha Christie's letter was published in *The Times* in September 1968.

Chapter 14. Florence testified that reading Shakespeare with Charles gave her some of the happiest moments of the marriage. The sonnet quoted is No 9: *Is It For Fear To Wet A Widow's Eye.*

DEATH OF AN ACTRESS

The disappearance of Gay Gibson, 1947.

A luxury liner steams across the equator off the coast of Africa. A beautiful actress disappears from her first-class cabin and a dashing deck steward is accused of her murder. Although the evidence against him appears damning, he vehemently protests his innocence. Found guilty and sentenced to death, remarkably he is saved from the gallows. Using recently-discovered police files, the full story is told for the first time with new evidence never brought to trial. Was he guilty, or does the new evidence point in a different direction?

MOVE TO MURDER

The murder of Julia Wallace, 1931.

A telephone message is left at a chess club, instructing one of its members, insurance agent William Wallace, to meet a Mr Qualtrough. But the address given by the mystery caller does not exist and by the time Wallace returns home he finds his wife Julia bludgeoned to death. The case turns on the telephone call. Who made it? The police thought it was Wallace, creating an alibi that might have come from an Agatha Christie thriller. Others believe Wallace innocent but disagree on what happened. What is your verdict in one of the most celebrated cold cases of all time?

1/21